THE WEEK

THE LIVES OF THE FAMOUS
AND THE INFAMOUS

EVERYTHING YOU NEED TO KNOW
ABOUT EVERYONE WHO MATTERED

EBURY
PRESS

10 9 8 7 6 5 4 3 2

Published in 2014 by Ebury Press, an imprint of Ebury Publishing
A Random House Group Company

Text © The Week 2014

The Random House Group Limited Reg. No. 954009

Addresses for companies within the Random House Group can be found
at www.randomhouse.co.uk

A CIP catalogue record for this book is available from the British Library

The Random House Group Limited supports the Forest Stewardship Council® (FSC®),
the leading international forest-certification organisation. Our books carrying the FSC
label are printed on FSC®-certified paper. FSC is the only forest-certification scheme
supported by the leading environmental organisations, including Greenpeace. Our
paper procurement policy can be found at www.randomhouse.co.uk/environment

To buy books by your favourite authors and register for offers
visit www.randomhouse.co.uk

Compiled and edited by Steve Tribe
Commissioning Editor: Carey Smith
Assistant Editor: Nicola Crossley
Text design by ClarkevanMeurs Design Ltd

Printed and bound by CPI Group (UK) Ltd, Croydon, CR0 4YY

ISBN 978 0 09195 866 4

Contents

Foreword

Unputdownable. Is that a proper word? I very much hope so, for that's exactly what this little book is. Unputdownable.

I had thought, when asked to write this foreword, that I'd find its contents all a bit too familiar, too well trodden. Every entry, at some time or another, has appeared in *The Week*: there isn't one here that I haven't edited over the years. But I couldn't have been more wrong. This book is addictive. If you need an antidote to boredom or *Weltschmerz*, this, dear reader, is it.

What's the secret? Why is this book so absorbing? The main reason is that the short obituary, the condensed life story, is such a powerful yet neglected art form in its own right. Here, in a handful of well-wrought paragraphs, are the hopes, fears, joys, disappointments, follies, tragedies, reconciliations, loves and hatreds attendant on human striving. And they are paragraphs that owe their excitement not just to the best obituary writers in the national press but also to the skills of *The Week*'s uncredited writers (mainly Caroline Law, until 2007, and mainly Tom Hodgkinson thereafter) in gathering together all the best bits from those different accounts and weaving them into a story.

But it's not only the pleasure contained in these stories that's so compelling, it's the pleasure to be found in diversity, in juxtaposition, in the astonishing variety of human experience and achievement that unravels before you in these pages where poets, politicians, pilots, prostitutes, polo players, puppeteers, prisoners, plutocrats, psychopaths, polar explorers and high-school principals all jostle for attention. Some famous, some infamous, some unknown. Their collective life stories, covering most of the twentieth century and most of the twenty-first (so far), form a weird and wonderful historical tapestry covering the big social, cultural and political events of our age.

Perhaps most enjoyable of all, however, is the encounter with the bizarre and unexpected aspects of people's lives – aspects that never make it into the historical record. Which famous violinist had his first name chosen for him by his parents with the express purpose of embarrassing his anti-Semitic landlady? Which famous serial murderer attended literary lunches attended by Charlie Chaplin and his own last victim? Which politician included the question 'Why is there only one Monopolies commission?' in his party's election manifesto? You won't have to go far into this book before you discover the answers to these and other memorable 'would-you-believe-it?' questions.

So if you cannot enjoy this book, dear reader, I'm afraid there is something wrong with you, and you should seek help. But, fear not, it won't come to that. As I said, it's unputdownable.

Jeremy O'Grady
Editor-in-chief, *The Week*

The literary renegade who shot his wife

WILLIAM BURROUGHS

1914-1997

There was nothing in William Burroughs's background or upbringing to suggest his future notoriety. He was born in a fashionable district of St Louis in 1914, the grandson and namesake of the inventor of the adding machine. He studied at Harvard (where he attended T.S. Eliot's lectures) and, briefly, at medical school in Vienna, before returning home and drifting into a series of increasingly dead-end jobs, as a reporter, a barman, a private detective, and even a pest exterminator. Eventually, after failing an army medical, he gravitated to New York where he first experimented with drugs, quickly falling prey to addiction.

After a spell farming in Louisiana and Texas, where he grew his own opium and marijuana, Burroughs moved to Mexico in the company of his wife, Joan Vollmer. Although Burroughs was mostly homosexual, the bond with his wife appeared to be a close one. She too suffered from addictions, and the relationship was to end tragically. One September afternoon in Mexico City in 1951, when the two of them were attending a drunken party, Burroughs turned to Joan and said, 'It's time for our William Tell act. Put that glass on your head.' She did so; but Burroughs shot an inch too low, the bullet entering her head and killing her instantly. Before the authorities could investigate, Burroughs skipped bail and fled the country.

The killing of his wife was the defining moment of Burroughs's life, as he explained in the introduction to his novel *Queer*. 'I am forced to the appalling conclusion that I would never have become a writer but for Joan's death,' he said, going on to explain how it had brought him into 'contact with the Invader, the Ugly Spirit, and manoeuvred me into a life-long struggle, in which I had no choice but to write my way out.' Writing his way out resulted most famously in *The Naked Lunch*, a book he himself described as 'necessarily brutal, obscene and disgusting'. The book, summed up by Ed Vulliamy in *The Guardian* as 'a plotless wordscape of sexual violence and drug abuse', grew out of his years in Tangiers, where he lived in a male brothel in the company of 'Opium Jones'.

The book, banned in America, was first published in Paris in 1959. It appeared in Britain in 1964, when Burroughs was living in a basement flat in Notting Hill Gate. Although *Lady Chatterley's Lover* had been published two years earlier, no one seemed ready for the horrors of this new novel. The review in the *Times Literary Supplement* was published under the headline 'Ugh' and sparked a 13-week correspondence. The most memorable contribution came from Edith Sitwell: 'I do not wish to spend the rest of my life with my nose nailed to other people's lavatories,' she wrote. 'I prefer Chanel No. 5.' Another fierce critic was the publisher Victor Gollancz, who accused Burroughs of purveying 'bogus-highbrow filth'. Burroughs for his part was equally

> **The Naked Lunch, 'a plotless wordscape of sexual violence and drug abuse', grew out of his years in Tangiers, where he lived in a male brothel in the company of 'Opium Jones'.**

scathing of the London literary scene, dismissing it as 'sordid' and accusing English writers of eking out a living by appearing on each other's radio programmes.

Nonetheless, *The Naked Lunch* assured Burroughs's position as the pre-eminent literary renegade of his generation. The poet Robert Lowell acclaimed the book, and critics such as Mary McCarthy enthusiastically invoked shades of Swift. It was also admired by many for its avant-garde style of 'fold in and cut up writing', as Burroughs called it, a technique which John Calder, who published *The Naked Lunch* in Britain, explained in *The Independent*. Instead of being composed sequentially, 'sections were simply picked up from the floor or out of the drawer, put together as they came to hand and published that way.' Some sections even went into other books.

Has Burroughs's claim to be a writer of significance survived the test of time? *The Times* didn't think so. He might have seemed shocking at the time, it argued, but his ideas were shallow and even his celebrated cut-up technique, post *Finnegans Wake* and Gertrude Stein, 'was perhaps not so revolutionary and exciting as was made out'. But the novelist J.G. Ballard disagreed. Burroughs's 'weird genius was the perfect mirror of his times, and made him the most important and original writer since World War II', he wrote in *The Guardian*. 'Now we are left with the career novelists.'

One area in which he undeniably did leave his mark was on the 'beat generation' of writers – people like Jack Kerouac and Allen Ginsberg. His central theme of power as the manipulation of pleasure and pain by gangsters, judges, psychiatrists and policemen also made him a favourite with the 1960s hippies and 1970s punks, to whom he became an honorary godfather. And in later years, noted James Campbell in *The Guardian*, when Burroughs was living in a windowless locker room in New York known as 'the Bunker', it became fashionable for rock stars to seek him out. Mick Jagger, David Bowie, Frank Zappa and Patti Smith 'all sang for their supper at the Burroughs table'.

And yet Burroughs was not an orthodox rebel. His work may have been a warning against the nature of power, said *The Times*, but he also 'saw human beings as irrevocably addicted to victimisation by their overlords'. And though much of his work was fuelled by drugs, once cured of his addiction in London in the 1950s, he spoke out against the dangers of hard drugs. But his obsession with sex remained throughout his life. In 1995, after the publication of *My Education: A Book of Dreams*, one reviewer dismissed him as a 'dirty old man'. 'I wish I was a *dirtier* old man,' Burroughs responded. 'I'm ashamed to go 24 hours without thinking about sex. It's alarming. It really is.'

The cotton-picker who dreamt of being a star

TAMMY WYNETTE

1942-1998

Tammy Wynette was 'everything a country singer should be,' said *The Times*. With her big hair and rhinestone dresses, she looked the part; but more importantly, she lived it. Her love-life was punctuated by violent and stormy relationships, and she was once accused of setting to music 'every cross word and flying plate'. Right up to the end, her story read like a tragic, heroic country song. Yet she overcame her troubles to become the most successful female country singer of all time, selling over 30 million records.

Born in 1942, on a Mississippi farm, she was named Virginia Wynette Pugh. Her father died of a brain tumour when she was nine months old, and soon afterwards her mother left to find work in an aircraft factory. Wynette, said the *Daily Telegraph*, was brought up by her Baptist grandparents, who put her to work picking cotton – 'the hardest work I've ever done', she later recalled. The family was so poor that she had to make her clothes out of flour bags, using the white ones for undergarments and the coloured ones for dresses. Her grandmother took her to church, where she learned to sing and harmonise, and she became convinced that she wanted a career in music.

But nothing in her life went smoothly. At 17, she married a local boy called Euple Byrd and was thrown out of high school. She quickly produced two daughters, but her husband was a chronic philanderer. Left alone with the children, she lapsed into depression and was given electric shock treatment. After giving birth to another daughter, who suffered from spinal meningitis and screamed continuously, Wynette decided she'd had enough. She stuffed the kids into her beaten-up station wagon and told Byrd she was leaving. When he asked where she was going, she told him Nashville, to be a star. 'Uh-huh,' he replied, 'dream on!'

Wynette's big break came when she turned up at the offices of Billy Sherill, a producer at Epic records. He said he liked the 'teardrop' quality in her voice, told her to change her name, and had her record his song, 'Apartment Number Nine'. It was a major hit in 1967, and Sherill and Wynette became life-long writing partners. More hits followed, including her biggest, 'Stand By Your Man' (1968), which she co-wrote with Sherill in half an hour. The song, which urged downtrodden wives to 'give him two arms to cling to', annoyed many feminists, but Wynette was unrepentant, said *The Guardian*. 'Although I consider myself more independent than many of the "sisters" who criticised the song,' she once said, 'I am emotionally dependent on men, and I wouldn't want it any other way.'

In 1969, after divorcing her second husband, an unsuccessful musician, she married her childhood idol, the country star George Jones. The couple made numerous albums together. They built a country and western theme park, with guitar-shaped lakes and chandeliers made out of wagon wheels, and drove a white Pontiac with 4,000 silver dollars embedded in the dashboard, bull-horns on the front bumper and door handles made from real pistols. But their bliss was short-lived. Jones had a weakness for drink and an explosive temper. Once, at the end of her tether, Wynette confiscated the

> **She stuffed the kids into her beaten-up station wagon and told Byrd she was leaving. When he asked where she was going, she told him Nashville, to be a star. 'Uh-huh,' he replied, 'dream on!'**

keys to all 27 of their cars, only to discover that he had hot-wired the lawn mower and driven straight to the nearest bar. They separated in 1975, after Jones chased her round the house with a loaded rifle, but continued to record together for years afterwards. Wynette said the break-up inspired her. 'I write better when I'm depressed.'

There followed an affair with Burt Reynolds, which ended when she accidentally poisoned him with a banana pudding, and a 44-day marriage to a property developer. Finally, in 1977, she married George Richey, an old friend who had written songs for her, and found the stability she had been seeking. But her troubles still weren't over. The following year, she was mysteriously abducted by a masked assailant, who tied her hands and drove her 80 miles before attempting to strangle her. She was severely beaten and then abandoned. No one was ever charged with the kidnapping. In 1982 Wynette entered the Betty Ford clinic to cure her addiction to painkillers, and two years later went bankrupt because of bad investments. Yet she remained as feisty as ever. In 1992, Hillary Clinton said on TV: 'I'm not some little woman standing by her man like Tammy Wynette, staying home and baking cookies.' Wynette was furious, and not until Burt Reynolds interceded on Hillary's behalf was the remark forgiven. Before she died, Wynette's first husband, Euple Byrd, came to see her in concert in Alabama. After the show he asked her hesitantly if she might sign his autograph book. Wynette smiled sweetly and agreed. 'Dream on,' she wrote. 'Dream on.'

The life and loves of the man whose voice defined the twentieth century

FRANK SINATRA

1915-1998

Frank Sinatra was the original pop star, said Mark Steyn in the *Sunday Telegraph*. Not because of his music, which transcended fashion, but because of the adulation he inspired.

Born in Hoboken, New Jersey, in 1915, he was the only child of Italian immigrant parents. His mother Dolly was a formidable figure, whom Frank nicknamed 'the Force'. A midwife and back-street abortionist, she nagged her husband into hen-pecked impotence, but she doted on young Frank. When, inspired by Bing Crosby, he decided he wanted to be a crooner, she bought him his first microphone, and encouraged him to sing in local clubs.

Sinatra's big break came in 1940, when he was signed up by big-band leader Tommy Dorsey, whose trombone-playing taught him about breath control. His first big hit, 'I'll Never Smile Again' was with Dorsey. By 1942, he felt confident enough to launch a solo career – he pulled it off in style. At the Paramount theatre, New York, the bobby-soxers went wild, screaming and fainting in front of their hero. Sinatra made people feel he was singing just for them, and they loved him for it. His timing, too, was fortunate. As he later reflected, 'It was the war years, and there was a great loneliness. I was the boy in every corner drugstore, the boy who'd gone off to war.'

By 1943, there were 2,000 Sinatra fan clubs in the USA, and over the next nine years 'the Voice' had 86 hits and sold ten million records a year. However, Sinatra's career took a nose dive in 1949, thanks to his links with the mob and his high-profile affair with Ava Gardner. But Sinatra hustled his way back, and was performing into his seventies. He also became a hero to many pop stars. As Bruce Springsteen put it, 'His voice was filled with bad attitude and sex, and a sad knowledge of the world.'

A brush with Mario Puzo: His links with the mob

Outside Frank Sinatra's Palm Springs estate was a sign that read: 'Forget the dog, beware of the man.' It was, said Kitty Kelly in the *Daily Mail*, a fitting notice for a man always dogged by his mafia connections. Brought up among the hoods and hoodlums of smalltown America, he never lost his admiration for the Mob. As he said himself: 'I was a saloon singer and the joints I played were owned by the mob. You didn't meet many Nobel prize winners in those places.'

> **His mother Dolly nagged her husband into hen-pecked impotence, but she doted on young Frank.**

Perhaps more than anything, it was Mario Puzo's book *The Godfather* that tarred Sinatra with the Mafia brush. He was always thought to be the model for Johnny Fontaine, a fading crooner who uses mafia connections to force Hollywood to give him plum roles – most famously, by leaving a horse's head in a producer's bed. Sinatra once encountered Mario Puzo in a restaurant and became puce with anger, screaming abuse. Puzo fled, with Sinatra shouting after him: 'Choke. Go ahead and choke, you pimp.'

Sinatra's mob links put paid to his political ambitions. He backed Kennedy's presidential campaign, but, when Kennedy won, he was advised to put some distance between himself and Sinatra. And when the president was due to visit Palm Springs, Sinatra was so sure he would stay with him that he installed a 'hot line' telephone and ordered a helicopter pad. When Sinatra heard that Kennedy was going to stay with Bing Crosby instead, he flew into a furious rage and tried to smash up the helipad with a sledgehammer.

Creating the world's biggest fast-food chain

RICHARD McDONALD

1909-1998

When, in 1940, Dick McDonald and his brother Maurice opened their first drive-by burger joint in San Bernardino, California, they little imagined that one day McDonald's would become the world's biggest fast-food chain; or that they would be blamed for corrupting the world's eating habits.

The brothers, said *The Times*, had migrated from New Hampshire to California in the late 1920s with just one aim: to make $1 million by the time they were 50. They began by working in the Hollywood film industry, but by the late 1930s decided to change tack, and opened a hot dog stand in Arcadia, outside LA. It was a success and they began looking around for new ventures. This was the time when the car was king – and they hit upon the idea of feeding people in a way which didn't require them to get out of their Chevrolets. The result was the San Bernardino 'car-hop'. A car-hop, explained Christopher Reed in *The Guardian*, was a young woman in a short skirt, who brought customers their orders as they waited in their cars. After 1945, however, as motorways proliferated, the brothers decided their customers needed an even faster service, and opened a new style of eatery in which customers drove in, chose from a menu and collected their orders on paper plates at the next window. The menu was simple: Hamburger, 15 cents; Cheeseburger, 19 cents; Fries, 10 cents; Malts (milkshakes), 20 cents. Dick – the marketing genius of the two – coined the slogan 'Millions Served' (later amended to 'Billions Served'), and designed the Golden Arches in the shape of an 'M' to sit on the roof of the restaurant. This, said Daniel Jeffreys in the *Daily Mail*, was the beginning of the end: the 'golden age' when families sat together in American diners was being 'stomped underfoot'. The McDonalds had created 'an unstoppable monster, a Godzilla of low culture that gave birth to the phrase "junk food". In his wake Dick McDonald has left a world that will never recover the innocence lost when it first tasted a Big Mac.'

> **The McDonalds had created 'an unstoppable monster, a Godzilla of low culture that gave birth to the phrase "junk food"'.**

Initially the new self-service concept was slow to catch on, but by 1954 the brothers had managed to open eight new sites. The following year they sold their US franchise to a milkshake machine salesman called Roy Kroc for $2.7 million – the equivalent of $24 million today. In 1961, Kroc bought the world rights. Dick McDonald remained a consultant until the 1970s when he and Kroc fell out over Kroc's claim that the burger chain was his creation. Today there are 34,000 outlets in 119 countries, including Japan, China and Russia. It is said that a new McDonald's will open somewhere in the world every three hours. There are some local variations. In India, the burgers are made from lamb; in Israel, there's a choice between kosher and non-kosher. But the restaurants are near-identical, said Jeffreys: any sense of a country's history 'is destroyed by the smell of cooking oil and the sight of Mr McDonald's name in letters 28ft high'.

Auschwitz survivor who married Anne Frank's father

ELFRIEDE FRANK

1905-1998

Life could hardly have seemed bleaker to Elfriede 'Fritzi' Markovits as she travelled home on the train returning Auschwitz survivors to Holland. She and her daughter Eva had survived the war, but the fates of her husband Erich and son Heinz were unknown. Her worst fears were later confirmed by the Red Cross: Heinz had died of exhaustion after a forced march from Auschwitz and Erich had perished just three days before the end of the war.

A chance meeting on the train, however, was to provide Fritzi's life with a new purpose. Her daughter Eva recognised the father of one of her friends, Anne Frank. Otto Frank and Fritzi became friends and drew strength from each other. 'By the tragedy in both our lives,' Fritzi said, 'together we found new happiness.' Back in Amsterdam, Otto discovered the diary which his daughter Anne had written while in hiding. He read out extracts to Fritzi and they decided it was too important to keep to themselves. It was published in 1947. Following its success, they found themselves inundated with mail which they spent up to eight hours a day replying to, said Laura Stadler in *The Independent*. Otto and Fritzi married in 1953, and devoted the rest of their lives to educating the world about the Holocaust.

Elfriede Markovits was born in Vienna but fled Austria with her husband,

Erich Geiringer, and their two children after the Nazi invasion. They settled in the Jewish quarter of Amsterdam across the street from the Frank family and it was there that her daughter Eva made friends with Anne. But when Germany invaded Holland in 1940, the family were forced into hiding. For safety, they split up and Elfriede found herself alone with Eva. In May 1944, on Eva's 15th birthday, they were raided by the Gestapo. Desperate to save Eva, Fritzi grabbed the arm of a Dutch Nazi. 'My daughter is not Jewish,' she pleaded. 'I had an affair with a non-Jew, my dentist. She's not really Jewish.' They were taken in filthy cattle truck to Birkenau, the largest of the Auschwitz camps. Elfriede, fearing that Eva would be sent straight to the gas chambers with the other children, made her wear her large coat and stylish hat despite the boiling heat. It probably saved Eva's life.

'My daughter is not Jewish,' she pleaded. 'I had an affair with a non-Jew, my dentist. She's not really Jewish.'

In the long months in the camp, Elfriede suffered starvation, disease and torture but, said the *Daily Telegraph*, she managed to stay with her daughter, often giving Eva her own meagre rations. Only once were they separated, for two months. When they were reunited, Eva hardly recognised her mother. 'A pitiful figure with a shaved head jerked upright and stared at me in disbelief. Her gaunt face mouthed "Evertje" and then she grasped hold of my hand … we lay cuddling each other for days.' They comforted each other by planning what they would do when free again, imagining warm baths with soap, clean sheets and glorious menus. They were eventually liberated by the advancing Soviet army on 27 January 1945. The war had left them devastated and exhausted but, as Eva later said, 'our deep, deep bond pulled us through.'

'I'll save your life, but first I'll sing you a little song'

GENE AUTRY

1907-1998

'Them bandits have beaten my mother, ravished my girl, burned down my house, killed my cattle and blinded my best friend. I'm goin' to get 'em if it's the last thing I do. But first, folks, I'm gonna sing you a little song.' That, said the *Daily Telegraph*, just about sums up the plot of the average Gene Autry movie. It was a plot recycled in countless B-movies with names like *Tumbling Tumbleweeds* or *In Old Santa Fe* (in which Autry was billed as a 'tuneful cowpuncher'). In total he made 90 feature films (or 'horse operas' as he jokingly called them) and, in most, Autry appeared with his sidekick Frog (Smiley Burnette), and his trusty 'hoss' Champion. Champion hit the British headlines in 1939 when, as part of a publicity tour, Autry rode him up the steps into the Savoy Hotel.

Autry's songs were generally unrelated to the plots of his films, but the musical format proved such a crowd-puller that even John Wayne at one time felt obliged to appear as 'Singin' Sandy'. Critics were baffled by it. How, asked one, could 'such a weak and colourless actor and only a passable action performer' be so popular? Even Autry himself was puzzled, said Dennis Gifford in *The Independent*. 'I'm no great actor, I'm no great rider, I'm no great singer. But whatever it is I've got, they seem to like it.' Autry was also successful on radio and records and was best known, perhaps, for the song 'Rudolph The Rednosed Reindeer', which he recorded in 1949. But whatever he sang, said the *Daily Telegraph*, he was careful to look the part of a Westerner. 'The owner of 300 pairs of cowboy boots, and an equal number of cowboy suits, he helped establish Western clothes as the standard dress for Country singers.'

Autry's image as the screen cowboy was not entirely bogus. His father had been an itinerant cattle farmer and, as a boy, Autry had helped to drive cattle to the railway station. It was his grandfather, however, 'the singin' baptist minister', who set him on his singing career when he co-opted him into the church choir. One of the first stars to allow his name to be used for advertising purposes, Autry invested his money shrewdly and built up a considerable fortune. Besides TV and radio companies, he owned petrol stations, oil wells, hotels and part of the California Angels basketball team. But fame and wealth never turned his head. As he himself wrote in his autobiography, *Back in the Saddle Again*, he was always 'just an average guy'.

> **How could 'such a weak and colourless actor and only a passable action performer' be so popular? Even Autry himself was puzzled.**

The code-cracking genius who helped foil the Nazis

TOMMY FLOWERS

1905-1998

Tommy Flowers played a crucial role in cracking Nazi Germany's most sophisticated codes during the Second World War. Working with the wartime intelligence team at Bletchley Park, he built a code-breaking machine called Colossus, a device that not only had a profound effect on the course of the war, but is widely accepted as being the world's first working computer. 'The work at Bletchley may not in itself have won the war,' said *The Times*, 'but it undoubtedly made it shorter, perhaps by two years or more.'

The early code-breaking, overseen by mathemetician Alan Turing, was all done by hand, and famously succeeded in cracking the Enigma code, providing vital information on the everyday movements of German forces. But Flowers was involved in a perhaps even more remarkable achievement, said the *Daily Telegraph*: 'the breaking of the enciphered teleprinter communications used by Hitler to talk to his generals'. These higher levels of intelligence were vastly harder to crack. The code-breakers initially used a mechanical computing machine known as Heath Robinson to help them. But when this failed, Turing, who knew of Flowers' earlier work with telephone systems for the Post Office, suggested he be called in.

A year later, in December 1943, Flowers presented the first working prototype of Colossus. The size of a small room, and weighing a ton, Colossus could process 5,000 characters a second, dramatically improving both the speed and accuracy of the decryption process. It was decisive in stopping Rommel from taking Egypt after decoding a message from Hitler to the Afrika Korps, which was then passed to General Montgomery. An improved model of Colossus went on to be invaluable in the preparations for D-Day.

By the end of the war, 11 Colossi were in operation. All but one were destroyed on Churchill's orders; the last remaining machine was taken to GCHQ in Cheltenham, where it remained in use until the early 1960s. Flowers returned to the Post Office and continued his work on electronic telephone systems, which led to the development of modern direct dialling. He was appointed MBE for his war work, but his vital contribution to the breaking of the Nazi codes remained a secret, even to his family, until the early 1970s. In 1980, he met Boris Hagelin,

> **Colossus not only had a profound effect on the course of the war, it is widely accepted as being the world's first working computer.**

inventor of the German coding machines, said the *Daily Mail*. 'I never regarded Herr Hagelin's machine as an enemy,' he remarked. 'It was just an interesting problem. It is a great pleasure to see someone I had "known" for so many years without having met.'

Tight-fisted millionaire who lived on £5 a week

FRANK FARMER

1925–1999

When pensioner Frank Farmer made one of his rare visits to the bank, he was he was taken for a tramp and thrown out. 'It was an understandable mistake,' said Paul Bracchi in the *Daily Mail*: he was after all dressed in an old raincoat tied together with binding string and a worn-out pair of wellingtons. But what the staff did not realise was that the scruffy old man was a multi-millionaire property tycoon. Indeed, he owned the building he had just been ejected from.

Only after his death did the strange history of the eccentric recluse from Staffordshire begin to emerge. His property business was established by his father. Together with his late brother Walter, Frank Farmer – known by his middle name, Alan – built up the portfolio of properties, believed to be worth up to £5 million. A man of few words, he became a virtual hermit after the death of Walter in 1980. Few ever guessed at his fortune. He apparently survived on no more than £5 a week; he was so tight-fisted that once he even sent an employee back into a bank to find an elastic band that had fallen off a wad of notes. After he suffered a heart attack, he refused to buy a walking stick, but would steady his progress with a 'totally unsuitable' five-foot-long fence post.

His six-bedroom farmhouse near the market town of Tutbury, which was 'marooned in a sea of weeds and rusty old cars', was unheated and illuminated by just three lightbulbs (he would move between them by the light of a candle). Rare visitors to his house would find him of an evening sitting in his car on his driveway, reading the papers by the interior light.

Farmer was unmarried. His fortune passed to two first cousins he hardly knew.

Playwright who shocked the critics with her 'feast of filth'

SARAH KANE

1971-1999

In 1995, when the Royal Court Theatre staged *Blasted*, a play by unknown 22-year-old Sarah Kane, nothing had prepared the audience for what was to come. The play, set on a Bosnian battlefield, features scenes of fellatio, homosexual rape, masturbation, defecation, eye-gouging and baby-eating – 'a disgusting feast of filth', according to the *Daily Mail*'s Jack Tinker. Yet, as furious headlines demanded that it be banned, audiences flocked to see it. It was later performed all over Europe where there was an intense curiosity about what Kane's work 'said about modern Britain', said Michael Billington in *The Guardian*. The publicity catapulted Sarah Kane to instant notoriety and won her commissions to write further works in a similar vein.

Her next play, *Phaedra's Love*, was a modern version of the ancient Greek tale of Phaedra, who falls for her stepson, Hippolytus, and commits suicide when he rejects her. In the hands of Euripedes and Racine, the gore was kept offstage. In Kane's version, however, Hippolytus is a terminal depressive who masturbates into his socks; Phaedra gives blow jobs; Theseus rapes his daughter to enthusiastic cheers; Hippolytus's penis is cut off and sizzles on a barbecue. 'It's not a theatre critic that's required here,' wrote the *Daily Telegraph*'s Charles Spencer, 'it's a psychiatrist.'

Kane was born in Essex, where her father was East Anglian correspondent for the *Daily Mirror*. Her parents were obsessive Christians. 'It was spirit-filled, born-again lunacy,' she later said. The theatre gripped her from an early age; she gained a First in drama at Bristol university and, after graduating, moved to London where she lived on state benefits and wrote monologues.

She had wide support. To Harold Pinter, she was 'facing something true and ugly and painful'. Mark Ravenhill in *The Independent* claimed 'she had a sensibility that would have been recognised by Shakespeare, Sophocles or Racine.' Shortly before her suicide at the

'It's not a theatre critic that's required here,' said the *Daily Telegraph*, 'it's a psychiatrist.'

age of 28, she began to appeal to a wider audience. *Crave*, performed at the Edinburgh Festival in 1998, impressed her erstwhile critcs with its lyricism, yet Kane felt they had missed the point: 'People think that *Crave* is the most uplifting and hopeful thing I've written, yet it ends in suicide and despair.'

The man who convinced Einstein there was a God

YEHUDI MENUHIN

1916-1999

Yehudi Menuhin was, quite simply, the most famous musician on Earth, said Norman Lebrecht in the *Daily Telegraph*. His name was synonymous with greatness, even to people who never listened to classical music. And yet he was neither the world's greatest violinist, nor the most commanding presence on a concert stage. Technically, he was outshone by such geniuses as Fritz Kreisler and Jascha Heifetz. But he had perhaps the greatest quality of all: charisma.

Menuhin was born in New York to prosperous Russian Jewish immigrants. They named him Yehudi ('Jew') to make a statement to an anti-Semitic landlady. At the age of 3, he heard Louis Persinger, leader of the San Francisco Symphony Orchestra, and demanded a violin of his own. He was given a toy one, but smashed it when it wouldn't 'sing'. Menuhin's emerging talent was spotted by his tyrannical mother, said Tony Palmer in *The Guardian*, who subordinated everything to her son's career. His sister, Yaltah, was shorn and locked in a cupboard when she protested about the regime. Yehudi was not allowed to ride a bicycle for fear of injuring his fingers; he did not even cross a road alone until he was 18. His other sister, Hephzibah, once mourned for the young Yehudi, who had been 'so repressed, so beaten, so thwarted and humiliated'.

Menuhin hit the headlines at the age of 10, when he performed Beethoven's Violin Concerto in Carnegie Hall, New York. On being told his soloist's age, the conductor Fritz Busch complained: 'one doesn't hire Jackie Coogan [a child actor] to play Hamlet'. But he soon revised his opinion, telling Menuhin: 'You can play anything with me, any time, anywhere.' By the time of Menuhin's Berlin debut in 1929, news of the prodigy had spread, and the police had to be called in to control the crowd. Albert Einstein, who was in the audience that night, hugged Menuhin after the concert, saying, 'Now I know there is a God in Heaven.'

Menuhin began touring in earnest, but his mother stayed close to his side, refusing to relinquish control over his life. She even arranged his first marriage, to a beautiful Australian called Nola Nicholas. But Nola couldn't stand her mother-in-law's constant interference and the marriage foundered. It was, perhaps, to escape his mother that Menuhin moved to England in the 1950s, with his second wife, the ballet dancer Diana Gould.

Menuhin began to make gramophone records in 1928. What remains perhaps his most famous recording took place in London in 1932, when the 16-year-old

On a plane back from Warsaw, he started writing on a sick bag: 'Oh, it's just my ideas for a solution to the Northern Ireland crisis,' he explained.

recorded Elgar's Violin Concerto, with the composer conducting. After a short rehearsal and discussion of the finer points at the Grosvenor House Hotel, Elgar declared himself satisfied and went off to the races. He described the violinist as 'the most wonderful artist I have ever heard'. Menuhin himself had no patience for either the process or the results of recording music – 'I don't listen to music that's already canned,' he once said, 'just as I don't eat canned food.' He nevertheless made countless records during his long career. Once, on an ocean liner, he heard a recording of the concerto, and wished he could have played it so well. Later, he discovered that it was his own recording, made with Wilhelm Furtwängler in 1947.

But Menuhin's greatness was not confined to performance. As a boy it had been Yehudi who settled disputes in the family; later he fulfilled a similar role in music and politics. It was his intention, he said, to leave the world a better place than it was when he entered it, and he believed music could be used to that end. During the war he played over 500 concerts for Allied troops. Then, in July 1945, with Benjamin Britten, he toured the recently liberated Nazi death camps. At Belsen, the skeletal inhabitants lined up before him. 'I shall not forget that afternoon as long as I live,' he later wrote. Neither did the survivors, several of whom, in the years that followed, came to see him backstage.

But two years later, Menuhin, never afraid 'to pit conviction against received wisdom', enraged his Jewish brethren by performing with the Berlin Philharmonic. His aim, he said was to rehabilitate German music and the German spirit. In 1950 he played in Israel but ambivalent about Israeli nationhood, he later gave benefit concerts for Palestinian refugees. The violinist Tasmin Little recalled in *The Independent* how, on a plane back from Warsaw, he started writing on a sick bag: 'Oh, it's just my ideas for a solution to the Northern Ireland crisis,' he explained. Menuhin's interest in politics never left him. On the Tuesday before he died, he wrote to Britain's then Chancellor, Gordon Brown, congratulating him on his Budget.

In music, too, he built bridges. He played Indian ragas with the sitar player Ravi Shankar and duets with the jazz violinist Stephane Grapelli. In 1963 he founded the Yehudi Menuhin school of music in Surrey, where he waived fees for promising pupils from low-income families. Nigel Kennedy was one of them. Small, fastidious and deeply spiritual, Menuhin was a follower of Indian mysticism and a devotee of yoga. When he died, he said, he wanted 'whatever will reunite me most quickly with the sources of life accompanied by folk music and dance. Back to the earth, under a tree or in a river. That is what I choose.'

Editor of *Vogue* who hated snobbery

LIZ TILBERIS

1947-1999

Liz Tilberis was something of a maverick in the fashion world, said *The Times*. The editor of two of the world's glossiest magazines seemed too down-to-earth for such a glamorous profession, but her kindly exterior concealed a fighting spirit and a ruthless will to succeed.

Born Elizabeth Kelly, the daughter of an eye surgeon, Liz was always a rebel, said Avril Morrison in *The Independent*. At Malvern Girls' College she refused to be confirmed, stating: 'I don't believe in God.' Later, she was expelled from Leicester Polytechnic for having a boyfriend in her room. But Liz, who had been devouring *Vogue* since the age of 12, was determined to study fashion. Applying for a place at the Jacob Kramer Art College in Leeds, she was interviewed by Andrew Tilberis. Noting the Leicester report, he said, 'We don't have hookers here,' and dismissed her work as the output of a boarding-school dilettante. But when she embarked on a long, enthusiastic speech he changed his mind. They married in 1971.

In 1969, Tilberis entered a *Vogue* talent contest. She didn't win, but it led to her being given a job. Starting at the bottom, she gradually worked her way up. In many respects, said Sally Brampton in *The Independent*, she revolutionised the fashion pages. Images of languid models would be combined with pictures of laughing women, children, even dogs. At the same time, she fought against the elitism and snobbery inherent in the magazine, and virtually invented the notion of affordable chic. As editor from 1987, her greatest coup was persuading her friend, Diana, Princess of Wales, to pose for the cover.

Tilberis, who was devoted to her husband and their two adopted sons, was attractive, but never claimed to be a stunner. 'Fashion editors who look too good make models feel bad' was her motto. When she moved to New York in 1992 to revitalise *Harper's Bazaar*, she was a size 14 – 'which is practically illegal in our business', as she put it in her autobiography, *No Time to Die*. The press referred to her as 'bovine'.

> **'Fashion editors who look too good make models feel bad' was her motto.**

In 1993, Tilberis was diagnosed with ovarian cancer. But, her spirit undiminished, she went on working, campaigned to raise cancer awareness, and chose not to move back to England, where she had never felt appreciated. In England, she said, she was dismissed as 'just' the editor of a fashion magazine. In New York, on the other hand, 'they call me Million Dollar Liz. I'll take Manhattan.'

No-nonsense approach of a brave pilot

GROUP CAPTAIN PADDY GREEN

1914-1999

Group Captain Paddy Green was a wartime fighter pilot who demanded the highest standards from his men. A tough, no-nonsense officer, he didn't suffer fools gladly, said the *Daily Telegraph*, and once even reprimanded a young pilot for failing to shoot him down.

Early in 1943, Green was commanding a squadron in North Africa. On one exercise, Flying Officer Rob Sprag, a burly South African with a devil-may-care approach, mistook Green's Bristol Beaufighter for an enemy Ju 88, and opened fire. Green took evading action, and fired a recognition signal. But it was the wrong one, and Sprag closed in, all guns blazing. Just as the plane was escaping for a second time, he realised to his horror that it was another Beaufighter. Back on the ground, Green gave his junior a firm dressing-down. 'You're a bloody bad pilot,' he barked. 'You should be ashamed I'm still able to talk to you. From where you came up behind me you should have destroyed my Beau with your first shot. The wrong identification is forgivable, bad shooting isn't.'

Green was born in South Africa in 1914. Educated at Harrow and Cambridge, he was a skilled athlete who won a bronze medal with the British bobsleigh team in the 1936 Winter Olymplics. In wartime, as a Spitfire pilot with the No 92 (East India) Squadron, he covered the evacuation of Dunkirk and took part in the Battle of Britain. In 1942, he appeared in *The First of the Few*, a flag-waving film about the birth of the Spitfire. Ironically, he played an enemy bomber pilot. A valiant flyer, who survived the war despite numerous injuries, he was credited with 11 confirmed kills and was awarded the DSO in 1943.

Bookshop legend famous for her lunches

CHRISTINA FOYLE

1911-1999

Christina Foyle was one of literary London's most eccentric figures, said the *Evening Standard*. She ran her vast bookshop, W&G Foyle Ltd, like her own personal empire, maintaining it as a time capsule, unaltered for 50 years. A woman of steely determination (she once wrote to Hitler to ask if, rather than burning books, he would sell them to her) she was also the driving force behind the famous Foyle's literary luncheons.

Foyle's was founded in 1904 by Christina Foyle's father, William, and his brother, Gilbert, the two sons of an East End grocer. Miss Foyle, as she was known by her staff, joined the family firm at the age of 18. She worked surrounded by authors: Arthur Conan Doyle was a family friend; Arnold Bennett was a regular customer, who showed her the ancient £5 note he always carried to give to the first person he spotted reading one of his books.

It was encounters like these that inspired the young woman to tart up the literary luncheons, said Quentin Letts in the *Daily Mail*. Held monthly, originally in the old-fashioned surroundings of the Dorchester Hotel, speakers at these 'quirky, kitsch and slightly boozy' affairs included some of the biggest names of the day: from A.A. Milne to Charlie Chaplin, from

J.B. Priestley to Edith Sitwell. The food was invariably chicken or salmon, and the audiences of up to 2,000 were largely made up of little old ladies in hats. In the 1940s, the acid-bath murderer John Haigh was a regular ticket-holder, as was his last victim, Mrs Durand-Deacon. In 69 years, Foyle missed only two lunches. When her husband died, she sent a note simply announcing: 'Miss Foyle has a cold.'

Speeches were usually short and funny. An exception was Sir Walter Gilbey, who droned on for 90 minutes. A man at the top table fell asleep, so someone hit him with the toastmaster's gavel. 'Hit me again,' the man cried, 'I can still hear Sir Walter.' At another lunch, said the *Daily Telegraph*, the theme was convicts. Foyle borrowed a waxwork effigy of the murderer Charlie Pearce and sat it next to the chairman. At the end of the lunch, one guest tried to shake the dummy's hand, having mistaken it for the Secretary of State for Scotland. 'Nearly right,' someone remarked, 'but I think you'll find the Secretary of State less lively.'

At the lunches, Foyle, a tiny, latterly grey-haired figure with a reedy, little-girl voice, kept in the background. But in the shop, her style was 'not so much autocratic as profoundly feudal', said the *Evening Standard*. Following her father's death in 1963, she insisted on preserving its eccentricities – not always to the benefit of the customer. Books were displayed by publisher rather than by author, making them notoriously difficult to find. A high turnover of staff, including large numbers of foreigners, made matters still worse: one customer who asked where to find *Ulysses* was told he was on his lunch break. The last straw for many was the demented sales procedure, which involved carrying chits from one desk to another. As one customer commented, it was as though Kafka had gone into the book trade. The inevitable stream of perplexed book buyers led a rival to run an advertisement outside the shop reading: 'Foyled again? Try Dillons.'

As an employer, Foyle, who was married but childless, had a terrible reputation. Employees were kept on the shortest of contracts and paid the most meagre of wages. One day in 1956, said the *Evening Standard*, she sacked 40 women for talking too loudly in the post room. As recently as 1932, she threatened to close the business rather than be forced by an industrial tribunal to reinstate two employees. But to the end, Foyle remained unrepentant about her methods. On the fall of another iron lady, she commented: 'It's a shame about Mrs Thatcher. Luckily, they can't chuck me out – I own the place, you see.'

Maverick who brought lunacy into politics

LORD DAVID SUTCH

1940-1999

Screaming Lord Sutch was one of Britain's best-loved eccentrics, said the *Daily Telegraph*. A born entertainer, he gained a taste for publicity as a rock star, before emerging in politics as the leader of the Official Monster Raving Loony Party (OMRLP). Although he never won a seat in Parliament, his zany antics made him better known than many MPs, and for 30 years his 'manic grin', rosette-encrusted jacket and leopardskin top hat were a 'staple part of election-night entertainment'.

David Edward Sutch was born in Kilburn in 1940. His father was killed in the Blitz and his mother, to whom he was devoted, worked as a cleaner. Having left school at the age of 15, Sutch ran a window-cleaning business before being seduced by the glamour of the rock 'n' roll scene. He auditioned at the Two I's coffee bar in Soho and in 1960 formed a band, the Raving Savages. Sutch was Britain's first long-haired pop star, said the *Independent*, and his act was an outrageous Gothic affair, largely plagiarised from the American performer Screamin' Jay Hawkins. On stage, he would emerge from a coffin before setting fire to his hair and launching into a frenzy of ghoulish songs accompanied by such schlock-horror props as axes and fake human entrails.

As a live performer, Sutch was always in demand, but chart success eluded him (in 1998, one of his albums was voted the worst ever recorded). Frustrated by the pop world, in 1963 he turned his attentions to politics, standing for election for the National Teenager Party in Stratford-upon-Avon, the seat left vacant by John Profumo's resignation. He gathered 209 votes. Going on to challenge prime ministers at every election for 30 years, Lord Sutch – he changed his name by deed poll in 1977 – stood for the Go to Blazes Party and the Green Chicken Alliance before forming the OMRLP in 1983.

To the bemusement of the public, Sutch always insisted that he was serious about entering Parliament. He was certainly a 'shrewd' campaigner, said the *Daily Telegraph*. 'Why is there only one Monopolies Commission?' his manifesto demanded. And many voters warmed to his slogan: 'Vote for Insanity – You Know It Makes Sense!' In retrospect, his ideas were not as absurd as people thought. Several of the policies he formed in the mid-1960s – passports for pets, votes for 18-year-olds and all-day licensing – have since been adopted by mainstream parties. And though he invariably lost his deposit, Sutch's election results were not without significance. In Bootle in 1990, the OMRLP scored more votes than David Owen's Social Democrats, signalling the end of that party. In the aftermath, Sutch suggested an alliance between the parties, and even offered Owen the leadership. Owen, he recalled 'gave a sad little smile and turned it down'.

> **'Why is there only one Monopolies Commission?' his manifesto demanded. 'Vote for Insanity – You Know It Makes Sense!'**

Despite a troubled private life – he was prone to depression and is thought to have taken his own life – Sutch never lost enthusiasm for his party. On the resignation of Margaret Thatcher in 1990, he commented: 'Thatcherism may come and go, but Loonyism, which we believe represents the true spirit of the British people, will go on for ever.'

Muscle-bound film star who refused to do his own stunts

VICTOR MATURE

1913-1999

Victor Mature was the original Hollywood 'beefcake', said the *Daily Mail*. His muscular physique won him legions of female fans, but the critics were always derisive. It didn't worry him unduly. When he was turned down for membership by the Los Angeles Country Club on the grounds that he was an actor, he replied: 'Hell, I'm no actor – and I've got 28 pictures and a scrapbook of reviews to prove it.'

Victor John Mature was born in Kentucky in 1913, the son of an Austrian scissors grinder. Aged 20, he made his way to Hollywood with 11 cents in his pocket and one ambition: to become a film star. After a succession of odd jobs, he was employed by the Pasadena Community Playhouse. He appeared in some 60 plays, before being spotted by film producer Hal Loach. Mature was a sensation in his first film. For his five-minute appearance in *The Housekeeper's Daughter* (1939), he received over 20,000 fan letters.

But it was his stage role in *Lady in the Dark* in 1941 that 'ensured his Hollywood success', said *The Times*. Described as 'the most beautiful hunk of a man you ever saw', he won rave reviews and was signed up for a long-term contract at 20th Century Fox. The studio's publicity machine immediately went into overdrive, dubbing him 'the irresistible male' and 'He-Man of the Year'.

But behind the tough exterior, Mature was, in his own words, a 'devout coward', who refused to do his own stunts, said the *Daily Mail*. When Cecil B. DeMille told him he had to wrestle with a lion during the making of *Samson and Delilah* (1949), Mature baulked. 'He's harmless, he doesn't have a tooth in his head,' pleaded DeMille. Mature replied: 'Mr DeMille, I don't give a damn. I don't even want to be gummed.' Later, DeMille again tried to cajole him into working with a lion, with the assurance that the creature had been raised on milk. 'So was I,' said Mature promptly. 'But now I eat meat.'

Samson and Delilah was a box-office hit – but it probably destroyed Mature's chances of ever being cast in a serious film. Groucho Marx spoke for many when he quipped: 'No picture can hold my interest when the leading man's bust is bigger than the leading lady's.' Thereafter, Mature was largely confined to appearing in trashy, though lucrative, biblical epics. But he had never been precious about the acting profession, and had a gift for self-mockery. 'Actually, I'm a golfer,' he once told an interviewer. 'I never was an actor. Ask anybody – particularly the critics.' And he would disarm difficult directors by saying, 'I have two looks. Which do you want, Number One or Number Two?'

> **DeMille tried to cajole him into working with a lion, with the assurance it had been raised on milk. 'So was I,' said Mature. 'But now I eat meat.'**

But Mature, whose five marriages all ended in divorce, was no fool, said *The Independent*. He invested his earnings in a number of successful business enterprises and in 1962 was able virtually to retire from the film industry. He moved into a luxurious ranch near San Diego, where he played golf nearly every day of the week. 'I loaf very gracefully,' he commented. 'There's a lot to be said for loafing if you know how to do it gracefully.'

Outcast who became 'one of England's stately homos'

QUENTIN CRISP

1908-1999

Quentin Crisp was made famous by the publication of his memoir, *The Naked Civil Servant*. He became a sought-after raconteur, actor and gay icon, said *The Guardian*. But the only cause that Crisp adopted was the right to be himself.

Crisp, who was born Denis Pratt in 1908, believed that homosexuality was in the genes, said the *Daily Mail*. How else, he argued, could you explain the fact that at the age of 6 he would 'float around' in his mother's dresses, declaring: 'Today, I am going to be a beautiful princess?' His parents tolerated his behaviour, but he had a rude awakening at the age of 11, when he was sent to prep school. '[It] was like going to jail,' he recalled. 'And as in jails, it's not the warders you're frightened of but the other inmates.' Having failed to hold down proper jobs, Crisp abandoned all attempts at being 'normal' in his early twenties. He began frequenting seedy cafés in Soho and developed the full-blown persona – lilac eye-shadow, frilly silk blouses and bouffant hair – that became his trademark. 'The time comes for everyone to do deliberately what he used to do by mistake,' he later explained. 'If you are effeminate by nature, you have to find some way of telling the world that you know you are, otherwise they keep telling you.'

It was, he said, a form of 'martyrdom'. He was regularly thrown out of public places, spat upon in the street and beaten up.

During the war, Crisp, who was exempted from army service on the grounds of 'sexual perversion', found a job as an art school nude model, which kept him in work for the next 30 years. As such, he was an employee of the Ministry of Education, which gave him the title of his 1967 autobiography. Its success turned him, as he put it, into 'one of England's stately homos'. It was made into a television film in 1975. He starred in his own critically acclaimed West End show and became a regular guest on chat shows and at smart parties. But fame had its price. From the day after the TV screening, the phone in his Chelsea bedsit rang constantly with death threats. 'Do you wish to make an appointment?' was his response to the anonymous callers.

In the late 1970s, Crisp visited New York and decided to make it his home. Here, among so many oddballs, he didn't stand out. Living in a cramped bedsit on the Lower East Side, he made cameo appearances in a number of films, including playing Elizabeth I in *Orlando*, and held court in local restaurants, regaling members of the public with his unpredictable views. He found Oscar Wilde 'pitiful', described Princess Diana as a 'fag hag' and became increasingly irritated by gay politics. 'I think that gay people have gone too far,' he told *The Independent*. 'When I was really young, you never mentioned it. Now you never talk about anything else.' He felt that the constant call for gay rights was divisive, and angered militants by publicly stating that homosexuality was 'horrible' and 'like having an illness'. 'In England I am frowned on by real people and accepted by gay people,' he said. 'Here I am accepted by the real people and frowned on by the gay people because I cannot deal with the shrillness with which the gay people cope with their fate.'

> 'If you are effeminate by nature, you have to find some way of telling the world that you know you are, otherwise they keep telling you.'

Footballer with 'artistry in his feet and integrity in his soul'

SIR STANLEY MATTHEWS

1915-2000

Sir Stanley Matthews was a sportsman with 'artistry in his feet and integrity in his soul', said the *Daily Mail*. Nicknamed the 'Wizard of the Dribble', he was one of Britain's greatest footballers who, in his heyday, drew crowds around the block wherever he appeared. Other players may have matched his skill, but none have been held in such affection or esteem.

Matthews was born in 1915 in Hanley in the Potteries. His father – a fearsome amateur boxer known as 'the Fighting Barber of Hanley' – bought him a pair of running shoes for his fourth birthday and instilled in him a lifelong passion for physical fitness: he trained rigorously throughout his life, and even in his eighties was up at 6am to do his exercises.

Matthews first made his mark as a sprinter, said the *Daily Telegraph*, but his ball skills were such that by the the time he was 6 or 7, local boys would make a detour just to watch him play. At school, his team won 'by embarrassing totals such as 18-0' and, at the age of 14, Matthews joined Stoke City as a ground boy. For £1 a week, he made tea, cleaned boots, and played for the juniors on Saturdays. The atmosphere was rigidly hierarchical. 'One morning, I went into the dressing room and said, "Good morning", Matthews recalled, 'and the senior players threw me into the bath with my clothes on to teach me a lesson.' He became professional at the first possible opportunity – the day he turned 17 – and his wage went up to £5 a week, with a £1 bonus for every win. When Stoke were promoted to the First Division in the 1933–1934 season, the club's directors celebrated by giving each player a three-piece suit. In the days before TV, Matthews' reputation was such that his mere presence on the wing could add 10,000 to the gate, but he was never paid more than £20 a week.

Matthews, who retired shortly after his 50th birthday, played more than 700 league games; he made 84 international appearances and won 55 England caps. He was, said *The Independent*, the last surviving member of the team that – at the insistence of the Foreign Office – gave the Nazi salute at the Berlin Olympics of 1938, before thrashing the Germans 6-3. 'A lot of fuss was made,' Matthews later said, 'but it was the result that mattered.' After the war, during which he joined the RAF, Matthews returned to Stoke City, but two years later was transferred to Blackpool for £11,500 and a bottle of whisky. It was with Blackpool that the small, wiry Matthews made his most famous appearance in the 1953 cup final. With 20 minutes to go, Blackpool were 1-3 down to Bolton when Matthews sprung into life, and turned the game around to give Blackpool a 4-3 victory. The game went down in history as the Matthews Final.

By the mid-1950s, his reputation was such that defenders who tried to foul him could expect to be jeered by their own supporters. In 1961, he rejoined Stoke City and in a 1962 match against Chelsea at Stamford Bridge, in front of 60,000 Chelsea supporters, Matthews, then 48, was fouled by Chelsea's hard man Ron Harris. The stadium fell silent. 'It was very strange,' recalled the Chelsea player John Hollins. 'One minute our supporters were right behind the team, willing our players on, then they went silent. It was as though they felt that the promotion didn't amount to much if we had to foul Stan Matthews to get it.' In his 33-year career Matthews was never booked, said the *Express*, and he would never have dreamed of resorting to the antics that are all too common in today's game. 'I'll tell you how different it was when I started,' he said. 'Before the war, if you got sent off you were booed by your own fans. If you got sent off while playing for England you never played for England again.' In 1965, he became the first player to be knighted. 'I'm no hero,' he said with typical modesty. 'Doctors and nurses are heroes. I'm just an ordinary man.'

The first woman
to be awarded
the George Cross

DAPHNE PEARSON

1911-2000

In May 1940, Daphne Pearson was working at the sick quarters of the RAF base in Detling, Kent. At about 1am on 31 May, she was woken by the sound of a plane in distress, said the *Daily Telegraph*. She got up at once, pulled on her clothes and dashed outside in time to see it slam into the ground.

'A guard told me to stop but I said, "No"', she recalled. 'I ran on, opening the gate for an ambulance to get through.'

As she approached the aircraft, others appeared on the scene. 'Leave him to me,' she yelled. 'Go and get the fence down for the ambulance.' Single-handedly, she dragged the injured pilot away from the blaze and had just got him behind a ridge when the petrol tanks blew up. Pearson threw herself on top of him to shield him from flying splinters, and placed her helmet over his head. The plane was loaded with bombs and, moments after the pilot was stretchered away, another vast explosion shook the ground. Undaunted, Pearson rushed back to the wreckage to look for the plane's wireless operator, but he was dead. She then returned to the base, and helped treat the wounded through the night. The next morning, she was on duty as usual at 8am.

In July 1940, she was awarded the Empire Gallantry Award, becoming the first woman to receive an award for gallantry during the Second World War. It was converted to a George Cross in 1941. Sir Winston Churchill praised her action in the House of Commons.

After the war, Pearson, a vicar's daughter, studied horticulture and worked at the Royal Botanical Gardens in Kew.

Oscar-winning actor who avoided the limelight

ALEC GUINNESS

1914-2000

Alec Guinness was the last of the great character actors, said John Mortimer in *The Independent*. A master of disguise with a gift for acute observation, he immersed himself so thoroughly in each character that no hint of the actor could be seen. His versatility was most famously displayed in the classic comedy *Kind Hearts and Coronets*, in which he played eight members of the D'Ascoyne family bumped off by Dennis Price on his way to becoming the Duke of Chalfont. With typical modesty, Guinness later described his performance as 'pretty cardboard'.

'Yet if Guinness seemed capable of adapting himself to almost any role,' said the *Daily Telegraph*, 'his own personality remained elusive.' An intensely private man, he managed to write two volumes of autobiography without giving away anything of himself. Even his parentage remains something of a mystery. His friend John le Carré claimed: 'He was the illegitimate son of a prostitute who was once called upon to service the male members of the Guinness family when their yacht sailed into port. His mother subsequently found herself pregnant, and named her son in the hope that he might be the product of an aristocratic liaison.' But blood tests – taken by the Guinnesses, who longed to claim him when he became famous – showed that he was not. Guinness himself believed that his father was a Scottish bank director named Andrew Geddes, whom he met four or five times as a child, but the question was never resolved. 'I have to admit that my search for a father has been my constant speculation for 50 years,' he wrote in his autobiography.

By the age of 14, Alec had lived in 30 different lodgings, mainly along the south coast of England. 'Each,' he recalled, 'was hailed as 'home' until such time as my mother and I flitted, leaving behind a wake of unpaid bills. When he was 5, his mother married a Scots army captain named Stiven, who held a loaded revolver to the boy's head on one occasion, and suspended him upside down from a bridge on another. So it was a relief when, at the age of 6, he was sent to boarding school. At the age of 17, he took a job in a London advertising agency where he wrote copy extolling the merits of lime juice and razor blades. But he spent every spare penny on theatre tickets and, 18 months later, plucked up the courage to contact his idol, John Gielgud, for advice on becoming an actor. Gielgud sent him to Martita Hunt for lessons.

In 1933, Guinness applied to the Fay Compton Studio, and was awarded a scholarship. 'I lived on less than 30 shillings a week in a squalid little room on Westbourne Road,' he recalled. 'Walking everywhere, often carrying my shoes to save the leather, I was remarkably healthy and looked uncomfortably thin.' In 1934, his funds ran out and he once again turned to Gielgud for help. Gielgud gave

> **His versatility was displayed in _Kind Hearts and Coronets_, in which he played eight members of the D'Ascoyne family. Guinness described his performance as 'pretty cardboard'.**

him a part in his production of _Hamlet_. Rehearsals, he remembered, were fraught. 'What's happened to you,' thundered the great man. 'I thought you were rather good. You're terrible. Oh, go away! I don't want to see you again.' Gielgud subsequently modified his opinion, and Guinness's performance as Osric was widely praised. Numerous roles followed – until his burgeoning career as a juvenile lead was interrupted by war. He joined the Navy as an ordinary seaman, and within a year received a commission.

'I gave my best performance during the war – trying to be an officer and a gentleman. A small part, but a very long run.'

After the war, Guinness appeared in his first major film role, as the ebullient Herbert Pocket in David Lean's *Great Expectations* (1946). Two year later, Lean cast him as Fagin in *Oliver Twist*. He proved a natural screen performer, said Sheridan Morley in the *Daily Mail*. He said that he could never get into a part until he had learnt the character's walk – a technique he mastered when he was out of work before the war. 'I had nothing to do, so I just followed people around and began to imitate their walks.' Unlike many of his theatrical contemporaries, he understood that when acting in front of the camera, 'less is more'. Guinness continued to work on stage, but it was on screen – in such classics as *The Man in the White Suit* and *Tunes of Glory* – that he excelled. In 1957, he won an Oscar for his portrayal of the half-mad Colonel Nicholson in *The Bridge on the River Kwai*. The film made him an international star, said *The Times*, but he retained his anonymity. He often told the story of how he handed in his coat to a hotel cloakroom and, when he offered to give his name, was pleased to be told that it would not be necessary. The coat was later handed back with the ticket still attached and the inscription 'Bald with glasses'.

> **'A sweet-faced boy told me proudly that he had seen *Star Wars* more than 100 times. Looking into the boy's eyes, I thought I detected little star shells of madness beginning to form.'**

In later life, Guinness, who married the playwright Marula Salaman in 1938, became a devout Catholic. He converted after an encounter in France during the making of the 1954 film *Father Brown*. Walking back to the hotel one evening, and still wearing his cassock, his hand was seized by a small boy who called him *Mon Père* and trotted along beside him, chatting in French. The trust which the Church inspired in the boy made a profound impression. Each morning, Guinness recited a passage from the Psalms – *Cause me to hear your loving kindness in the morning*. 'I think it is a wonderful line,' he said, 'and I say it when I wake up every day.'

Guinness's hatred for *Star Wars*

'Many under the age of 35,' said *The Times*, 'will think of Sir Alec not as the star of Ealing Comedies, of David Lean's epics or even in the television role of the quiet spy, George Smiley, but as Obi-Wan Kenobi in *Star Wars*.' It was not how he would have wished to be remembered. He loathed making the film, described the dialogue as 'absolute rubbish' and grew tired of gormless adolescents asking him to say 'May the Force be with you' in ringing tones. But he could do little to separate himself from the role. 'In March 1997, 20 years after it was released, a refurbished version of the film was put out. As I left a Chinese restaurant one evening, the dapper little maître d' bowed low and, full of Chinese smiles, said: "Sir Guin, now that *Star Wars* is being shown again, you will be famous once more."'

As time went on, he began to worry about the film's cult appeal. 'The bad penny first dropped in San Francisco, when a sweet-faced boy of 12 told me proudly that he had seen *Star Wars* more than 100 times. Looking into the boy's eyes, I thought I detected little star shells of madness beginning to form and I guessed that one day they would explode. "I would love you to do something for me," I said. "Anything! Anything!" the boy said rapturously. "Well, I said. "Do you think you could promise never to see *Star Wars* again?"'

However, the film did make him fabulously rich. Halfway through making it, the producers ran out of money and, in return for waiving his fee, Guinness was awarded a two per cent stake in the profits. This, it has been estimated, made him $120 million. John Mortimer recalled meeting him in a gents' club and admiring his jacket. '"Feel it," he said. "What do you think it's made of?" It was very soft and I guessed "cashmere". "No," his voice rumbled, deeply amused. "Mink." I'm still not sure if he was joking.'

A life dedicated
to an anarchic fox

IVAN OWEN

1927-2000

Ivan Owen was the man behind Basil Brush, the anarchic fox glove-puppet whose 'Boom! Boom!' catchphrase, raucous laugh and club-bore jokes entertained millions of television viewers throughout the 1970s.

Owen devised Basil's character in 1963, said the *Daily Telegraph*. He was a suburban fox with social pretensions, and Owen modelled his aristocratic, slightly caddish tones on those of the British film star Terry Thomas. The puppet itself, with its tweed cape and cravat, was created by Peter Firmin, who later worked on *The Clangers* and *Ivor the Engine*. Basil made his screen debut in 1964, said Anthony Hayward in *The Independent*, and four years later was given his own show – which went on to run for 12 years, drawing audiences of 13 million.

The format was simple, said *The Times*: star guests would come on to the show, only to be upstaged by Basil's monstrous ego. At the end of the programme, one of a series of straight men, including Rodney Bewes and Derek Fowlds, would patiently try to read a story to the fox, 'only to have their tales constantly interrupted with a stream of awful gags and quick-fire one-liners'. The proceedings were, of course, entirely orchestrated by Owen.

But the puppeteer himself remained completely unseen. Believing that Basil's success depended on his own invisibility, Owen rarely gave interviews, and never allowed himself to be photographed. 'The children believe in Basil and never see me, and with so little magic in the world, it would be a shame to appear and kill it,' he said. But adults were also entranced by Basil's irreverent asides. When asked who his favourite TV personality was, Lord Carrington replied, 'Basil Brush, of course, because he says things to people I would love to say.' Basil became an international phenomenon, and Owen, who was married with three children, a millionaire.

Born in 1927, Owen grew up in south London, the son of an architect. He studied drama at Lamda, and made his stage debut at Watford Rep in 1949. By the late 1950s, however, he had moved backstage to become a floor manager for the BBC. 'I'm a failed actor who set out to be another Laurence Olivier,' he once said. 'Now Basil expresses the person I suppose I must be. He wants to be Laurence Olivier.'

> **Asked who his favourite TV personality was, Lord Carrington replied, 'Basil Brush, of course.'**

Red-brick novelist who nurtured a generation of writers

SIR MALCOLM BRADBURY

1932–2000

Sir Malcolm Bradbury, the writer and academic, founded the acclaimed creative writing course at East Anglia University. 'Bradbury wrote as others breathe,' said the *Daily Telegraph*, producing a steady stream of criticism, biographies, novels, short stories and dramas. An extremely erudite writer, he was also gifted with the popular touch. 'He was an intellectual who wrote episodes of *A Touch of Frost*; a pipe-smoking academic who adapted for television the novels of Tom Sharpe.'

Born the son of a railway worker in Sheffield in 1932, Bradbury was a sickly, bookish child who had to undergo a heart operation at an early age. 'Before' and 'After' photographs of the procedure appeared in *The Lancet*, and he was not expected to live beyond 50. He went to West Bridgford grammar school and Leicester University, before taking up a series of teaching posts at universities in Britain and the USA. With his first novel, *Eating People Is Wrong* (1959) and, later, *The History Man* (1970), Bradbury established himself as one of the leading social satirists of the age, said *The Times*. 'He came to be the exemplar of a radical, sceptical spirit which was proudly non-Oxbridge, exposing social mores to a specifically grammar-school and red-brick university-educated sensibility.' *The History Man* is the work for which he will be best remembered, said the *Daily Telegraph*. 'In Howard Kirk, the libidinous left-wing lecturer for whom teaching is a means to manipulate young minds and bodies, Bradbury created one of the great anti-heroes of the age.'

Arguably, however, Bradbury's greatest achievement was setting up the influential creative writing course at East Anglia University in 1970. Inspired by similar courses in the USA, Bradbury and Angus Wilson created an atmosphere that was 'creative, contemporary and exciting', said *The Times*. They made East Anglia a mecca for students 'in search of something less dogmatic and hidebound, more creative and forward looking'. The course was not an immediate success: indeed, there were no applicants until the late summer of the first year, when Bradbury received a telephone call from a graduate of Sussex University who had based his thesis on a Marxist-Freudian interpretation of Enid Blyton's Noddy books. The writer's name was Ian McEwan who, by the end of his first year, had written 20 stories and sketched out the contents of his first two novels.

'I can well believe it,' said Erica Wagner, literary editor of *The Times*. 'I was a writer before I arrived on Malcolm's course but I believed in myself more after I left it. He was a generous, stimulating teacher. To have the belief of a man such as Malcolm was like being given an extra spine.' There

> **'I was a writer before I arrived on Malcolm's course but I believed in myself more after I left it. To have his belief was like being given an extra spine.'**

was 'a liberating feeling' about Malcolm's seminars, said Kasuo Ishiguro, another graduate of the course, in *The Guardian*. 'You could turn up with almost any kind of writing – an intense Joycean monologue, a gritty slice of northern realism, a piece of soft porn – and he would insist the group look at it with seriousness and evaluate it on its own terms.'

Bradbury's oldest and closest literary friend was David Lodge, who paid tribute in *The Times*. 'Our literary careers were so intertwined that I feel some support has been cut away,' he mourned. 'Writing just will not be as much fun any more.'

The model whose cartoon alter ego helped win the war

CHRISTABEL LEIGHTON-PORTER

1913-2000

Christabel Leighton-Porter was described by Winston Churchill as 'Britain's Secret Weapon'. For she was the inspiration for Jane, the curvaceous heroine of the *Daily Mirror*'s cartoon strip who lost her clothes – though not her virtue – in every adventure. Jane became a forces sweetheart and when she first appeared nude in 1944, the sight was credited with inspiring the British 36th Division in Normandy to gain six miles of enemy territory in a single day. 'She was worth two armoured divisions to us,' said one serviceman. 'Three if she lost her bra or pants.'

Created by Norman Pett, Jane first appeared in 1932. At first, Pett used his wife, Mary, as a model. But when the *Daily Mirror* asked him to make the strip more racy, and his wife turned her attention to golf, Pett was forced to look for a more curvaceous model. He found her in 1939, when he spotted Leighton-Porter in a life class. The more risqué strip – in which Jane was forever shutting her skirt in doors, or plunging naked into freezing seas – created a sensation, said the *Daily Mail*. 'Suddenly, I became a sweetheart all over the world,' Leighton-Porter recalled. 'One admiral told me that there wasn't anybody on the ships from the lowest ranking to the highest in the fleet, who didn't have a drawing of Jane in his pocket or on his bunk.' Throughout the war, Jane's 'escapades raised spirits on the Home Front and proved a tonic for the troops', said the *Daily Telegraph*. She was painted on the sides of Spitfires, ships carried bundles of the cartoons to soldiers fighting overseas and the RAF adopted her as its mascot. Leighton-Porter, who spent the war making morale-boosting appearances, received up to 60 marriage proposals a week. (The fact that she was already married to Arthur, an RAF pilot, was kept a closely guarded secret.) She was named 'Britain's Perfect Girl' at the London Palladium, and appeared in a stage show based on the cartoon. This was a great success, although the Lord Chamberlain, as the official censor, was concerned about the amount of clothing removed. Leighton-Porter tried to convince him that she could take her bikini off and still preserve her modesty by covering her chest with her hands. 'I see,' said the Lord Chamberlain, looking sceptically at her embonpoint. 'You must have very large hands.'

Soon after the war, said the *Mirror*, Jane was axed – prompting a wave of complaints. Pett dashed off a sketch showing her peeking from behind a curtain, captioned: 'Give us a break, boys, I've lost my panties.' Over the next few days, the newspaper's offices were deluged with knickers sent in by readers. The cartoon was reinstated and ran until October 1959. It was revived in 1985, and the final Jane strip appeared in 1990.

Leighton-Porter, who remained in constant demand for public appearances, was devoted to her alter ego. 'Now the war is over,' she once said, 'I wouldn't have missed it for the world.'

> **Leighton-Porter tried to convince the official censor that she could cover her chest with her hands. 'I see,' said the Lord Chamberlain, looking sceptically at her embonpoint. 'You must have very large hands.'**

Concert pianist who became the Clown Prince of Denmark

VICTOR BORGE

1909-2000

Known as the Clown Prince of Denmark, Victor Borge was one of the most popular musical entertainers of the 1950s and the 1960s. A pianist-cum-comedian, his one-man show – *Comedy in Music* – ran on Broadway for a record-breaking 849 performances; his records sold in their millions, and he conducted in front of many of the world's leading orchestras. But in his view, his greatest accomplishment, said *The Times*, was that 'I can make people happy.'

Born in Copenhagen in 1909, Victor Borge was the son of a professional violinist. He excelled at the piano from early childhood, and studied at the Danish Conservatory, as well as in Berlin and Vienna. Having made his debut at the age of 13, Borge made his living as a concert pianist until 1934. Then he discovered that his talent for comedy could bring him a good income from the variety halls. But Borge's one-liners were eventually to drive him from his country. He made the Nazis a butt of his jokes – 'What's the difference between a Nazi and a dog? The Nazi lifts his arm' – and when the Germans invaded in 1940, Borge was forced to flee to the USA with just $20 in his pocket. Settling in New York, he found a job doing warm-up routines on radio. He was spotted by Bing Crosby's chief writer and, in 1942, Borge was named 'best new radio performer of the year'. Soon the Great Dane had gained a massive following.

Borge delighted in pricking the pomposity of classical musicians, said the *Daily Telegraph*. 'Do you want some modern music?' he would ask. 'Or would you rather stay?' Preparing to play a piece by Aaron Copland, he told the audience: 'This is a sonata he wrote very early. [Pause] He should have stayed in bed.' His humour ranged from the slapstick to the surreal. In one sketch, he strode on stage, walked briskly towards the podium, and, without stopping, climbed from the piano stool onto the piano itself. He then looked around, as if he had just come to his senses, got off the piano and announced to the audience: 'This instrument was designed on the plans of a famous swimming pool.' Sitting down, he went to strike a chord, but, the lid being down, his hand hit the wood. 'No water,' he finally murmured.

> '**Do you want some modern music?' he would ask. 'Or would you rather stay?'**

Borge was received at the White House by every American president since Roosevelt and honoured in numerous European countries. 'After being knighted five times,' he quipped, 'I became a weekend.'

Awe-inspiring dancer who founded the Royal Ballet

NINETTE DE VALOIS

1898-2001

Dame Ninette de Valois was the driving force in British ballet for more than 70 years, said the *Daily Telegraph*. Tenacious, far-sighted and benevolently autocratic, she founded the company that became the Royal Ballet and brought together one of the dance world's most magical partnerships, that of Margot Fonteyn and Rudolph Nureyev. Such was her personal reputation that colleagues, critics and teachers alike stood in awe of 'Madam', as she was invariably known; many were terrified of her.

She was born Edris Stannus at Baltiboys, Co Wicklow, in 1898. Her father, an Irish Protestant, was a soldier and landowner; her mother collected and made glassware. Edris's ambition – and determination – became apparent at an early age: after seeing another girl dance at a party, she insisted on performing an Irish jig. 'She carried it off with complete confidence, anxious only lest the pianist should fail to accompany her properly.' When her family moved to England, Ninette was taught 'fancy dancing' by the fashionable Miss Wordsworth. She joined a dance troupe – Miss Lila Field's Wonder Children – at the age of 11, said the *Daily Mail*, and, two years later, saw Anna Pavlova dance her famous solo, *The Dying Swan*. Awestruck, Edris wrote down the movements and taught herself the dance, step by step. By the time she was 14, she had, she later claimed, performed *The Dying Swan* 'on the end of every pier in England'.

In her late teens, Edris began to make her name as a classical ballerina, and in 1923 she was invited to join Diaghilev's prestigious Ballet Russes, based in Monte Carlo. In those days, ballet dancers were expected to adopt exotic foreign names; and just as Alice Marks decided to call herself Alicia Markova, so Edris Stannus became Ninette de Valois. Three years later, she returned to London determined to set up her own company. She opened a school, grandly called the Academy of Choreographic Art and gained the support of the impresario Lilian Baylis, who 'liked her face' and agreed to house the fledgling company at the Old Vic. In 1931 it moved to Sadler's Wells, where de Valois steadily increased its reputation with the help of such dancers as Anton Dolin, Markova and Fonteyn. Constant Lambert was the musical director. During the war, the company toured the provinces, bringing ballet to the people, and in 1946, it settled in Covent Garden. On 20 February, the company performed its now legendary *Sleeping Beauty*. The

At 13, she saw Anna Pavlova dance *The Dying Swan*. Awestruck, she wrote down the movements and taught herself the dance, step by step.

production turned Fonteyn – who received a record-breaking 47 curtain calls – into an overnight star. But the overall credit, as everyone knew, rested with de Valois. In 1956, the Sadler's Wells Ballet Company was granted a royal charter as the Royal Ballet.

In addition to her work building a national ballet, said *The Guardian*, 'de Valois lived a happy parallel life as the wife of Dr A.B. Connell, whom she married in 1935.' (He died in 1987.) With no interest in material possessions, they lived quietly in a small house in west London. To his patients, Ninette de Valois was simply 'the doctor's wife'. On Thursday afternoons, she would stand in for his receptionist, taking messages and running errands. To her regret, the union was childless. But 'her colleagues, her dancers – her children, as they could not help regarding themselves – loved her, especially towards the end when she needed them most.'

Reluctant author behind *The Hitchhiker's Guide to the Galaxy*

DOUGLAS ADAMS

1952-2001

Douglas Adams, who died of a heart attack aged 49, wrote one of the bestselling books of the 1980s. *The Hitchhiker's Guide to the Galaxy* – dubbed a 'trilogy in four parts', until a fifth instalment was added – sold over 14 million copies, and spawned a TV series, a stage play and several computer games.

The book opens with a mild-mannered suburbanite named Arthur Dent being rescued from Earth just before it is demolished to make way for a hyperspace bypass. With the help of an interstellar travel writer, he hitches a lift on a Vogon spacecraft and, with the Hitchhiker's Guide to the Galaxy at his side, embarks on a picaresque journey through the universe on which he meets a host of improbable aliens, and discovers the answer to life, the universe and everything: 42. He never learns what the actual question is.

Adams was only 25 when he wrote the original radio series but, said the *Daily Telegraph*, 'some 20 years on, *Hitchhikers* bears comparison with the work of Lewis Carroll and P.G. Wodehouse as a classic of light comic fiction.'

Born in Cambridge in 1952, Adams was the son of a nurse and a management consultant who divorced when he was five. He did not speak until he was 4 – his teachers wondered if he was educationally subnormal – but sold his first stories to the *Eagle* comic at the age of 13. Educated at Brentwood School, he developed a passion for Monty Python and went up to St John's College Cambridge, hoping to write scripts for the Footlights Revue. Standing 6ft 5in in his socks, his ambition, he said, was to be John Cleese. 'It took me some time to realise the job was in fact taken.' On leaving university, Adams worked with another Python, Graham Chapman, on a TV series that was never made, and tried, without success, to make it as a gag-writer for Radio 4's *Weekending*. He was eventually reduced to taking odd jobs to make a living, including a stint as bodyguard to the Qatari royal family, which consisted mainly of sitting outside London hotel rooms. One night, the door of an adjacent room opened and a young lady emerged. 'It's all right for you,' she told him. 'At least you can read while you're on the job.'

Then, in 1977, Adams pitched *The Hitchhiker's Guide to the Galaxy* to BBC Radio. He had first come up with the idea in 1971, while touring the continent with a copy of *The Hitchhiker's Guide to Europe*. The radio show was a hit, a bestselling book followed, and Adams's life was never the same again. 'It was,' he said, 'like being helicoptered to the top of Mount Everest or having an orgasm without the foreplay.' Adams wrote numerous books after the *Hitchhiker* series, including *Last Chance to See*, which reflected his fascination with ecology and evolutionary science. None, however, were as successful as his early works. The problem was perhaps that he was not a natural writer. He did not enjoy the process – hating the loneliness of sitting in front of a computer screen – lacked self-confidence, and suffered from repeated bouts of writer's block. At one point, Adams's editor set up her office in his kitchen in an attempt to encourage him to finish a book; on another occasion, a publisher locked him into his hotel room. 'I love deadlines,' Adams once said. 'I love the whooshing noise they make as they go by.'

> **Standing 6ft 5in in his socks, his ambition, he said, was to be John Cleese. 'It took me some time to realise the job was in fact taken.'**

The charismatic actor who fathered twelve children by five women

ANTHONY QUINN

1915-2001

It was easy to mock Anthony Quinn as an actor, said Mark Steyn in *The Spectator*. The star of *Zorba the Greek* and Fellini's *La Strada* was 'rough, raw, primal, lusty, throaty and stubbly'. As a performer, he was 'the life-force who forces a little too much life on you, who pisses on subtlety, sprays mouthfuls of ouzo on nuance and rubs the prickle of his three-day beard on ambiguity before throttling it in a bear-hug'.

He was born in Chihuahua, Mexico, in 1915, of Irish-Aztec ancestry. Following his birth, Quinn's parents fled from Pancho Villa's revolution and settled in California. His father found work in the film business but was killed in a car accident when Quinn was just 9 years old. Thereafter, Quinn became the breadwinner, working as a cement mixer, a boxer and the foreman in a mattress factory. At 14 he was supervising 150 workers on an apricot farm.

Having abandoned plans to become an architect, Quinn turned to acting. His breakthrough came when he was cast in Cecil B. de Mille's *The Plainsman* (1936) in which he played a Cheyenne Indian. He won the part by talking gibberish at the audition which convinced the casting director that he was an authentic Native American. Thereafter he specialised in playing parts which required any degree of 'ethnicity': he was a sheikh in *The Road to Morocco*, a Filipino guerrilla in *Back to Butaan*, Inuk the Eskimo in *The Savage Innocents*, the French painter Gauguin in *Lust for Life* (a role for which he won an Oscar, despite being on screen for just six minutes), and a Bedouin tribesman in *Lawrence of Arabia*.

But it was the role of Zorba that turned him into an international superstar, said *The Times*. 'The disadvantage, of course, was that ever afterwards he was called upon to play Zorba the Italian, Zorba the Romanian, Zorba the Mexican, Zorba the Arab, and even once or twice Zorba the American-Greek.' Quinn claimed to have invented Zorba's famous sliding dance himself. 'He had broken his foot the day before shooting began, and found that if he dragged it along, it would not cause too much pain,' said *The Guardian*. 'I just held out my arms, in a traditional Greek stance, and shuffled along the sands,' Quinn explained. 'Soon Alan Bates picked up on the move… We were born-again Greeks, joyously celebrating life. We had no idea what we were doing, but it felt good.'

Quinn had married de Mille's adopted daughter, Katherine, in 1936, but he was prone to bouts of infidelity, bedding some of the most glamorous women in Hollywood, including Rita Hayworth, Lana Turner, Carole Lombard, Ingrid Bergman and Greta Garbo. He fathered 'at least eight sons and four daughters' by five different women and had his last two children when he was in his eighties. Their mother was a former secretary more than 50 years his junior, prompting an admiring tabloid to run the headline 'The Mighty Quinn!'

> **He was 'the life-force who forces a little too much life on you, who pisses on subtlety, sprays mouthfuls of ouzo on nuance and rubs the prickle of his three-day beard on ambiguity before throttling it in a bear-hug'.**

Newspaper publisher who brought down a president

KATHARINE GRAHAM

1917-2001

One hot afternoon in the summer of 1963, Katharine Graham woke from a nap to find her husband lying dead in the next room, said Cole Moreton in the *Independent on Sunday*. He had killed himself with a shotgun. Three days later, the 46-year-old housewife, who had no experience of running a newspaper, announced that she would be taking over her late husband's job as publisher of the *Washington Post*. 'What I essentially did was to put one foot in front of the other, shut my eyes and step off the ledge,' she later recalled. 'The surprise was that I landed on my feet.'

Katharine Graham became a legend in the world of newspaper publishing. But she was not brought up for a career in business, said *The Times*. Born in New York in 1917, she was the daughter of Eugene Meyer, a Wall Street financier whose assets included the *Washington Post*. Katharine was expected to devote her life to marriage and motherhood, and in 1940, after a brief spell working as a reporter, she married a dynamic young man named Phil Graham. Within a few years, Graham had taken over the reins of his father-in-law's newspaper. He increased its circulation, consolidated this success with the acquisition of *Newsweek*, and forged friendships with some of the most influential figures of the day, including John F. Kennedy. Katharine, meanwhile, devoted herself to raising their four children and being a good society wife. 'I really felt I was put on earth to take care of Phil Graham,' she said. 'He was so glamorous I was perfectly happy just to clean up after him.'

In 1957, Phil Graham suffered a nervous breakdown. He made a temporary recovery, before spiralling out of control in the early 1960s. He drank heavily, embarked on an affair with a young journalist and, in one of his worst moments, began to strip naked at a meeting of the Associated Press. Following his suicide, Katharine, who once described herself as a 'doormat wife', vowed never again to allow her life to be run by a man. Finding herself sole owner of the *Washington Post*, she determined to take control and carry on where her husband had left off. At first, the 'new boss' was seriously daunted by the male-dominated world of newspaper publishing, said Moreton. Before her first Christmas party at the *Post*, she rehearsed greeting her guests by saying 'Merry Christmas' over and over again. But within a decade, she was being hailed as the most powerful woman in the world.

In 1972, Graham defied the government by publishing the Pentagon Papers – top-secret documents about America's illicit activities in Vietnam. The following year, she risked ruin by backing the *Post*'s

> **'Jeeeeeesus!' Nixon's campaign manager screamed down the phone. 'All that crap, you're putting it in the paper? It's all been denied. Katie Graham's gonna get her tit caught in a big fat wringer if that's published!'**

Watergate investigation – a story no other paper would touch. The Nixon administration did everything possible to quash the story, said the *Daily Telegraph*. The president forbade anyone in his government from talking to the *Post*, and Graham was warned by a friend with White House contacts 'not to be alone'. On one occasion, the journalist Carl Bernstein rang John Mitchell, Nixon's campaign manager, with evidence that he was linked to a fund used to gather dirt on the Democrats. 'Jeeeeeesus!' Mitchell screamed down the phone. 'All that crap, you're putting it in the paper? It's all been denied. Katie Graham's gonna get her tit caught in a big fat wringer if that's published!' But Graham was unmoved by the threats, and stood behind her staff. Following Nixon's resignation in 1974, the paper was covered in glory, and the story was turned into a film, *All the President's Men*. But Graham was not featured. The film's producer, Robert Redford, 'imagined I would be relieved', she said, 'but to my surprise, my feelings were hurt'.

Graham had a reputation for steeliness – Redford described her as having a 'tight-jawed blue-blood quality' – yet she was not at all stuffy, said Maureen Dowd in the *New York Times*. Her great passion was for the movies – anything from teen romances to action thrillers – and she was known for sneaking out of the office to go to the cinema. Once, a friend called to ask: 'Do you want to go see the French President?' 'Where's it playing?' Graham asked. 'I meant Pompidou,' the friend replied.

Luftwaffe pilot who introduced the Germans to sex

BEATE UHSE

1919-2001

Beate Uhse was probably the most famous woman in Germany, said *The Guardian*. Credited with almost singlehandedly revolutionising her nation's attitude towards sex, she was the driving force behind Europe's first and largest chain of sex shops – Beate Uhse AG – a company whose brand recognition in Germany is on a par with that of BMW or Mercedes.

Uhse was born in Eastern Prussia in 1919. Her father was a farmer; her mother a gynaecologist. A tough, passionate and adventurous girl, she left school at 16 to become a pilot. She got her licence two years later, married her instructor and, at the age of 24, joined the Luftwaffe as a transport pilot. Her husband was shot down by the British; her parents were killed by the Russians; and in 1945, as the Red Army marched on Berlin, Uhse escaped in a plane, with her baby in tow. They settled in Schleswig-Holstein, said *The Times*, where she made ends meet by trading door-to-door in toys, coffee and other goods, before 'stumbling into her unlikely career'. Wherever she went, Uhse found that local women were ignorant about sex and fearful of becoming pregnant. She decided to help them, and began by printing a leaflet explaining the 'rhythm method'. It sold 32,000 copies, said the *Daily Telegraph*, and customers began writing to her, asking for condoms, sex education books and stimulants. The mail-order business expanded – but not without difficulty. She was attacked by the Churches, and subjected to endless police raids; charges were brought against her 2,000 times. But Uhse was unrepentant, said *The Guardian*. She felt she was performing a public service, and not without reason, for the Germans had a lot to 'unlearn'. The Nazis had preached that contraception was the greatest evil, and even in the 1950s many men believed it was 'cleaner' to have sex with a blonde than a brunette. 'I am convinced I did a lot of good,' she said. 'I helped to make the Germans less repressed; repression had led to Nazism.'

In the 1960s, the company began selling pornographic magazines and videos, as well as an array of sex toys. Uhse opened her first sex shop – the Institute of Marital Health – in 1962. Clean, well lit and cheerful, the shops 'eschewed the trappings of sleaze', said *The Times*, and proved a 'winning formula'. In 1999, when the company went public, turnover exceeded DM300m. Feminists claimed that the company was exploiting women.

Even in the 1950s many men believed it was 'cleaner' to have sex with a blonde than a brunette.

But Uhse dismissed her critics: 'With my underwear and sugar-coated pills,' she said, 'with creams and juices, with confectionery and condoms, I have managed to patch up millions of broken marriages over the years.'

Brilliant art historian who told Churchill of Hitler's death

SIR ERNST GOMBRICH OM

1909-2001

E.H. Gombrich was the pre-eminent art historian of the twentieth century. A revered scholar and theorist, he was also the author of a bestselling book, *The Story of Art* (1950), which made art history accessible to millions. The son of a lawyer, Gombrich was born in Vienna in 1909. His mother Leonie, a talented pianist who played with Schoenberg, counted Gustav Mahler among her friends. She also knew Sigmund Freud, 'whom she did not much like, although she admired his brilliance at telling Jewish anecdotes,' said Charles Hope in *The Independent*.

After the First World War, Vienna was hit by severe food shortages. Gombrich became so malnourished that he was sent by Save the Children to Sweden, where he lived for nine months with a carpenter who specialised in making coffins. Upon his return, he attended the Theresianum Secondary School, where, at the tender age of 14, he wrote a thesis on changing approaches to art from Winckelmann onwards. After graduating from Vienna University in 1936, said the *Daily Telegraph*, he came to Britain and joined the Warburg Institute. He was able to help his parents leave Austria in 1938, but with the outbreak of the Second World War, he was regarded as an enemy alien and his movements were subjected to restriction.

Nonetheless, he got a job at the BBC, 'an experience to which he was to ascribe his acquisition of the flawless English that was to characterise his writings', said *The Times*. For six years, he monitored radio broadcasts from Germany and, in 1945, realised that the playing of a Bruckner symphony prior to an 'impending announcement' had tremendous significance. The piece had originally been written to commemorate Wagner's death: now it was being played to mark the death of Hitler. Gombrich himself broke the news to Churchill.

After the war, he held a variety of research and teaching posts, eventually becoming director of the Warburg Institute. *The Story of Art* first appeared in 1950 and was immediately recognised as a remarkable achievement, said *The Times*. 'Gombrich was a master of lucid English prose', and he succeeded in explaining complicated ideas to a wide range of readers. To date, the book has sold more than two million copies and been revised 16 times. Gombrich's other, more theoretical works such as *Art and Illusion* (1960) and *Meditations on a Hobby Horse* (1963) have also been enormously influential in academic circles. He was sceptical of contemporary art 'fads' and didn't have much time for lofty pronouncements about 'movements' such as 'the Renaissance' or 'Romanticism'. For Gombrich, art was best seen as a series of technical advances, said *The Times*. 'Stylistic change was born of individual technical accomplishment: Giotto's realistic rendering of space, Ucello's understanding of perspective.'

> **He never learned to paint and never collected art, 'saying that the best was available to him in the National Gallery'.**

Gombrich lived modestly in a terraced house in Hampstead, surrounded not by pictures but by musical scores, said *The Times*. He never learned to paint and never collected art, 'saying that the best was available to him in the National Gallery'. In a distinguished academic career, he held prestigious chairs at Oxford, Cambridge, Cornell and Harvard, and became one of the country's most honoured scholars. He was knighted in 1972 and made a member of the Order of Merit in 1988.

Schoolteacher who railed against the permissive society

MARY WHITEHOUSE

1910-2001

Mary Whitehouse was a schoolteacher from the West Midlands who began an unlikely second career in the mid-1960s as the self-appointed – and much derided – guardian of the nation's morals. Her critics dubbed her the Queen of Clean and the Archangel of Anti-smut, but Whitehouse was impervious to their sneers, said Dennis Barker in *The Guardian*. She thrived on the fight, and – convinced that she was following God's will – withstood criticism and even abuse with unfailing humour and grace.

The only person to ruffle her feathers was the man she referred to as the 'devil incarnate': Sir Hugh Greene, director-general of the BBC from 1960 to 1969. A lofty, 'patrician' figure, he repeatedly refused to meet the 'lower-middle-class Midlander'– or even acknowledge her letters – and for four years banned her from appearing on the BBC. There was something rather 'pathological' in Sir Hugh's attitude to Whitehouse, said the *Daily Telegraph*. At one point, he bought a naked portrait of her, adorned with six breasts, which he would throw darts at, 'squealing with pleasure as he made a hit'. By comparison Whitehouse seemed quite well adjusted. 'I never had any hang-ups about sex,' she said. 'As for being sexually repressed, nothing could be further from the truth.' She was, she insisted, neither 'narrow-minded or old-fashioned. But I am square, and proud of it, if that means a sense of values.'

She was born Mary Hutcheson in 1910 and raised in a church-going household in Chester, said David Winter in *The Independent*. She was educated locally, and studied art before becoming a teacher. From the beginning, she was true to her own beliefs. At 20, she fell deeply in love with a married man but ended the affair without consummating it when she saw his wife's forlorn expression. 'I just knew,' she recalled, 'that if I was the cause of so much unhappiness, our relationship could not be right.' In 1940, she married Ernest Whitehouse and, for the next two decades, devoted herself to bringing up her family in Wolverhampton. In 1960, she went back to work, teaching art and sex-education classes, in which she stressed the importance of chastity before marriage and fidelity within it.

'It was the Profumo scandal of 1963 that first disturbed this anonymous provincial existence,' said the *Daily Telegraph*. One day, Whitehouse found some girls pretending to have sex behind the bike sheds. They told her they were imitating Christine Keeler and Mandy Rice-Davies, whom they had seen on TV the night before. Appalled, Whitehouse began planning the 'Clean up TV campaign', which was launched in 1964 in Birmingham. The event attracted 2,000 enthusiastic supporters and was widely covered by the media. The following year

> **Her campaigns ranged from the 'prescient' to the absurd, such as trying to ban the Chuck Berry song 'My Ding A Ling' because it encouraged masturbation.**

saw the launch of the National Viewers and Listeners' Association, with Whitehouse as head, presiding genius and public voice. Within a year, she claimed to have won the support of 'half a million housewives, the chief constables of Britain, MPs, bishops, leaders of all churches, city councils and people of standing throughout the country.' Almost overnight, the hitherto unknown teacher had become a household name.

For the next 30 years, Whitehouse waged war on smut wherever she found it, said *The Times*. Her campaigns ranged from the 'prescient' – child pornography – to the absurd, such as trying to ban the Chuck Berry song 'My Ding A Ling' because it encouraged masturbation. But she was fearless in the face of ridicule. In 1971, for instance, she was invited to speak at Leicester University, only to be greeted by a torrent of obscenity. Undaunted, she stood and endured it for over an hour. She was routinely pelted with eggs; she often received death threats; and one pornographer named his most hard-core magazine after her.

But Whitehouse also scored some notable victories: she brought a lawsuit against the magazine *Oz*, and had the editor of the *Gay News* convicted of blasphemy. And as the tide began to turn against the permissive society, she was joined by some unlikely bedfellows. Speaking at a debate on pornography at the Cambridge Union, she was loudly supported by a group of lesbians in boiler suits, who punched the air, shouting, 'Right on, Mary!' She won the debate by 331 votes to 151.

In the end, Whitehouse was able to do little to stem the tide of sex and violence. But she comforted herself with the idea that without her efforts things would 'have gone on and on and become even more extreme'.

The quiet Beatle who shunned the mainstream

GEORGE HARRISON

1943-2001

George Harrison was the lead guitarist with The Beatles, the pop group that shook the world for nearly a decade. The youngest quartet, and known as 'the Quiet One', he often felt overshadowed by the songwriting talents of Paul McCartney and John Lennon. But his contribution to music history is inestimable, said Sean O'Hagan in *The Observer*. Although he was not the band's defining force, The Beatles 'as we know and remember them, would not have existed without him. "We were economy-class Beatles," he once said of himself and Ringo – but it was never that simple.' Harrison was the guitarist whose riffs made Lennon and McCartney's songs better, the peacemaker who kept the band together, and the serious musician who led the band away from mainstream pop.

Harrison was born in Liverpool in 1943, the son of a bus driver. A bright child, he passed his 11-plus and won a place at the Liverpool Institute. But he was never academic, and had few interests, until he caught on to the skiffle craze. He talked his mother into buying him a second-hand guitar and, with a dedication to his craft that would mark his later life, taught himself to play, often practising until his fingers split. Then, on the school bus, he befriended another Liverpool Institute schoolboy, Paul McCartney.

'I discovered Paul had a trumpet and he found out I had a guitar so we got together.'

The following year, Paul introduced George to his friend John Lennon, who had formed The Quarrymen. Already a mature, acid-tongued 17-year-old, Lennon resisted the idea of performing alongside a scruffy boy of 14. But he changed his mind when he heard Harrison play. Harrison was formally accepted into the group on 6 February 1958 – a few days short of his 15th birthday. From the start, Harrison was the 'baby', stuck between the competing egos of Lennon and McCartney. 'I couldn't be bothered with him at first,' Lennon said. 'He used to follow me around like a bloody kid. It took me years to start considering him as an equal.'

The band started out in local clubs and discos. Then, in 1960, they secured a residency at the Indra Club in Hamburg's red light district. 'The whole area was full of transvestites and prostitutes and gangsters, and I was in the middle of that, aged 17,' Harrison recalled. They played eight hours a night, honing their skills as a professional beat group, until Harrison was deported for being underage.

Back in Britain, The Beatles were discovered by Brian Epstein, and signed by EMI. Soon, 'Beatlemania' was sweeping the country. At first, Harrison behaved like a conventional star. He bought fast cars, married a model – Patti Boyd – and invested in a nightclub. On his 21st birthday, he received 60 sacks of mail, containing 30,000 presents and cards. But as time went on, he tired of being sidelined by Lennon and McCartney, and came to loathe Beatlemania, finding it trivial and exhausting. 'It was a very one-sided love affair,' he said. 'The people gave their money and their screams, but The Beatles gave their nervous systems, which is a much more difficult thing to give.' It was no coincidence that the first song he wrote for the band was entitled 'Don't Bother Me'.

In 1965, Harrison discovered the sitar. 'I listened to Indian music for the next two years and hardly touched the guitar except when recording.' His deep-seated interest in Indian music and mysticism not only defined The Beatles' look and sound in the late 1960s, said The Times, but was an influence on popular culture everywhere. Meanwhile, Harrison persevered with his songwriting, said Ray Connelly in the Daily Mail. His compositions included 'Taxman', the 'sublime' 'While My Guitar Gently Weeps', and 'Something', described by Frank Sinatra as 'the most beautiful love song of the last 50 years'.

In 1969, to Harrison's evident relief, The Beatles split. Not long afterwards, he released a triple album of songs rejected by Lennon and McCartney. *All Things Must Pass* completely overshadowed the other Beatles' first solo efforts, selling millions of copies. It was a revenge of sorts. But the 1970s was a difficult decade, said the *Daily Telegraph*. His solo projects waned, his charity concert for Bangladesh turned into an administrative nightmare, and his wife, for whom he had written 'Something', left him for his friend and collaborator, Eric Clapton. Patti Boyd inspired Clapton to write his two classics, 'Layla' and 'Wonderful Tonight'.

In the late 1970s, Harrison mortgaged his mansion, Friar Park in Henley, to fund *Monty Python's Life of Brian* – a film no one else would touch. His company, Handmade Films, went on to make a string of hits, including *The Long Good Friday*, *A Private Function* and *Withnail and I*. In the 1980s, Harrison returned to music: he joined the Traveling Wilburys, toured with Clapton and released a hit single, 'Got My Mind Set On You' (1987). But he always resisted calls to reform The Beatles – 'not while John's still dead' – and kept out of the public eye. 'I'd like to play in some out-of-the-way place where the emphasis is on enjoying the music rather than some superstar mob on stage,' he said. 'Somewhere where your myth and your past isn't attached to what you're doing now. Like we did before we were famous.'

Following Lennon's murder in 1980, Harrison became increasingly concerned for his family's safety. 'Before John's death the gates of Friar Park always stood open,' said the Beatles archivist Mark Lewisohn. 'But afterwards they were always closed.' In 1999, his worst fears were realised when a lunatic named Michael Abram broke into the house and stabbed Harrison ten times in the chest. He was saved by his second wife, Olivia, who knocked Abram out with a lamp-stand. In the ambulance, someone asked Harrison if he knew who his attacker was. 'He wasn't a burglar,' he replied, 'and he certainly wasn't auditioning for the Traveling Wilburys.'

Shortly before his death, Harrison wrote one final track, 'Small World, Big Friends', with his son, Dhani. Noted for gallows humour, he credited it 'RIP Ltd 2001'. 'I think people who truly can live a life in music are telling the world: you can have my love, you can have my smiles,' Harrison once said. 'Forget the bad parts, you don't need them. Just take the music, the goodness, because it's the very best, and it's the part I give most willingly.'

Insecure actor who found fame in *Yes, Minister*

SIR NIGEL HAWTHORNE

1929-2001

The actor Nigel Hawthorne laboured for years in obscurity before finding fame as the unctuous civil servant Sir Humphrey Appleby in *Yes, Minister*. It was once said of him that he spent the first 20 years of his career being ignored, and the rest of it being discovered. But Hawthorne enjoyed his late flowering, saying: 'I didn't really know who I was until I was middle-aged.'

Hawthorne was born in Coventry in 1929, said *The Times*, but moved with his family to South Africa when he was 2. He was educated at the Christian Brothers College in Cape Town, a bleak establishment run on the philosophy of beating wickedness out of boys and beating knowledge into them. Almost daily canings did nothing for Hawthorne's self-confidence. Nor did the fact that during his late teens, he realised that he was a homosexual. The situation further alienated him from his authoritarian father, who told him: 'All homosexuals should be shipped to a desert island and shot.' After a year at Cape Town University, Hawthorne dropped out to become an actor. In 1951, he moved to England with just £12 in his pocket, convinced he would find happiness in London. But his first foray onto the British stage proved a disaster. He failed to get an agent, and endless auditions led only to rejections. Penniless, dejected and deeply lonely, he lived in a tiny bedsit, surviving mostly on sultanas. 'I must have smelled of failure,' he once said. Eventually, he won the role of understudy to Leslie Phillips in a West End comedy. But although the play ran for 19 months, Hawthorne never once appeared on stage.

In 1957 he gave up and returned to South Africa, convinced he would never make it as an actor. But on arriving in Cape Town, he discovered that the theatre was going through a golden age, and was soon cast in several leading roles. He returned to London in the early 1960s, said *The Guardian*, and, after a period in revue, joined the Joan Littlewood Company in time to tour with *Oh! What a Lovely War*. Within a few years, he had established himself as a solid character actor. Leading roles, however, continued to elude him – largely because he still lacked confidence. All this changed in 1973. Cast as a ditherer in *The Philanthropist*, he realised that his own lack of forcefulness was holding him back. 'I'd been going for 24 years and wondering the whole time what I was doing wrong,' he recalled. 'That taught me to be a little more positive.' His career began to blossom, and in the late 1970s he won the part in *Yes, Minister* which made him a household name. At the same time, he found happiness in his private life. 'I found neither love nor success until I was 50,' he said. 'But when I met [long-time partner Trevor Bentham] it seemed as though everything fell into place.' *Yes, Minister* was shown in more than 50 countries, and became known as

> **Endless auditions led only to rejections. Penniless, dejected and deeply lonely, he lived in a tiny bedsit, surviving mostly on sultanas. 'I must have smelled of failure,' he once said.**

Margaret Thatcher's favourite television programme. At the height of its popularity, she invited Hawthorne to tea at Downing Street and insisted on filming a scene with the cast. Yet for all his success, Hawthorne remained wracked with insecurity, and needed medication to calm his nerves before filming in front of a studio audience.

In the 1990s, Hawthorne appeared in the West End and on Broadway in *Shadowlands*. His portrayal of C.S. Lewis reduced the press-night audience to tears and won rave reviews. Nevertheless, Hawthorne lost the film role to Anthony Hopkins. Two years later, he played George III in Alan Bennett's *The Madness of George III*. And when the play was turned into a film Bennett insisted that Hawthorne should star. The film was a hit, and Hawthorne was nominated for an Oscar. But Hollywood never suited him, said Ross Benson in the *Daily Mail*. He had worked with Sylvester Stallone in *Demolition Man*, and hated every minute of it. 'Stallone was never punctual, he strutted around the set with a producer on one arm and a bimbo on the other, and rarely spoke to me,' he said, adding, 'There is so much latitude for mediocrity in Hollywood.' To make matters worse, in the run-up to his appearance at the 1995 Oscars, he was publicly 'outed' as a homosexual by the US press. Hawthorne, a private man who had always distanced himself from the more radical elements in the gay community, was deeply shocked by the experience. 'The headlines were appalling, really disgusting things like The Madness of Queen George and Sir Bumphrey,' he recalled.

In the late 1990s, Hawthorne was persuaded to play King Lear – a part he had hitherto refused to take on. His original instincts proved correct: the reviews were savage, and he vowed never to go on stage again.

Hawthorne was knighted in 1999. But he was too modest to set much store by the honour. 'I have my K, which is very nice,' he said, 'but it is only for pretending, not real bravery.' The same year, he was diagnosed with cancer. His last public appearance, said Hugh Davies in the *Daily Telegraph*, was at the memorial service for fellow actor Michael Williams. After the service, Hawthorne was beset by fans and, although frail and tired, stopped to chat and sign autographs. 'It was a cold afternoon and he looked frozen. But he kept at it for half an hour or more. Then, when everyone was done, he left, walking slowly up the road, nodding his head, as if in delight. This was the last we saw of him.'

Intellectual giant who paved the way for the Welfare State

LORD YOUNG OF DARTINGTON

1915–2002

Michael Young was 'one of the most inspired innovators of his time', said the *Daily Telegraph*. A man of indefatigable energy and enthusiasm, he helped millions of people through projects ranging from the Open University and the Consumers' Association to Linkage, a scheme to bring together old people with no grandchildren and young people without grandparents.

Young was born in Manchester in 1915. His father was an impoverished Australian violinist, his mother an Irish artist. He was sent to several different schools where he found himself 'hunted and harried' by endless rules, regulations and corporal punishment. At one, he was so miserable that he vowed he would murder the sadistic senior master if he ever met him in later life. 'So far,' he wrote half a century later, 'I haven't. Perhaps a fellow-sufferer has forestalled me.' When Michael was about 6, his parents decided to split up, and for a time there was talk of putting him up for adoption. This incident, said his son Toby Young in *The Guardian*, left him with a 'crippling fear of abandonment' – and a lifelong compassion for the underprivileged and unwanted. 'All the organisations he set up, from the Consumers' Association in 1956 to the National Association of Sick

Children in 1993, were designed to provide a home for people otherwise left out in the cold.'

In 1929, Young was sent to Dartington Hall, a new progressive school for children of the intelligentsia, where he was much happier. He studied economics at London University, and qualified as a barrister at Gray's Inn, although he never practised. Instead he joined Political and Economic Planning, a think-tank conceived at Dartington in 1931 by 'people who were determined', he wrote later, 'that something should be done to relieve the miseries of the world'. He became its director in 1941 at the age of 26. (Asthma made him unfit for war-time service.) Four years later, having joined the Labour Party's research department, he single-handedly wrote the influential manifesto – Let Us Face the Future – which led to the formation of the Welfare State and the foundation of the NHS. Most men would have capitalised on this success by launching a career in politics. But Young was becoming increasingly interested in sociology and, in 1952, he enrolled at the LSE to research housing conditions in London's East End. The result, Family and Kinship in East London, warned of the danger of exporting communities wholesale to greenfield sites, and became a classic of its kind. This was followed by numerous other books, including The Rise of the Meritocracy, 1870–2033, which sold 500,000 copies, helped kill off the 11-plus and introduced a new word into the English language. Contrary to some interpretations, the meritocracy was not something Young endorsed. A committed egalitarian, he considered it just another form of elitism.

He also launched a host of other non-profit-making organisations, said Vincent Brome in The Independent, from the National Extension College to the Mutual Aid Centre. 'Whatever field he toiled, he sowed dragon's teeth and armed men seemed to spring from the soil to form an organisation to correct the abuses he had discovered,' wrote Lord Annan. 'Were consumers conned by manufacturers and advertisers? Let them form an association to test the products and appraise their work in Which? [magazine].' Tenacious, stubborn and tireless, he worked 65 hours a week, even in old age, fathered his sixth child at 80, and only retired at 84. Brome once travelled with Young on a 180-mile road trip to visit a Czechoslovakian prisoner. They made the journey in a souped-up Austin Mini. 'To see him crouched over a wheel travelling at 90mph and simultaneously discussing the solipsistic principle of metaphysics left an indelible imprint on my mind. It enshrined the intellectual man of action with an inexhaustible zest for living.'

Flame-haired politician with 'a masculine strength of will'

BARBARA CASTLE

1910-2002

Barbara Castle was one of the most remarkable female politicians of the 20th century, and a towering figure in the British Labour movement, said Anne Perkins in *The Guardian*. A clever, sexy redhead with a fiery temper, she dominated politics at a time when most party bosses were shameless chauvinists, and thus inadvertently 'paved the way for Margaret Thatcher to capture the commanding heights of government'.

There were 'striking similarities between the two women', said the *Daily Telegraph*. Both were single-minded conviction politicians; both were very feminine, and flirted shamelessly with male colleagues; both were careful with their appearance (as a minister, Castle had her hair done every day). And neither was averse to using feminine wiles to help them achieve their own ends – in Castle's case, even resorting to tantrums and hot tears. 'In my political life,' she noted in her diary, 'I always found men vulnerable to a little femininity and many are unable to cope when it is combined with some mental ability and with what is considered a masculine strength of will.' Castle certainly exhibited a fearsome dedication to any project she undertook. 'Think, think, think,' she said she had once been told. 'It will hurt like hell at first, but you'll get used to it.'

Barbara Betts was born in Bradford in 1910, the daughter of a tax inspector. She grew up in a fiercely socialist household, which was often packed with refugees from fascism, or the families of striking miners. Her father was a member of the Independent Labour Party and edited a controversial news sheet called the *Bradford Pioneer*. An aspiring teacher, he taught himself languages at the breakfast table and translated Lorca's poems into English. Her mother was a William Morris Socialist. Barbara composed her first election address at the age of 8. Written just after the First World War, consisted of a ten-word promise: 'Citizens! Vote for me and I will give you houses!' After attending Bradford Girls' Grammar School – where she preached socialism to the daughters of mill owners – Barbara won a scholarship to St Hilda's College, Oxford. But she failed to thrive at the university. Finding the atmosphere stifling, she poured her energies into the local Labour Club, and graduated with a disappointing third.

After a period selling crystallised fruit in a Manchester department store, Betts moved to London where she found work as a journalist and entered local government. Shortly afterwards, she fell in love with William Mellor, the socialist intellectual and one-time editor of the *Daily Herald*. He was married and wasn't in any position to get a divorce, as he made abundantly clear. ('I never expected a man to come and tell me his intentions to my daughter were strictly dishonourable,' commented Frank Betts.) Nevertheless, they embarked on a ten-year affair, which ended only with his sudden death in 1942. She also had a close relationship with Michael Foot, said Anne Perkins, with whom she claimed to have read *Das Kapital*, word by word, page by page. (Later, Foot hinted that they had shared more than Marx in front of the gas fire in her Bloomsbury flat – but Castle angrily denied there had ever been an affair and Foot, expressing mild surprise, 'loyally retracted'.) In 1937 Betts and Foot launched *Tribune*, an influential left-wing paper financed by Sir Stafford Cripps, whose stated mission was to recreate Labour as a truly socialist party.

At the Labour conference of 1943, Betts made a passionate speech about the Beveridge report, warning party leaders: 'We want jam today, not jam tomorrow.' Her comments caused a 'sensation', said *The Times*, and were picked up by Bill Castle, night editor of the *Daily Mirror*, who made her the next day's front-page story. Betts was hailed as the 'voice of youth' (although she was 32) and given a job as the *Mirror*'s housing correspondent. The following year, as the V1s rained down on London, she and Castle were married. Nye Bevan and Jennie Lee were two of the four guests at their wedding breakfast. Despite affairs on both sides, the marriage lasted until his death in 1979. Castle was devastated. 'How does one come to terms with such a loss?' she wondered. 'Keep him alive by endlessly remembering… or move on briskly… or just go numb and wait for death? I fluctuate between the three.'

In the 1945 election, Castle was elected member for Blackburn. The 'fiery young redhead', as she described herself, had made it. As soon as she got to Westminster, Stafford Cripps appointed her his PPS at the Board of Trade. When Cripps became chancellor, Castle was kept on by his successor, Harold Wilson. It was the beginning of one of the most important relationships of her life. Wilson was deeply impressed by her talenrs – 'She was good at whatever she touched' – and would act as her political patron for many years to come. A staunch Bevanite, Castle opposed cuts in public spending to fund the Cold War, and spent years battling for left-wing causes. She said she was driven by fury.

When Wilson came to power, Castle was appointed Minister for Overseas Development. She later became the first female Minister for Transport – despite not holding a driving licence – where she was famous for introducing the Breathalyser. The Equal Pay Act, Serps and child benefit – paid to the purse not the wallet – were other notable legacies. Despite her fierce support for socialism, she fell out badly with the Left over her plans to limit trade union power in 1969. The proposals – contained in a paper named *In Place of Strife* – sparked a major row within the party and with the unions and were ultimately defeated. By that time, she had lost the support of many former comrades. Even Foot turned against her. In 1976 Castle was sacked by James Callaghan – an old enemy – who told her she was too old. But even after leaving the Commons in 1979, she kept up the fight, as an MEP and later in the House of Lords.

Later on, Castle – in failing health and robbed of her eyesight – was a thorn in the side of New Labour. At the party conference of 1999, she savaged the Government for fixing pensions to inflation. That, she said in a ten-minute speech, amounts to a 1.1% rise. 'A pension increase of 72p – a fair price for a bag of peanuts.' When asked what kept her young, she replied: 'Dogs and politics. Dogs make you walk, politics make you think. Only boredom makes you old.'

One-eyed actor who found fame as Rumpole of the Bailey

LEO McKERN

1920-2002

Leo McKern was one of the 'soundest and widest-ranging actors in Britain', said Adam Benedick in *The Independent*. He excelled in classical roles, and was a regular West End lead in British and European drama. But to the wider public, he was best known as Horace Rumpole, 'the ageing, grumpy, henpecked and endearingly down-at-heel barrister in John Mortimer's TV series *Rumpole of the Bailey*'. Although he regretted being typecast, McKern had great affection for his alter ego. 'With Rumpole,' he once said, 'one comes to be reconciled to the fact that it isn't half a bad thing to be stuck with.'

McKern 'was generous always in calling me the "only begetter" of Rumpole,' said John Mortimer in the *Daily Mail*, 'but the character was born as a partnership in which the actor had just as much to play as the writer.' McKern was perfect in the role: he had a 'gruff voice which, touchingly, could be as sweet as honey'. And although short, and rather fat, he was dextrous and as light on his feet as a dancer. On set, he told jokes, recited rude limericks and could 'roll a hat up his sleeve until it fell magically on his head'. He was, 'quite simply', the 'only Rumpole'. But for all their similarities – not least a liking for claret – McKern was not Rumpole, said Adam Benedick. For one thing, he lacked the barrister's 'philosophical patience' and 'steadiness of purpose'. 'I'm not as loyal as Rumpers,' he once observed. 'I would have left She Who Must Be Obeyed years ago.'

Born in Sydney in 1920, McKern left school at 15 to work in a refrigerator factory, only to lose his eye in an industrial accident. Later, he used his disability to great advantage, adjusting his glass eye to any direction to give his countenance a 'peculiar and sometimes teasing ambiguity'. Off stage, he would tap it absent-mindedly with a Biro, or, in restaurants, drop it into his pasta to alarm the waiting staff. He enlisted during the war – and found army life so boring that he joined an acting troupe. With the return of peace, he fell in love with an actress named Jane Holland. When she decided to try her luck in England, McKern followed. They were married in 1946, and found lodgings in a Hampstead bedsit; money was so tight that in the freezing winter of 1946–1947 they were forced to sell their gas heater to buy food. McKern worked as a meat porter, before joining the Old Vic in 1949.

> **He would tap his glass eye absent-mindedly with a Biro, or, in restaurants, drop it into his pasta to alarm the waiting staff.**

The following year he acted alongside Donald Wolfit in the first revival of *Tamburlaine* for 300 years. Many stage roles followed, including *Peer Gynt*, A Common Man in Robert Bolt's *A Man for All Seasons* and *Toad of Toad Hall*. Kenneth Tynan described McKern's Iago as 'squat and squalid as a poisonous bug, yet equipped with a mask of profound concern that would deceive a saint'. The tragedy, said Mortimer, is that McKern never played Lear. The 'irascible, wilful old monarch who achieves wisdom, gentleness and finally peace, when near to madness, would have been a natural part for Leo, and it would have broken the hearts of many audiences'.

Palestinian terrorist rumoured to be in the pay of Israel

ABU NIDAL

1937-2002

A bu Nidal was for many years the world's most feared terrorist, said *The Independent*. Directly reponsible for ar least 900 deaths, he was America's Public Enemy Number One until supplanted by Osama bin Laden in 2001. Abu Nidal portrayed himself as a fervent Palestinian nationalist, but his acts were so harmful to the Palestinian cause that some speculated he might be in the pay of the Israelis, said the *Daily Telegraph*. He pursued a bloody campaign against mainstream Palestinian leaders and murdered considerably more Arabs than Jews. In 1982, one of his gunmen seriously wounded the Israeli ambassador to London, giving Israel the pretext it needed to begin its bloody invasion of Lebanon.

Abu Nidal, a *nom de guerre* meaning 'Father of the Struggle', was born in Jaffa in 1937. The son of prosperous landowners, he enjoyed a privileged upbringing until the 1948 Israeli war of independence, when Jaffa was incorporated into Israel. His lamily lost its possessions and fled to the West Bank. Like many young men of his generation, he was drawn into the struggle against the encroaching Israeli enemy. He became a member of the Ba'ath party in Jordan, whence he was expelled for his part in a failed plot to kill King Hussein. In Saudi Arabia, he joined a secret cell of Fatah, a guerrilla organisation founded by Yasser Arafat. Displaying an enthusiasm for armed operations, Abu Nidal soon became known for his willingness to indulge in risky hit-and-run attacks. In 1972 he was thought to be behind the kidnapping of the Israeli athletes at the Munich Olympics, which resulted in the deaths of all the hostages.

In the 1970s, Abu Nidal was posted to Iraq as the Palestine Liberation Organization's representative in Baghdad. With the encouragement of Saddam Hussein, he broke away from the organisation – accusing it of being too moderate – and joined a plot to assassinate Arafat, whose influence he had come to resent. For this he was tried in his absence in a PLO court and sentenced to death. Abu Nidal set up a rival group, the Fatah Revolutionary Council (FRC), which soon established a reputation for ruthlessness even among Palestinian militants. Most of the violence was directed towards those on the Palestinian side. In 1978, for instance, FRC gunmen assassinated the PLO's representative in London. His crime: holding secret talks with Israeli doves. But Nidal's real genius, said *The Independent*, was in creating the myth that whenever anything happened anywhere, the FRC was somehow behind it. Hunted across the Middle East by his Palestinian enemies as well as Western intelligence, Abu Nidal was constantly on the move, and rarely slept in the same

> **Abu Nidal's real genius was in creating the myth that whenever anything happened anywhere, the FRC was somehow behind it.**

place twice. He was reported dead five times, on at least some occasions faking his own death to get out of a tight corner. All of this only added to his mystique in the *souks*.

In 1983 Abu Nidal was expelled from Iraq (because Saddam needed US support for his war with Iran) and settled in Syria. From there, he sought to undermine Palestinian and Jordanian attempts to further the peace process with Israel by carrying out a series of bloody attacks, including the bombing of the British Airways offices in Madrid and Rome in 1985. He was also responsible for the machine-gun attack on an Istanbul synagogue in 1986, in which 22 people died. As the decade wore on, Abu Nidal became increasingly unstable. His violence became so cruel and senseless that even his own men objected, and tried to overthrow him. He regained conrtol with a bloody purge in which some 600 people were murdered, said David Hirst in *The Guardian*. 'He would order executions in the middle of the night when, after a heavy bout of drinking, his paranoia and vindictiveness were at their worst.' Sometimes, while his agents waited for the death sentence to be confirmed, they would bury prisoners alive, with a steel tube in their mouths to allow them to breathe. When the order came, a bullet was shot down the tube, which was then removed.

Eventually Abu Nidal was expelled from Syria and moved to Libya, where, it is rumoured, he masterminded the Lockerbie bombing. Later, Abu Nidal returned to Iraq, where he was reported to have killed himself in August 2002, although some claimed he was murdered by the Iraqi secret service. In his final years, Abu Nidal had become 'little more than a hired gun', said the *Daily Telegraph*. He was utterly without principles, which is probably why he thrived. 'His death will be mourned by very few.'

Head of the WAAF who was immortalised on screen

DAME FELICITY PEAKE

1913-2002

Air Commodore Dame Felicity Peake was an aeroplane-mad child who took up flying as a hobby in 1935; later, at the age of 33, she became Director of the Women's Auxiliary Air Force, with 98,000 women under her command. 'Her rise was phenomenal,' said *The Times*, 'though there were times when it was neither easy nor effortless.'

Felicity Hyde Watts was born in 1913, the daughter of a director in the family textile firm. Educated at St Winifred's, Eastbourne, she spent most of her schooldays 'playing games or being excused lessons to draw or paint'. After coming out as a debutante, she met Jock Hanbury on a cruise to the West Indies. He shared her passion for flying, and they gave each other flying lessons as a wedding present. Three years later, with war in the air, they both decided to join up. But the Forces were looking for women with an aptitude for repairing engines or skilled in telephone or communications work. None of this had formed part of Hanbury's education. Persistence, however, paid off: the authorities relented when she explained that she had a motorcycle that she could, and did, repair herself. In April 1939, she joined the No. 9 ATS company of the RAF. On 1 September, she was appointed company assistant (the equivalent of pilot officer); a month later, she became one of the war's earliest widows when her husband was killed while on a night-flying exercise.

In 1940 Hanbury was posted to Biggin Hill as second-in-command of the 250 WAAF personnel on the base. Set in the rolling Kent countryside, it was to become the most heavily attacked RAF base in the country. Hanbury's experiences there were later portrayed in the film *The Battle of Britain* (1969), with Susannah York playing the young WAAF officer. On 3 August, said the *Daily Telegraph*, she survived a surprise attack by German bombers that left 39 dead. Obeying orders, Hanbury had sheltered in a trench. 'The vibrations and blasts were such that one felt one's limbs must surely come apart,' she recalled. Then she went to see how the airwomen were coping. Scrambling through the debris, she came across a NAAFI girl lying on the ground, and was about to help when someone shouted, 'Don't bother, she's dead.' Hanbury had never seen a dead person before. 'I remember thinking I must have a good look at her, as I might have to get used to this kind of thing.' Later, on her way back, she saw that someone had covered the girl with a blanket. 'Somehow this had a greater effect on me than when I had seen her the first time. It seemed so final, almost casual. I tried to put the picture out of my mind.'

In 1941 she became the first woman in the war to be appointed MBE (military). The following year she was sent to work at the Air Ministry, where she met her second husband, Air Commodore Harald Peake. She later worked at Bomber Command, and in 1946 she became the first professional head of the WAAF, a role she held until 1949. In retirement, Peake worked as a trustee of the Imperial War Museum, and devoted much of her time to the RAF Benevolent Fund.

The Forces were looking for women with an aptitude for repairing engines or skilled in telephone or communications work. She explained that she had a motorcycle that she could, and did, repair herself.

Principled politician whose career stalled over Europe

LORD JENKINS OF HILLHEAD

1920-2003

L ord Jenkins of Hillhead was a giant of British politics for almost half a century, said the *Financial Times*. As Home Secretary in the 1960s he was credited with ushering in the 'permissive society'; he was also considered one of the greatest Chancellors of the century. Following a stint as the first – and so far only – British President of the European Commission, he joined the 'gang of four' behind the foundation of the Social Democratic Party. Yet Jenkins was not merely a career politician; an old-fashioned man of letters, he wrote a number of highly regarded biographies, including a life of Churchill which has sold half a million copies.

A son of the Monmouthshire coalfields, Roy Jenkins was born in 1920 into what he described as the 'working-class squirearchy'. His father was a 'remarkable' figurre, said Dennis Kavanagh in *The Independent*. A miner who began work down the pit at 12, Arthur Jenkins won a scholarship to Ruskin College and spent time at the Sorbonne, before becoming MP for Pontypool. Great things were expected of his son Roy. From Abersychan County School he went to Balliol College, Oxford, to study PPE. There he met many of the figures who would shape British politics in the twentieth century, including Denis Healey and Tony Crosland. Jenkins made no attempt to exploit his working-class roots (and was later amused by the 'prolier than thou' attitude prevalent in the Labour Party). This was no bad thing: with his patrician drawl and fondness for croquet and vintage 'clawet', as he pronounced it, he would not have made a convincing working-class hero. One Oxford don called him 'Nature's old Etonian'.

Jenkins left Oxford with a first in 1941. During the war he served with the Royal Artillery, and as a codebreaker at Bletchley Park. At the age of 27 he won the Southwark Central by-election to become Britain's youngest MP. Two years later he was adopted for Stechford, Birmingham, a seat he would represent for the next 26 years. Jenkins whiled away Labour's years in opposition by writing books – notably *Mr Balfour's Poodle* (1954) – and journalism. Initially a Bevanite, he soon came under the influence of Hugh Gaitskell, who would remain his lifelong political hero (although they fell out briefly over Europe). Indeed, when Gaitskell died, Jenkins nearly gave up politics to edit *The Economist*. Forty years after his death, Gaitskell's picture was still on display in Jenkins's drawing room.

In 1964 Jenkins joined Harold Wilson's government as Aviation Minister. A year later he was appointed Home Secretary. As part of his mission to make Britain more 'civilised', he liberalised the laws on homosexuality, supported the bill to legalise abortion, and reformed the criminal justice system by, among other things, abolishing flogging in prisons. In November 1967, following the devaluation of the pound, he replaced James Callaghan as Chancellor and became such a pivotal figure that in 1968, said *The Times*, many thought he could replace Wilson as Prime Minister. The PM certainly sensed danger: in one paranoid outburst he blamed the Government's troubles on the 'ambitions of one member of this Cabinet to sit in my place'. But Jenkins was too busy at the Treasury to mount a coup; in any case, he did not have a taste for the 'ruthless infighting of politics'.

Following Labour's defeat at the polls in 1970, Jenkins was elected deputy leader under Wilson. Again his time looked ripe, said *The Guardian*. But it was not to be. Politics was changing: the post-war boom was coming to an end, and the parties were 'retreating to the dogmatisms of the past. For Jenkins, the inside track was gradually closed off'. He was deeply concerned by the growing influence of the left-wing unions, and refused to bow to the growing anti-Europeanism in the party. To do so, he reasoned, would be to betray his principles and destroy his reputation as a man of integrity. So, in the decisive vote in 1971, he led 68 rebels into the Tory voting lobby, defying a three-line whip and a five-to-one vote at Labour's annual conference. The following year, he resigned over the decision to hold a referendum on Europe. 'It has all worked out for the best,' noted Wilson. 'Roy will go off and write books, and we will all have a more comfortable life.' Nevertheless, when Labour won the 1974 election, Jenkins returned to the Home Office. He led the 'yes' campaign to victory in the Europe referendum, but 'it was only a momentary shaft of light in the encircling gloom'. When Wilson retired in 1976 Jenkins came third in the first round of the leadership election, and withdrew to become President of the EC.

Three years later he returned to British politics 'with a bang', said *The Times*. In a BBC Dimbleby lecture entitled *Home Thoughts from Abroad*, he made a clarion call across party politics for a strengthening of the centre which appealed both to One Nation Conservatives and many mainstream Labour voters. Two years later the SDP was launched, its purpose being to 'break the mould' of British politics. Eager to get back into the Commons, Jenkins fought and won a by-election at Hillhead in Glasgow, and in the 1983 election the Liberal/SDP alliance won 26 per cent of the vote to Labour's 28 per cent. But the role of party leader did not suit Jenkins's urbane style, said *The Scotsman*, and he stepped down, making way for David Owen. Jenkins has often been credited with forcing Labour to modernise and move to the centre. But, to his critics, the opposite was the case. By dragging many 'sensible' MPs away from the party, argued Denis Healey in *The Independent*, he merely shifted the balance of power further to the left and made the party's recovery more protracted. 'The SDP did not create New Labour: it delayed it.'

> **Jenkins has often been credited with forcing Labour to modernise and move to the centre. But, to his critics, the opposite was the case. 'The SDP did not create New Labour: it delayed it.'**

After losing his seat in 1987, Jenkins went to the House of Lords. He became Chancellor of Oxford University, and Chairman of the Royal Society of Literature. Active into old age, he wrote his masterpiece – his life of Churchill – at the age of 80. 'If he was not like an old man, he was most emphatically not like an old politician,' said Robert Harris in the *Daily Telegraph*. Untouched by bitterness, he spoke warmly of his old foes, including Wilson, and in 2002 he and his wife Jennifer had lunch with James Callaghan followed by tea with Denis Healey. He did, of course, have a couple of bêtes noires – notably his old SDP rival David Owen. Arriving for lunch at the Jenkins house in Oxfordshire, Harris's wife once announced that she had almost reversed her car over Owen on Hungerford high street. 'Almost!' exclaimed Roy. 'Don't you ever come into this house and say that you *almost* ran over David Owen.'

Urbane historian with a flair for making enemies

LORD DACRE OF GLANTON

1914-2003

Hugh Trevor-Roper – Lord Dacre of Glanton – was one of the best-known historians of his generation, said *The Times*. His most famous work, *The Last Days of Hitler*, sold half a million copies and has never been out of print. He later achieved notoriety when, as a director of *The Times*, he authenticated the Hitler Diaries, which Rupert Murdoch had bought for serialisation. Trevor-Roper, a poor reader of German, had looked at the documents only briefly in a Swiss vault and based his conclusion on the testimony of two German experts. He soon realised his mistake, but it was too late. When the diaries were exposed as a fraud, he became a laughing stock. 'For the past three weeks,' he wrote in the spring of 1983, 'I have felt like an Arabian adulterer, pinioned in the sand and awaiting the next, perhaps fatal, volley of shots.'

Hugh Trevor-Roper was born in 1914 in Northumberland, the son of a country doctor. He won a scholarship to Charterhouse, got a First at Christchurch and went on to become an Oxford don, producing his first work, a study of Archbishop Lord, in 1940. By the time the book came out, he was in uniform, said the *Daily Telegraph*. Commissioned into the Territorials, he later served with Military Intelligence, which left him with 'a keen and enduring fascination for conspiracies and the world of secrets'. At the end of the war, he was asked to investigate rumours that Hitler had survived the Berlin bunker. This formed the basis for his best-selling *The Last Days of Hitler*, a portrait of the Führer's 'court of toadies and madmen'.

After the war, Trevor-Roper returned to Oxford. A thin man, 'donnish in appearance', he was an 'urbane and fluent' writer, said *The Independent*, with a flair for making enemies. 'Indeed, he enjoyed vendettas, as well as friendships ... Among his victims were Lawrence Stone (over the Elizabethan aristocracy); Arnold Toynbee (who dared to have a theory of history); and A.J.P. Taylor (over that "ridiculous book on the origins of the second world war").' In the 1960s, he gave short shrift to modish requests for courses on African history. 'Perhaps in the future there will be some African history to teach,' he observed. 'But at present there is none, or very little.' His own books covered subjects as diverse as the European witch-craze of the 17th century and the Philby affair.

> **He gave short shrift to modish requests for courses on African history. 'Perhaps in the future there will be some African history to teach,' he observed. 'But at present there is none, or very little.'**

In 1980, Hugh Trevor-Roper migrated to Cambridge to become Master of Peterhouse. He saw it as a come-down after Oxford: holding a party there, he said, was like 'inviting the beau monde to Biggleside'. This didn't endear him to colleagues, some of whom, said Philip Hensher in *The Independent*, rejoiced at the debacle over the Diaries. Indeed the story goes that one 'sparring partner', who had just acquired two dogs, named them Hitler and Diaries just for the pleasure of calling them repeatedly while walking past Trevor-Roper's house. Even so, his tenure was a success, said the *Daily Telegraph*. He raised large benefactions, built a new library and made progress in reforming the tutorial body. Towards the end of his time there, he felt able to write to a friend: 'The Fellows of Peterhouse have now been brought to order, if not to life.'

Tempestuous diva who fought racism and loved Bach

NINA SIMONE

1933-2003

Nina Simone was a legendary singer whose voice defied categorisation, said the *Daily Telegraph*. 'She took from blues, jazz, folk and classical music, and sang from the soul.' Deeply political and fiercely independent, she played a major role in the civil rights movement, and her songs dealt with persecution, both emotional and racial. 'All my life, I've wanted to shout of my feeling of being imprisoned,' she said.

She was born Eunice Kathleen Waymon in Tryon, North Carolina, in 1933, the sixth of eight children. Her father was a barber and church deacon; her mother a Methodist minister. Both were musical, and by the age of four Eunice was playing hymns on the church organ. Her talent was spotted by her mother's white employer, who paid for her to have piano lessons. In return, Eunice gave recitals in the local library; her parents, being black, were only allowed to stand at the back. The teenager seemed destined for a career as a great classical musician, and the entire community clubbed together to send her to the Juilliard School of Music in New York. But her classical training came to an abrupt halt at the age of 21, said *The Times*, when she was refused a scholarship by the Curtis School of Music in Philadelphia. For the rest of her life she was convinced she was turned down on racial grounds. 'I never got over it,' she said later. 'I had never thought about being black before.'

Out of necessity she took a job playing the piano at a bar in Atlantic City and, fearful of her family discovering she was performing in such an ungodly environment, she changed her name to Nina Simone. The bar owner had thought he was employing a vocalist, and after one night he told her: 'Tomorrow you sing, or you're out of a job.' So she sang – and proved such a hit that three years later she was performing jazz and blues at Carnegie Hall. 'I'm where you always wanted me to be,' she wrote to her parents, 'but I'm not playing Bach.' Simone had a succession of hits in the late 1950s and the 1960s, including renditions of 'I Love You Porgy', 'My Baby Just Cares For Me' and 'I Put A Spell On You'. She was a friend of Martin Luther King, said *The Independent*, and in 1963 wrote the 'vitriolic' 'Mississippi Goddam', in response to the deaths of four children in the bombing of a Baptist church in Alabama. Her 1969 song 'Young, Gifted And Black' became an anthem of the movement to end segregation.

In the early 1970s, Simone left America, saying that, as a black person, she had 'paid a heavy price' for fighting the establishment, and that racial inequality in the USA was 'worse than ever'. For the next 25 years she moved around the globe, living in Barbados, Liberia, Egypt and Turkey before finally settling in the south of France. Her personal life, however, was always troubled. Her second husband, Andrew Stroud, beat her. She had an affair with Earl Barrow, the prime minister of Barbados, but he was married. And in Liberia she was so badly assaulted by a lover that she was hospitalised. Simone herself was a prickly character, wont to fight with her audiences and even walk out if she felt they weren't being sufficiently appreciative. She had numerous battles with the music industry, which she despised, and once pulled a knife in a meeting. In 1995 she was arrested in France after shooting at her rowdy teenage neighbours with an air rifle.

Despite suffering from depression and various physical ailments, Nina Simone continued to perform, last appearing in Britain in 2001. But she admitted she was only in it for the money. 'I came to despise popular songs and I never played them for my amusement,' she wrote in her autobiography. 'Why should I when I could be playing Bach, Czerny or Liszt?'

Champion polo player forced to disguise herself as a man

SUE SALLY HALE

1937-2003

Sue Sally Hale 'belonged with Joan of Arc and George Eliot in the select company of women who had to pretend to be men in order to succeed', said Rupert Cornwell in *The Independent*. Her chosen field, however, was not warfare or literature, but 'the exotic world of polo'.

Born in Los Angeles in 1937, Hale was given her first horse at the age of 3. Her father, Grover Jones, a successful Hollywood screenwriter, died when she was 4, and Hale's mother, a ballerina, married the film stuntman Richard Talmadge. Hale spent much of her childhood swimming, riding her pony and playing cowboys and Indians in Pacific Palisades. 'I was wild,' she later recalled. 'I grew up like a wild Indian. I ran around with a feather in my hair.' At 13 she qualified for the Olympic swimming trials, said the *Daily Telegraph*, but Hale's heart was set on another sport. She had grown up watching men practising on the polo grounds of the Riviera Country Club near Santa Monica, and wanted nothing more than to play the game herself. However, polo in the California of the 1950s was an all-male affair, and Hale had to go to extreme lengths in order to realise her dream.

As soon as she was proficient in the sport, Hale began disguising herself as a man in order to play in polo tournaments. She would flatten her chest with tape, apply mascara to her upper lip to simulate a moustache, wear oversized men's shirts and pull her hair up under her helmet, said Richard Goldstein in the *New York Times*. As soon as a game was over, Hale would disappear into the locker-rooms, re-emerging moments later as a fragrant Californian housewife. 'It was a kick to clean up and then mingle unrecognised with the guys I'd just played against on the field,' she told the *Los Angeles Times*. Only her team-mates knew the truth about her identity.

The masquerade was kept up for two decades, as Hale's efforts to gain admission to the United States Polo Association (USPA) were repeatedly rebuffed. Eventually her fellow players decided that enough was enough, and wrote to the USPA demanding that women be allowed to compete in tournaments. Under threat of a lawsuit, the USPA caved in, and in 1972 Hale became the association's first female member. 'It was the greatest moment in my sports life,' she said.

In due course, Hale became the first female 'rated' player – someone expected to score in every game. Small, tough and stockily built, she could, as one commentator observed, 'ride a horse like a Comanche and hit a ball like a Mack truck'. She played through all five of her pregnancies; one of her daughters, Sunny, is currently ranked No. 1 in women's polo in America. After retiring from the game, Hale enthusiastically extolled the thrill of the sport in verse:

> Total exertion, the ultimate high
> A true test of self, The why for which over and over we try
> Sometimes unique, yet in the same breath quite bleak
> This game we play also out of which a living we eke.

As soon as a game was over, Hale would disappear into the locker-rooms, re-emerging moments later as a fragrant Californian housewife.

Film legend who refused to play the Hollywood game

KATHARINE HEPBURN

1907-2003

Katharine Hepburn was America's last connection with the golden age of Hollywood. In a career that spanned seven decades, she starred in nearly 50 films and acted opposite such legends as John Barrymore, Cary Grant, Humphrey Bogart and Spencer Tracy. She was nominated for an unprecedented 12 Oscars, and won four. Yet Americans didn't love her in the same way as they did, say, Marilyn Monroe. This may have been because Hepburn, with her high cheekbones, upper-crust New England accent and haughty demeanour, never played on a girlish vulnerability. Intelligent, proud and fiercely independent, she had, as she was the first to admit, been dealt a winning hand in life. 'All she had to do,' said David Hinckley in the *New York Daily News*, 'was play it.'

Katharine Hepburn was born in 1907 into a wealthy family in Connecticut. Her father was a surgeon; her mother a suffragette and crusader for birth control. They encouraged their children to swim, ride and climb trees, a regime that left Katharine, in her own words, 'very strong, and utterly fearless'. Her childhood, although privileged, was not idyllic. One morning when she was 13, she went to wake her 16-year-old brother Tommy, only to find him hanging from the rafters. It was Katharine who cut him down. The family could not accept that he might have taken his own life and Tommy was never spoken of again. After that, Katharine, who remained mystified by her brother's death, cut her hair and refused to wear dresses, seeking to fill the hole in the family left by the loss of the eldest son.

Hepburn made her professional stage debut in 1928 after graduating from Bryn Mawr, the exclusive all-female college. In the same year, she married a wealthy stockbroker named Ludlow ('Luddy') Ogden Smith. The marriage broke down after 18 months. In later life, Hepburn accepted that her overweening ambition was to blame. 'In those days it was me, me, me,' she recalled. 'I am horrified at what an absolute pig I was.' Following a period on stage in New York, where she earned a reputation for being difficult, Hepburn was offered a contract with RKO in 1932. Not caring a jot about cinema, she asked for what was then considered an outlandish $1,500 a week – and got it. Hepburn cut an unlikely figure in Tinseltown. She only wore trousers off set, rarely wore make-up and refused to give interviews. (Once she was nearly decapitated when she ducked behind a revolving aeroplane propeller to avoid a journalist.) Such behaviour earned her the nickname Katharine of Arrogance. Nor was she a conventional beauty, said the *Washington Post*. Hepburn described herself as having an 'angular face and body, and I suppose, an angular personality'. She had freckles, coppercoloured hair and a voice that reminded Tallulah Bankhead of 'nickels dropping in a slot machine'. She could, however, afford to be different, said the *Los Angeles Times*. Unlike the likes of Bette Davis and Joan Crawford, she was educated and independently wealthy. She had social graces, and she had class.

Hepburn won an Oscar for her third film, *Morning Glory* (1933), and rave reviews for her role in *Little Women* (1933). But these were followed by several duds which even the screwball comedy *Bringing up Baby* (1938), co-starring Cary Grant, could not redeem. Meanwhile, her performance in a play called *The Lake* inspired Dorothy Parker's famous remark that 'she ran the gamut of emotion from A to B'. In 1938 Hepburn was labelled 'box office poison'. Shortly after, she was turned down for the role she wanted most, Scarlett O'Hara. 'The part was practically written for me,' she told David Selznick. 'I just can't imagine Clark Gable chasing you for ten years,' he replied. Unbowed, Hepburn returned to New York to star in a new play, *The Philadelphia Story*. The part of Tracy Lord, the snooty heiress who mends her ways on the eve of marriage, was written with Hepburn in mind, and proved her salvation. 'The play was not about a spoiled socialite like Katharine Hepburn,' wrote the critic Andrew Sarris. 'The play was about Katharine Hepburn herself, and what the American people thought about Katharine Hepburn in 1939, and what Katharine Hepburn realised she had to do to keep her career going. *The Philadelphia Story* is, quite simply, the breaking, reining in and saddling of an unruly thoroughbred for the big races to come. It is Katharine Hepburn getting her comeuppance – and accepting it like the good sport she was.'

In 1942 Hepburn was cast in *Woman of the Year*, opposite Spencer Tracy. On set, she took one look at her co-star and said: 'You're not as tall as I thought you were.' 'Don't worry,' Tracy snapped, 'I'll soon cut you down to size.' And so he did. The pair bickered their way through several classic films, and began a relationship which would last until Tracy's death 27 years later. But whereas on screen they fought as equals, said Geoffrey Wansell in the *Daily Mail*, in real life, Hepburn allowed her lover to dominate her entirely, putting up with his alcoholism, his affairs and his refusal to divorce his wife. 'I tried not to disturb him, irritate him, bore him, nag him,' she said. 'I struggled to change all the qualities about me which I felt he didn't like. I can only say that I never would have left him… I was his.' Ill for several

> **She took one look at Spencer Tracy and said: 'You're not as tall as I thought you were.' 'Don't worry,' Tracy snapped, 'I'll soon cut you down to size.'**

years, he died in her arms 17 days after they finished making their final film together, *Guess Who's Coming to Dinner* (1967). Out of respect for his wife and children, Hepburn did not attend the funeral. But she refused to feel sorry for herself, or be cast as the martyr. 'Self-sacrificing women give me melancholia,' she said. 'My mother, who was an angel, said: "Please yourself; then at least you're sure somebody is pleased."'

Following Tracy's death, Hepburn gave some of her finest screen performances, including as Eleanor of Aquitaine in *The Lion in Winter* (1968), for which she received her third Oscar. (Her second was for *The African Queen*, during the making of which she braved malaria and dysentery.) Her last great performance was opposite Henry Fonda in *On Golden Pond* (1981), a rather sugary film that was really about two great actors grown old, and the passing of an era. Both stars won Oscars, Fonda's being awarded posthumously. In later life, Hepburn divided her time between her brownstone house in New York, which she had bought in the 1930s, and her family home in Connecticut, where she was still known simply as Dr Hepburn's daughter. She made her last film in 1994. In 1999, the American Film Institute voted her the greatest female film star ever. But Hepburn was not one for self-congratulation. 'I could have accomplished three times what I've accomplished,' she said. 'I haven't realised my potential. It's disgusting.'

The devastation wrought by a soldier with 'not much grey matter'

IDI AMIN

1925-2003

I di Amin was the former dictator of Uganda, and self-styled 'conqueror of the British Empire'. Initially considered an amiable buffoon, he became one of Africa's most reviled despots, responsible for the deaths of up to 500,000 of his own people. Amin seemed to relish his 'monstrous reputation', said the *Daily Telegraph*. A self-confessed cannibal, he reportedly boasted of owning a collection of human heads extensive enough to require its own deep freeze. Such was his cruelty that his enemies claimed he must be insane; but 'Amin survived too long, exhibiting too shrewd an instinct for manipulation, to be dismissed as a mere madman.'

Amin was, essentially, a British creation, said Richard Dowden in the *Independent on Sunday*. A corporal in the Kings African Rifles (KAR) he served his colonial masters loyally and, as independence approached, was promoted rapidly. Amin seemed happy in his role as 'well-trained faithful beast', and the British were reassured by his apparent lack of guile. 'Not much grey matter, but a splendid chap to have about,' said one British officer. Asked if Amin might try to seize power, the British high commissioner replied that he had just enough intelligence to know he couldn't run the country properly. But Amin was no fool, said the *Telegraph* and, in power, 'the stereotype mercilessly mocked its former masters'. His self-importance and penchant for ludicrous public statements caused merriment in the West, but the joke was a savage one, and 'it was not at Amin's expense, but at the expense of those who laughed'.

Born in Koboko, in the north-western part of Uganda around 1925, Amin was the son of poor farmers. He received little formal education and joined the Army in 1946. Six foot four inches tall, 'he was to play rugby for his country and held the light heavyweight boxing championship of Uganda for nine years,' said *The Independent*. His bravery in action attracted the attention of the British, and in 1957, he was sent on a course to become an effendi – a senior rank reserved for outstanding 'natives'. Amin's record was not unblemished: there were allegations that his men tortured and murdered villagers during a crackdown on cattle rustling. But six months before independence, it seemed unwise to court martial one of the Army's few native Ugandan officers, and so no action was taken.

Following independence in 1963, Amin made rapid progress due, in part, to the sponsorship of the new prime minister, Milton Obote. And when Obote decided to oust the president, King 'Freddie' of Buganda, Amin proved his loyalty by leading the attack on the palace. Although King Freddie's men were armed only with a few hunting rifles, the assault – and Amin's part in it – gained mythical status. However, towards the end of the 1960s, Obote began to feel he'd supped with the devil long enough and he plotted to dismiss Amin – only to find the tables turned and himself ousted in a coup in 1971. At first, the genial new leader seemed, to some observers, a breath of fresh air: he promised to root out corruption; Obote's political prisoners were freed; and King Freddie's body was brought back from England, where he had died in 1969, for burial. 'I have never encountered a more benevolent and popular leader than General Amin,' wrote one British commentator.

But in the streets of Kampala, there were rumours of terrible atrocities: people told of senior officers being herded into rooms into which hand grenades were thrown, and entire officer corps being ordered to their parade ground to be mown down by tanks. At the Makindye military prison, political prisoners were handed sledgehammers and ordered to beat each other to death. Thousands of people – including civilians – disappeared, as did two American journalists who tried to investigate reports of massacres. The country's rivers overflowed with human debris and, from time to time, body parts clogged up the hydro-electric dam at Lake Victoria, causing power cuts in Kampala. One of Amin's own wives was reportedly killed, mutilated and then sewn back up for identification by her children. Once, a minister heard the news of his own death on the radio; apparently, his scheduled assassination had been delayed by a bureaucratic backlog. Amin was terrifyingly impulsive. His decision to expel the Asian community in 1972 came to him, he said, in a dream. He acted on it the next day, giving 35,000 people just 90 days to flee. The move was popular among Ugandans, but since Asians made up most of the country's business class, it ruined the economy.

On the international stage, Amin took particular pleasure in baiting the British. During the Winter of Discontent, he launched a 'Save Britain Fund', offering to send vegetables to relieve the suffering and promising Ted Heath he'd organise a whip-round if 'you will let me know the exact position of the mess'. And at a reception for ministers of the Organisation for African Unity in 1975, the band struck up Colonel Bogey as Amin was carried in on a sedan chair borne aloft by four white businessman. In 1977, after Britain broke off diplomatic relations, he appointed himself CBE – Conqueror of the British Empire. To his long-standing enemy, Julius Nyerere, the president of Tanzania, he wrote: 'I wish to assure you that I love you very much and if you had been a woman I would have considered marrying you, although your head is full of grey hairs.'

In 1972, Amin caused international outrage by sending Kurt Waldheim a memo condoning the Holocaust. In 1976, Palestinians hijacked a plane bound from Tel Aviv to France and landed it at Entebbe airport. Amin protected the hijackers but one night, Israeli commandos flew in and rescued all but one of the hostages. Dora Bloch, an elderly Jewish woman travelling on a British passport, had been taken to a hospital in Kampala; after the raid, she was dragged screaming from her bed and executed. Amin's rule finally came to an end in 1979, after he made the mistake of declaring war on Tanzania; Nyerere countered by mounting an invading force on Uganda, and drove Amin into exile. He was given refuge in Libya by his long-time ally Colonel Gaddafi, before settling in a modest, nine-room villa in Jeddah, Saudi Arabia.

Unstarry opera singer whose life was cut tragically short

SUSAN CHILCOTT

1963-2003

The British soprano Susan Chilcott was one of the outstanding opera singers of her generation, said *The Independent*. After her Desdemona at Glyndebourne in 2001, she was described by one critic as an 'English rose in full bloom'; to Antonio Pappano, the musical director of the Royal Opera, she was simply the 'real thing'. But unlike so many leading ladies, Chilcott was 'blessed with a natural modesty', and never let such adulation go to her head. 'Asked about the glowing reviews and fans' adulation, her reply was invariably the disarmingly simple: "I am grateful."'

Born in 1963, Chilcott was brought up by her adoptive parents on their farm in the Mendips. She won her first prize for singing at the age of 3 and, although her parents were not musical, they were unstinting in their support as she pursued her chosen profession at the Guildhall in London. In 1991 she made her debut as Frasquita in *Carmen* with Scottish Opera. Her major break came three years later, as Ellen Orford in *Peter Grimes* at the Monnaie in Brussels.

Before her career took off, Chilcott had made ends meet by working as a cleaner in an old people's home, and even after she became famous she remained completely unstarry. She spent her free time at a cottage near her parents' farms, and thought nothing of joining in the hymns at the local church on Sunday mornings. It was all in sharp contrast to the grandeur of Covent Garden. 'One day I am digging potatoes, baking, putting my son's toys away,' she said. 'The next I am meeting Placido Domingo.' Chilcott developed cancer in 2001, and underwent a mastectomy. She had reconstructive surgery, and resumed her career last year after a bout of chemotherapy. But during her final illness, her thoughts were not of music, but of her son. 'Her love of opera goes without saying, but more than anything, her devotion was to Hughie,' her husband, David Sigall, told the *Sunday Telegraph*. 'In those final months motherhood kicked in above all else.'

> **She was described by one critic as an 'English rose in full bloom'.**

Reluctant heart-throb whose best work was on the stage

SIR ALAN BATES

1934-2003

Alan Bates was one of the greatest British actors of his generation. He came to prominence in the 'kitchen sink' theatre and cinema of the 1950s and early 1960s, said *The Times*, 'but his versatility and willingness to take risks ensured that he was never confined to one sort of character'. Having said that, he was particularly gifted at portraying 'brooding, troubled men wrestling with inner demons, whether in the plays of Simon Gray, or as Thomas Hardy's doomed Henchard in the BBC version of *The Mayor of Casterbridge*'.

Born in Derbyshire in 1934, Alan Bates was the son of a cellist who earned a living selling insurance. His parents encouraged him in his ambition to become an actor – announced at the age of 11 – and at 18, he enrolled at Rada. His contemporaries during that 'fruitful period for the academy' included Peter O'Toole, Albert Finney and Richard Briers. Within a year of graduating, Bates had won the role that would make his reputation, as Cliff in John Osborne's groundbreaking drama *Look Back in Anger*, at the Royal Court Theatre in London. He toured with the play on and off for two years, and was offered a seven-year Hollywood contract on the back of his success on Broadway. He turned it down: a private man, he had no interest in the trappings of fame and was never comfortable with his heart-throb status.

Nevertheless, Bates was to become a stalwart of 1960s cinema, said *The Guardian*. He played a 'Christ-like hobo' in *Whistle Down the Wind*, a working class anti-hero in *A Kind of Loving*, and a Swinging Londoner in *Georgy Girl*. He was also 'outstanding' as Ted, the tenant farmer in Joseph Losey's film of *The Go-Between*, scripted by Harold Pinter. One of his best-known screen moments was the nude wrestling scene with Oliver Reed in Ken Russell's *Women in Love*. Russell recalled that both actors were wary of doing the scene until they discovered, during a drunken visit to a pub lavatory, that they were both healthily endowed. 'However, between takes, Oliver gave nature a helping hand, so that on film it looks, mistakenly, as if he is the larger actor.'

For all his brilliance on screen, Bates was most comfortable in the theatre, and it was there that he gave some of his best performances. He enjoyed a long association with Simon Gray and Harold Pinter, which began with *Butley*, at the Criterion in 1971. Other successes included Gray's *Otherwise Engaged* (Queen's, 1975), *Life Class* by David Storey, at the Royal Court in 1974, and a 1983 revival of Osborne's *A Patriot for Me*. One of his finest TV roles was in Alan Bennett's *An Englishman Abroad*, in which he played Guy Burgess. More recently he was a glorious Farve in a version of Nancy Mitford's *The Pursuit of Love / Love in a Cold Climate*.

> **He was particularly gifted at portraying 'brooding, troubled men wrestling with inner demons'.**

Bates married Victoria Ward in 1970. They had twin sons, one of whom, Tristan, died suddenly of an asthma attack in 1990, aged 19. Two years later, Victoria died of grief. Bates was devastated: he spoke of his life being 'cut literally in half, with four becoming two, like a sniper in your garden'. In his son's memory, he established the Tristan Bates Theatre at the Actors' Centre in Covent Garden.

Aboriginal woman
whose story inspired
a major film

MOLLY KELLY

1917-2004

Molly Kelly was the Aboriginal woman whose incredible journey across 1,500 miles of the Australian Outback inspired the film *Rabbit-Proof Fence*, said Kathy Marks in *The Independent*. Released in Britain in 2002, the film highlighted the plight of the 'stolen generations' – the 100,000-odd mixed-race children who were taken from their parents and brought up in white society, in the hope of 'breeding out' their Aboriginality. 'Mum's legacy is the calming influence and quiet dignity of the desert women, and the stolen generations story,' said her daughter, Doris. 'She looked you straight in the eye.'

Born in Jigalong, in the north west of Australia, in around 1917, Molly Craig was the daughter of Maude, a Mardu Aborigine, and a white man named Thomas Craig, who was an inspector working on the rabbit-proof fence which stretched the length of Western Australia. The family settled in a 'blacks' camp', but in 1931, when Molly was about 14, she and two younger girls – her sister Daisy and their cousin Gracie – were abducted from their families and transported to an institution near Perth called Moore River. The abduction was part of the government's integrationist policy. Its leading proponent was A.O. Neville, who argued that removing mixed-race children from their mothers was no crueller than taking a pup from a bitch, 'no matter how frantic the momentary grief might be at the time'. At Moore River, the girls were beaten for speaking their own language and locked up at night. After just one day, Molly decided that they should escape. The younger girls were alarmed by the prospect of a long journey home; but Molly, strong-willed even then, reasoned that if they walked far enough in the right direction, they would eventually come across the rabbit-proof fence, which they could then follow back to Jigalong. It was a gruelling journey which the trio survived by begging food from sympathetic farmers, foraging and catching rabbits. When the younger girls became too tired and sore to walk, Molly carried them. The police launched a massive search for the girls, but Molly was clever, and made sure they only walked by night. Nine weeks later they were home.

> **The government argued that removing mixed-race children from their mothers was no crueller than taking a pup from a bitch, 'no matter how frantic the momentary grief might be at the time'.**

Some years later, Molly married an Aboriginal stockman, Toby Kelly, and had two daughters, Doris and Annabelle. Then, in 1940, she and her two daughters were taken back to Moore River. She ran away in 1941, carrying Annabelle, and leaving Doris with a relative. Annabelle was permanently removed a couple of years later, never to see her mother again; Doris eventually found her way back to her mother 21 years later. Her book, *Follow the Rabbit-Proof Fence*, published in 1996, was used as the basis for the film. Its success turned Molly and Daisy, by then elderly ladies living in adjoining houses in Jigalong, into celebrities. But Molly never regarded herself as anything very special. 'We only walked,' she told Doris. 'We go back. We go back to mummy and daddy.'

First woman to win the Polar Medal

VIRGINIA FIENNES

1947-2004

Lady Twisleton-Wykeham-Fiennes, known as Ginny, was 'the single most important thing' in the life of her husband, the explorer Sir Ranulph. She masterminded most of his adventures, accompanied him on many of them – she was the first woman to be awarded the Polar Medal – and made the roast chicken and apple crumble that haunted his dreams when he was starving in the frozen wastes of Antarctica, said the *Daily Express*. Unflappable (except when Ranulph left a frostbitten big toe on the side of the bath), witty and independent, Ginny was the ideal wife for an explorer. 'I'm not the type to throw myself on the floor and burst into tears each time he sets off,' she said. 'I just keep myself extremely busy.'

Born Virginia Pepper in 1947, she grew up in West Sussex. Ranulph lived nearby, and, as an unruly 12-year-old, would come over to play with the Peppers' electric train set. He was entranced by his hosts' 9-year-old daughter from day one. 'I can still see her big, sparkling blue eyes and her wicked smile,' he once recalled. They married in 1970. The honeymoon did not bode well – 'we were like two wild animals put in a cage', she said – but after a few tempestuous years, they worked out their differences and 'ended up sublimely happy' together.

Ginny accompanied Ranulph on six trips and spent two years with him in the field. In addition to receiving the Polar Medal for her work on radio communications, she was the first woman invited to join the famously macho Antarctic Club. But it was at logistics that Ginny excelled. Undaunted by bureaucracy, said *The Times*, and able 'to make big men quake in their boots with a flash of her bright blue eyes', she was fearless in the face of financiers and icebergs alike.

In 1990, the Fienneses moved from West Sussex to Exmoor, where Ginny bred award-winning Aberdeen Angus cattle (all of which she knew by name) and Welsh mountain sheep. She adored animals, especially her Jack Russell, Bothie, who went with her to the Antarctic and about whom she wrote a bestselling book, *Bothie the Polar Dog*.

Unflappable (except when Ranulph left a frostbitten big toe on the side of the bath), witty and independent, Ginny was the ideal wife for an explorer.

When asked the secret of their happy marriage, Ranulph said that Ginny was 'not only my wife but a sister and a friend'. Ginny retorted that it was 'probably because you're away all the time'.

Author who sent an 'urgent ticker tape from hell'

HUBERT SELBY JR

1928-2004

Hubert Selby Jr was the author of 'one of the great books of 20th-century American fiction', said *The Independent*. Published in 1964, *Last Exit to Brooklyn* – a collection of loosely linked stories about America's poor and dispossessed – caused the kind of fuss of which most fledgling writers would be proud. One critic described the author as 'mired in American slime', another called his book 'an urgent ticker tape from hell'. Selby himself was bemused by the furore. 'The events that take place are the way people are,' he said. 'These are not literary characters; these are real people. I knew these people.'

Hubert Selby Jr was born in Brooklyn in 1928, the son of a Kentucky coalminer turned merchant seaman. It was a tough district and Hubert soon began to call himself Cubby, having discovered that his given name commanded little respect in a neighbourhood where everybody else was called Mikey, Tony or Vinny. At the age of 15, he dropped out of high school to follow his father's footsteps into the merchant marines. While at sea, he contracted severe tuberculosis, and was told he had only a few months to live. Returning to New York, he underwent extensive surgery to remove sections of ten of his ribs, and spent three years in hospital, where he was put on a course of the experimental antibiotic Streptomycin. The side effects were catastrophic. 'It impaired my vision, destroyed most of my inner ear and fried my brain,' he said. He left hospital addicted to morphine, full of rage, and – having read voraciously during his illness – determined to write, because 'I did not want to die having done nothing with my life'.

For the next few years Selby supported himself with a series of dead-end jobs – as a clerk, an insurance adjuster and a freelance copywriter – while he wrote the short stories that would eventually form his first book. They were based on the tales he had heard and the people he had met, and made for harrowing reading. *Tralala*, for instance, features the brutal gang rape of a young prostitute in a car park, and was the subject of an obscenity trial when it was first published in 1961. *Last Exit to Brooklyn* was published in 1964 – and was denounced as the 'dirty book of the month'. Other reviewers, however, could see what Selby was trying to do; Allen Ginsberg, for instance, declared that the stories would 'explode like a rusty hellish bombshell over America and still be eagerly read in a hundred years'.

The book came out in Britain in 1966 – six years after the Chatterley trial – and its publishers were almost immediately taken to court. They lost the case when it was put to a jury (which was, at the judge's direction, all male), but won an appeal ably argued by John Mortimer, QC. *Last Exit* became a bestseller on both sides of the Atlantic; Selby spent the profits on heroin and alcohol, before going cold turkey and moving, rather improbably, to West Hollywood for the sake of his health. Over the course of the next 14 years he published three further novels: *The Room* (1971), *The Demon* (1976) and *Requiem for a Dream* (1978), all of which had similarly bleak themes, and were well received. For some years after that he 'laboured in obscurity', said *The Times*; however, his fame was reawakened in 1989, with the release of a film version of *Last Exit*, which proved almost as controversial as the original book.

In person, 'Cubby' Selby was a kind, 'self-effacing' man, and a believing Christian, said Catheryn Kilgarriff, the daughter of his English publisher, in the *Daily Telegraph*. When he came to give a sell-out talk in London in 2001, no one could believe that this chronicler of madness and despair 'had the bluest twinkling eyes, and the humblest demeanour. Everything about him was joyful, and so unlike his writing.'

Glamorous former head of St Paul's Girls' School

BARONESS BRIGSTOCKE

1929-2004

Baroness Brigstocke was the High Mistress of St Paul's Girls' School, the prestigious London day school, from 1974 to 1989, and the 'denizen of numerous boardrooms and quangos', said the *Daily Telegraph*. Tall, immaculately coiffed and 'strikingly elegant', she ran the school 'like a business', with herself as its charismatic CEO. 'Many girls found her a dazzling role model'; others complained that she took little interest in those pupils whose parents were neither influential nor famous. 'She doesn't know me from Adam,' was a common refrain. Nevertheless, she organised bursaries for poorer girls, and even paid the fees of four pupils out of her own pocket.

Heather Brown was born in Reading in 1929, the daughter of a former coalminer who ran a tobacconist's shop. She was educated at the Abbey School, Reading, and won a scholarship to Girton College, Cambridge to read classics. She had no intellectual pretensions, and dedicated much of her time at university to acting. Her parents, however, disapproved, and refused to pay for her to go to drama school, said *The Times*. Instead, she joined Selfridges as a management trainee, where she learned 'the vital skills of flattery after being reprimanded for nearly insulting Selfridges' best customer'. After eight months, she left to teach classics at Francis Holland School, and in 1952, married Geoffrey Brigstocke, a diplomat. 'I was so pleased to be Mrs Brigstocke with an "e" after years as Miss Brown without one,' she once said.

When Geoffrey Brigstocke was posted to America, she was glad to swap the 'drudgery' of the London teaching circuit for the 'glamour of Washington at the time of the Kennedys. She taught Latin at the National Cathedral School, where she eschewed convention by fraternising with the parents of her pupils and was known for charming the famous.' She even persuaded the First Lady to allow her daughter to join her nursery at the White House. Returning to the UK, she used her new networking skills to transform Francis Holland. Six months before she moved to St Paul's, her husband was killed in the DC10 aircraft crash in Paris.

A brilliant fundraiser, Mrs Brigstocke 'charmed cash out of governors and rich parents' to build new libraries, laboratories and an impressive theatre complex. During this time, she became 'unquestionably grand,' said Katharine Whitehorn in *The Guardian* – 'and outrageous'; she turned up to a party wearing towelling pyjamas ('I was fed up with looking like a headmistress'), danced an energetic can-can at a fundraising gala, and drove a large Daimler known to pupils as the 'Brigmobile'. Brigstocke's imperious manner won her enemies, however, and from time to time, stories about her were leaked to an eager press. On one occasion, she told younger members of staff not to wear knee-length boots, and was then seen sporting an expensive pair herself. On another, she lectured parents about taking their children out of school for holidays, before jetting off on a term-time skiing trip.

Brigstocke retired from St Paul's in 1989, and was raised to the peerage in 1993. She was killed in April 2004 in a traffic accident in Athens, where she had been attending meetings of the charity Home-Start International. She was survived by her four children, and her second husband, Lord Griffiths, whom she married in 2000. 'She had a wonderful sense of humour and was extraordinarily courageous,' he told the press. 'I had four marvellous years with her and I am absolutely devastated.'

The Teflon President who charmed America

RONALD REAGAN

1911-2004

Ronald Reagan turned to politics after a career in film, and became his country's 40th president, said the *Daily Telegraph*. He will be remembered for two 'striking achievements': helping to end the Cold War, and restoring America's confidence in itself, after the traumas and tragedies of the 1960s and 1970s. Reagan was an instinctive politician who perceived that the average American wasn't much interested in issues, said Tony Allen-Mills in the *Sunday Times*: what they wanted was a genial, optimistic leader who could help them feel better about themselves – and that is precisely what they got. Conveying the traditional values of thrift, hard work and free enterprise, 'with the intimacy of a next-door neighbour', Reagan was, as *Newsweek* once put it, 'America as it imagined itself to be'.

Ronald Wilson Reagan was born in Tampico, Illinois, where his alcoholic father worked as a salesman. The family was poor, and during the summers 'Dutch', as he was then known, worked as a lifeguard, and was proud of the fact that he saved 77 people from possible drowning. A sporty youth, and a star of his college drama club, he was advised to become an actor. Instead, he took a job as a sports commentator on Iowa radio – and proved such a gifted communicator that at one occasion he commented, as though live at the game, entirely from wire reports. In 1937, while in LA, Reagan wangled a screen test with Warner Bros, and was offered a contract. It was the beginning of a long, but not especially distinguished, career. He described himself as the 'Errol Flynn of the B movie'; in the main features he usually played supporting roles. (When he was elected president, Jack Warner barked: 'No. James Stewart for President; Ronald Reagan as his best friend.') Reagan's favourite film was *Knute Rockne, All American*, in which he played a football star named George Gipp who, on his death bed, urges his team to 'win just one for the Gipper'. His best film was perhaps *Kings Row*, in which he played a womaniser who has both his legs amputated by a sadistic surgeon. Waking up from the operation, he utters the famous line: 'Where's the rest of me?' His political opponents, however, preferred to draw attention to *Bedtime for Bonzo*, in which Reagan played second fiddle to a chimp. During his first election campaign, his Democrat rival sponsored nightly showings of the film, in an attempt to undermine his authority as a serious politician.

Reagan was brought up a New Deal Democrat; his views gradually moved to the right, however, thanks in part to the influence of his second wife, Nancy. (Reagan's first wife, the actress Jane Wyman, divorced him in 1948, saying she was bored by his increasing interest in politics.) He honed his political skills as president of the Screen Actors Guild in the 1950s, joined the Republican Party in 1962, and ran for governor of California four years later. 'What do we do now?' he famously asked his staff, after winning a surprise landslide victory. Reagan captured the Republican presidential nomination in 1980, at the third attempt. By reaching out to former Democrats like himself – 'the ones who drive the trucks and raise the kids, the farmers and firemen, craftsmen and cops' – he defeated Jimmy Carter to become, at the age of 69, his country's 40th

17 million jobs were created, and GNP nearly doubled. But the national debt nearly tripled and the trade deficit quadrupled. ('I don't worry about the deficit,' he quipped, 'it's big enough to take care of itself.')

president. Cultivating a laid-back cowboy image borrowed from his films, he conveyed three simple messages: America needed less government, lower taxes, and to tackle the 'evil empire' of the Soviet Union.

Less than three months into his presidency, Reagan was shot in the chest by John Hinkley. In the emergency room, he told his wife, 'Honey, I forgot to duck.' And as he was being wheeled into the operating room, he joked to the team of surgeons: 'Please tell me you're all Republicans.' The public was deeply impressed by his humour and courage, and from that moment his 'political position was probably impregnable', said *The Times*. In Washington circles, many were baffled by Reagan's total lack of neuroses, and impenetrable charm. ('Beneath the lava flow in warmth, there is something impervious as a glacier,' said an aide.) But the public liked him, and in the long term that popularity enabled him to survive scandals that could have brought down other presidents, including claims that he was being advised by an astrologer. In the short term, he used it to push a massive 25 per cent tax cut through Congress. During his eight years in government, 17 million jobs were created, and GNP nearly doubled. But thanks to vast increases in defence spending – he was determined that the arms race would bankrupt the Soviet Union – the national debt nearly tripled and the trade deficit quadrupled. ('I don't worry about the deficit,' he quipped, 'it's big enough to take care of itself.')

Reagan's second term was overshadowed by the Iran Contra affair, in which it was revealed that his officials had been selling arms to America's arch enemy Iran, and using the proceeds to fund right-wing Contra rebels in Nicaragua. It could have been Reagan's Watergate, said *The Independent*, but the Teflon President survived by denying knowledge of the Contra deals. His claim certainly rang true. Reagan was known to be vague about such details as the names of the foreign leaders whose countries he happened to be visiting, and was notoriously lazy: rumour had it that by 6pm every evening, he and Nancy were in their pyjamas, watching *Little House on the Prairie* over a TV dinner. Challenged on the story, he joked: 'Hard work never killed anyone but I figure, why take a chance?' Yet he was no dolt, said *The Guardian*: he did, after all, have the wisdom to respond to President Gorbachev's overtures, and when it came to discussing disarmament, went further than his advisers wanted.

Reagan left office, looking forward to many happy years on his ranch in California. But not long after he was diagnosed with Alzheimer's. In 1994, he wrote a letter to the American people, explaining that as a result of the slow decline ahead he would be retiring from public life. 'I now begin the journey that will lead me into the sunset of my life,' he told them. 'I know that for America there will always be a bright dawn ahead.'

Ron and Maggie: A Love Story

When Mrs Thatcher was elected in 1979, Reagan was the first foreign politician to offer his congratulations; she, however, refused his call for three days, considering that he was not sufficiently important. But Reagan refused to give up, and their friendship gradually developed in the 1980s, said Peter Riddell in *The Times*. It was an attraction of opposites. Thatcher was, as Sir Percy Cradock put it, 'the bossy, intrusive Englishwoman, lecturing and hectoring... thin on imagination, strong on analysis', whereas Reagan was a 'sunny, Irish ex-actor, his mind operating mostly in the instinctive mode, happy to delegate or over-delegate, hazy about most of his briefs, but with certain stubbornly held principles'. The fact was, they complemented one another. The genial president was relaxed enough to take Thatcher's hectoring; she, aware of his intellectual limitations, was not afraid to disagree with him, and often did – over the US invasion of Grenada, over the Falklands, and over possible threats to the British nuclear deterrent from his Star Wars programme. Usually, she got her way, much to the annoyance of his aides. She was, after all, one of his 'dearest friends', while he was the 'second most important man' in her life, after Denis.

Lexicographer whose work earned him death threats

ROBERT BURCHFIELD

1923-2004

In his *Who's Who* entry, Robert Burchfield listed as the first of his recreations 'investigating English grammar'. In fact, it was rather more than a hobby: as editor of the 6,000-page, four-volume *Supplement* to the *Oxford English Dictionary*, and chief editor of the Oxford English Dictionaries (from 1971 to 1984) he dedicated his entire working life to the study of the sources and development of the language.

A New Zealander from a non-academic family (the only book in the house was a socialist tract), Burchfield was educated at the Wanganui Technical College. In 1949 he won a Rhodes scholarship to Magdalen College, Oxford, where he studied under C.S. Lewis and J.R.R. Tolkien. Thanks to their shared interest in medieval literature, the latter became a close friend: Burchfield later described Tolkien as the 'puckering fisherman who drew me into his philological net'. Burchfield was persuaded to become involved in lexicography by C.T. Onions, a former editor of the OED. As a lexicographer, Burchfield displayed an 'enthusiasm for the new that sometimes enraged traditionalists', said the *Daily Telegraph*. He revelled in the flexibility of the language, and once described it as 'a monster accordion, stretchable at the whim of the editor, compressable ad lib'. He saw 'standard English' and 'received pronunciation' as only a local form of language which had embraced many different strands, and broadened the scope of the OED to include words from Anglophone countries including South Africa and the West Indies. Many of his inclusions were highly controversial: he had to go to court to include pejorative definitions of the word 'Jew' (he argued the dictionaries exist to define words as they are used, not as we would like them to be used) and fought legal battles to include trademarks, such as Yale and WeightWatchers.

Then there was the 'perennial debate over which new words had made it in, and who was credited with first usage', said Christopher Hawtree in *The Guardian*. 'Grotty' was credited to the John Burke novelisation of the 1964 Beatles film *A Hard Day's Night*, rather than to the film itself, 'sod's law' to the *New Statesman*, rather than to the article's author (Richard Boston). Meanwhile 'bate' meaning rage is last recorded by the OED in 1690, notwithstanding the currency given it by Anthony Buckeridge in the Jennings books – as in 'Watch out, old Wilkie's in a bate'. Much of this work was delegated to assistants, among them the young Julian Barnes, who was employed as an 'expert in sports and dirty words'. He delved through back issues of *Autocar* to nail down early instances of 'gearbox', and tried to persuade a reluctant Burchfield to include a word to describe a form of sexual congress. 'I'm afraid, you know, there isn't as much of this about as you seem to think,' he was told. Words, Burchfield discovered, can arouse terrible passions: once, he received a letter warning him that 'You won't know when or where, but you'll be dead'.

This, however, was nothing compared with the outcry which greeted his revision of the grammatical bible, *Fowler's Modern English Usage*. In the third edition, said Adrian Williams in *The Times*, Burchfield dared to suggest that sentences may properly begin with 'and' or 'but', that infinitives may be split without the sky falling down, and that a sentence may end with a preposition. The traditionalists were furious: one reviewer wrote that 'Burchfield's wildly descriptionist perversions of the classic prescriptionist masterpiece have assured him a place in Hell'. In response, Burchfield pointed to his prescriptionist entry for the personal pronoun 'I', which stated that the 'regrettable' use of between you and I 'must be condemned at once'.

Investigative journalist who embraced satire and socialism

PAUL FOOT

1937-2004

Paul Foot was a tireless champion of the underdog, and one of Britain's greatest crusading journalists, said Francis Wheen in the *Evening Standard*. 'A former public schoolboy turned Trotskyist, a cricket-lover who learned his politics from robust Glasgow Trade Unionists,' he worked on the assumption that most powerful people are up to no good, 'and took a boyish delight in having his suspicions confirmed'. Working variously at *The Guardian*, *Private Eye*, and the *Daily Mirror*, he exposed countless injustices, and helped bring about the release of, among many others, the Birmingham Six, and the Guildford Four. 'Campaigns like this get high praise when they are successful,' he reflected. 'While they are going they are always unpopular.'

Born in 1937, Paul Mackintosh Foot was a member of the establishment, 'albeit the left-leaning one', said the *Financial Times*. His uncle, Michael, became leader of the Labour party and his father, Hugh, was ambassador to the UN. Paul was educated at Shrewsbury, where his classmates included the future founders of *Private Eye*, Christopher Booker, Willie Rushton and Richard Ingrams. After National Service, Foot went up to Oxford, where he was reunited with his fellow Salopians, and collaborated with them on

Parson's Pleasure, a forerunner to *Private Eye*. Even at this stage, however, Foot 'manifested a greater seriousness' than his friends, said the *Daily Telegraph*: he was president of the Oxford Union, edited *Isis* and, on leaving the university, headed not for the bright lights of London, but for working-class Glasgow, where he took a job on the *Daily Record*.

There, one of his first assignments was covering the 1962 by-election in West Lothian, where Tam Dalyell was standing for Labour. 'How on earth is it,' demanded the young reporter, 'that the West Lothian Labour Party with six coal mines in the constituency can choose someone from Eton and King's College, Cambridge as their candidate?' I was 'somewhat flummoxed' by this question, recalled Dalyell in *The Independent*, until H.B. Boyne of the *Daily Telegraph* came to my rescue, gently observing: 'Perhaps for the same reason that the *Daily Record* chooses somebody from Shrewsbury and University College, Oxford, as their political reporter.' Foot's left-wing politics never sat easily with his social circle, said the *Telegraph*. While in Glasgow, his friend Candida Betjeman used to send him postcards, designed to embarrass him in front of his comrades, imploring him to come to the country at the weekend to make up a four at tennis. The conflict was further illustrated some years later, when he found himself on television, arguing forcefully with General Sir John Hackett. 'Come, come,' said Hackett, after a particularly vicious thrust, 'that's no way to speak to your godfather.'

After the *Daily Record*, Foot worked for *The Sun*, *Private Eye*, the *Socialist Worker*, and the *Mirror*, where he was hired specifically as an investigative journalist. That relationship – love-hate at the best of times – came to an end when Foot used his column to highlight the 'victimisation, union busting and general macho management' of the *Mirror* itself. The editor refused to publish the piece, and offered Foot sick leave, so that he could 'seek professional help'. In 1999 Foot suffered an aortic aneurysm, which nearly killed him. He recovered, however, and the following year, was named the *What the Papers Say* 'Campaigning Journalist of the Decade'. There was no great secret to being an effective investigative reporter, he said. 'You just have to keep asking questions.'

Barber who served in the trenches

ARTHUR BARRACLOUGH
1898-2004

Arthur Barraclough served on the Western Front during the First World War, according to the *Daily Telegraph* – an experience the 'lively Yorkshireman' recounted at length for the BBC's television series *The Trench* in 2002.

Barraclough was born in Bradford in 1898, one of a wool-comber's 13 children, and trained as a barber. He was accepted into the army on his 18th birthday, despite weighing less than eight stone and having flat feet, and arrived on the Front in January 1917, after just four months' training. He spent that winter living in dugouts like 'pig sties' – aware that across no man's land, German soldiers had beds and electric light. Before going over the top, the troops were offered a tot of rum. Pte Barraclough declined. Instead, although he was not a particularly religious man, he would steady his nerves by saying a prayer. 'Dear God, I'm going into great danger. Would you please guard me and help me to act like a man. Please bring me back safe.' It worked. 'I used to go out there without a fear,' he said. During his time with the Duke of Wellington's Regiment, he never knowingly killed an enemy, but was wounded three times, badly enough to have to be sent home twice.

Barraclough was discharged early to return to his job. He served in the Home Guard during the Second World War and retired to Morecambe in 1962. As the number of Great War veterans dwindled, film crews began calling on him with increasing frequency. He and his wife Mary were unfailingly polite to journalists; he always made a point of being smartly turned out.

Doctor who sought a 'good' death

ELISABETH KÜBLER-ROSS

1926-2004

Elisabeth Kübler-Ross revolutionised the way hospitals in the West treated the dying, said *The Independent*. Before the publication in 1969 of her book *On Death and Dying*, doctors often failed to tell patients with terminal diseases the truth about their condition, leaving them isolated and bewildered. But central to Kübler-Ross's approach was the notion that there are five stages of dying – denial, anger, bargain, depression and then finally acceptance. Medical students came to refer to it as 'dabda'.

Elisabeth Kübler endured what she described as the 'tragedy of being born a triplet' in Switzerland in 1926, said *The Times*. Being a triplet, she said, is 'peculiar because you can literally drop dead and nobody would know the difference'. After the war, she worked as a relief worker in Poland, and visited a Nazi concentration camp. There, she met a young woman who had been pulled out of a gas chamber at the last minute because it was so full the doors wouldn't close. Crossed off the list of the living, she had 'lingered, ghost-like, in the camp for years until its liberation, surrounded by death but not threatened by it'. She was profoundly struck by this, as she was by the butterfly patterns carved into the barrack walls by condemned children.

Returning to Switzerland, she studied medicine at the University of Zurich, where she met her husband, Emmanuel Ross. In 1958, she moved to the USA, to work in hospitals in New York, Colorado and Chicago. Shocked by the treatment of dying patients, she made a point of telling them the truth and of encouraging them to talk about their concerns. This eventually became the subject of many books. Her goal, said *The Independent*, was for people to live fully until their death, not 'lie there and vegetate', and she criticised medical schools for teaching 'everything about the liver, and nothing about the person'. The dying, she counselled, deserved to be treated not as a series of components, but with dignity and humanity. Meanwhile, her books became bestsellers, and served as inspiration for the hospice movement.

> **'I told God last night that he's a damned procrastinator,' she said.**

Having spent so many years campaigning for people to be afforded 'good' deaths, Elisabeth Kübler-Ross was herself denied one. She suffered a series of strokes and was ill for many years. 'I told God last night that he's a damned procrastinator,' she said in 2002.

Midget actress who starred as a Munchkin in Oz

TINY DOLL

1914–2004

Tiny Doll was the last surviving member of the Doll family of midget actors, best known for playing Munchkins in *The Wizard of Oz*, and for their appearance in the Tod Browning horror film *Freaks*.

Tiny Doll was born Elly Ann Schneider in Germany in 1914, the youngest of seven children, four of whom were midgets. In 1925 she travelled to America to join her siblings, Gracie, Daisy and Harry. At first, they performed under the name Earles, but changed it to Doll, after hearing someone in the audience saying, 'Look, they are just like dollies'.

The Dolls were primarily a circus act, but in 1932 Harry was cast in *Freaks*, as a misguided midget performer who spurns his devoted fiancée (played by his sister Daisy, the 'midget Mae West'), in favour of the evil Cleopatra, an able-bodied trapeze artist. The 'freaks' in the film were genuine sideshow stars, and included 'pinheads' (microcephalics), a pair of conjoined twins, Violet and Daisy, and Prince Randian, the 'human torso'. *Freaks* caused an outcry, and was banned in Britain until 1963.

When producers began looking for midgets to star in *The Wizard of Oz*, Tiny and her sisters were cast as Munchkin maidens, while Harry was given a bigger role as one of the Lollipop Guild. On set, however, the Dolls kept themselves apart from the 'whoring, drinking and pimping' of the other Munchkins, most of whom were non-professionals whose only claim to fame was their diminutive status. 'They were drunks,' recalled Judy Garland. 'They got smashed every night and the police used to scoop them up in butterfly nets.' In later life, Tiny Doll remembered the making of the film with great affection. Garland, she said, was 'very kind to us', and 'we were treated good – fed well and had breaks'.

The Dolls toured with the Ringling Brothers throughout the 1950s, but when freak shows went out of fashion, they lost their livelihood, said the *Daily Telegraph*. They eventually retired to Florida, where they lived together in a large house. In 1989 Tiny took part in the 50th anniversary celebrations of the making of *The Wizard of Oz*. Her death left only eight remaining Munchkins.

At first, they performed under the name Earles, but changed it to Doll, after hearing someone in the audience saying, 'Look, they are just like dollies'.

The unlikely icon of British rock 'n' roll

JOHN PEEL

1939-2004

John Peel did not have the normal attributes of a rock icon. Paunchy, balding and badly dressed, he looked more like a taxi driver than a DJ, and had little time for the glitter of the music industry. Yet he was, without doubt, the 'single most important figure in British music since the birth of rock 'n' roll', said Andy Kershaw in *The Independent*. Passionate about music of all forms, Peel resolutely championed records that other DJs considered too weird or obscure, and in the process gave first airings to some of the biggest rock acts in history, including Jimi Hendrix, Marc Bolan, The Fall, The Smiths and Pulp. He was immune to fashion, said Peter Hook in *The Guardian*: he just played what he liked, and people loved him for it. By 1998, when he was made OBE, he had become a national treasure: 'Perhaps the reason young people put up with me is that I don't pretend to be anything other than what I am,' he said: 'an overweight 60-something, with four children and a sore back.'

'The only affectation he could be accused of was his quasi-scouse accent,' said Cheryl Stonehouse in the *Daily Express*. Born John Ravenscroft (he changed his name when he joined Radio 1), he was the son of a wealthy cotton merchant, and grew up on the Wirral. After prep school he went to Shrewsbury, where his refusal to conform meant that he was regularly beaten. He had been expected to join the family firm, but at 14 his life changed for ever when he heard Elvis Presley's 'Heartbreak Hotel' played on the radio. 'I stared open-mouthed,' he recalled, 'I had never heard anything so raw, so elemental.' Encouraged by his house master, he began listening to rock 'n' roll in his study while other boys were doing their prep in the library. He left school at 16, and had numerous jobs – including teaching football to deprived children – before doing national service in the Royal Artillery. His final report read: 'At no time has this man shown any sign of adapting to the military way of life.' Peel took it as a compliment.

In 1960 Peel went to the USA, where he worked for an insurance company in Dallas for three years, before being employed as a DJ on WWR radio. In 1964 Beatlemania swept America: Peel adopted a Scouse twang, claimed friendship with the Fab Four and as a result became a celebrity, with his very own groupies. 'It was the glamour of the job,' he said. 'An enormous number of rather attractive young women were prepared to have some kind of clumsy and depressing sexual experience with me.' In the States, he met his first wife, Shirley, a troubled teenager whose parents failed to tell Peel of her real age: she was just 15. The marriage was not happy, and ended in 1973. The following year he married Sheila Gilhooly, dressed in the colours of his favourite football club, Liverpool. They settled in a farmhouse near Stowmarket, which they called Peel Acres, and had four children.

'Perhaps the reason young people put up with me is that I don't pretend to be anything other than what I am: an overweight 60-something, with four children and a sore back.'

When he first returned from the States in 1967, Peel spent six months working for Pirate Radio London, before joining Radio 1, said the *Daily Telegraph*. 'From the start, his approach as a DJ – to play music which he saw as innovative and of high quality, irrespective of its commercial potential – struck a chord with listeners.' He won a host of awards, and 'somehow, over more than three decades, managed to remain on the cusp of what was new, without ever appearing merely modish'. Some of the music he promoted was too recherché for a wider audience – he was often asked if he was playing the record at the right speed, and sometimes he wasn't – but much of it became mainstream. But it was his evident integrity and love of music that won him so many admirers. 'Often,' said Caitlin Moran in *The Times*, 'for a putative hipster stuck in Norfolk, or Walsall, or Ayr, he was the only person "like" them that they "knew".'

In 1998, Peel found an unexpected new role as the presenter of *Home Truths*, a celebrity-free show based around interviews with 'ordinary' people. To some it was unbearably sentimental and cloying, but Peel, with his dry wit and deadpan delivery, excelled in the role of sympathetic listener, said Richard Williams in *The Guardian*. 'He sounded just as much at home presenting the tale of a woman trapped by her lack of a birth certificate as he did introducing a demo tape by a new band whose music sounded to the untutored ear like a small truck crashing into a cage full of exotic birds.' One reason was that Peel was himself devoted to home and hearth. He was a shy and unassuming man. Since his death, said Andy Kershaw, 'people have asked me, "What was John Peel like away from the microphone?" I'll tell you. He was exactly the same as he was when he was in front of it.'

John Peel's own favourite record was the 1978 Undertones hit 'Teenage Kicks'. 'We're talking about a record that even now reduces me to tears,' he wrote in *The Guardian* in 2001. 'Sheila, my wife – I wanna hold her, wanna hold her tight – knows that when I die, the only words I want on my tombstone, apart from my nasme, are "Teenage Dreams, So Hard to Beat". What more do you need?'

The Bishop of Rome whose election heralded a different sort of papacy

POPE JOHN PAUL II

1920-2005

His Holiness Pope John Paul II was one of the most extraordinary and influential figures of the twentieth century, said the *New York Times*. His 26-year papal reign – the third longest in history – witnessed sweeping social and political changes around the world, the growth of the Roman Catholic Church from 750 million to more than one billion members, and the beginning of Christ's third millennium. John Paul II was not the traditional papal figure: an ascetic individual, who rarely left Rome. He was a big, charismatic bear-hugger of a man, with a hearty laugh, expressive eyes and labourer's hands, who had performed in plays, and climbed mountains, worked in a factory and lived through war. A tireless missionary, he criss-crossed the globe, spreading a clear set of Christian ideas and making impassioned pleas for human rights, disarmament, peace and justice for the poor and oppressed.

Uncompromising yet compassionate, John Paul II denounced communism, totalitarianism, materialism, and the worst excesses of Western capitalism, while steadfastly resisting any change in church doctrine on issues such as abortion, birth control, and the ordination of women. He was often criticised for ecclesiastical authoritarianism, and for his refusal to modernise, but his personal popularity was quite astonishing: during a visit to the Philippines in 1995, he drew the largest crowd in human history, when five million people turned out to hear him celebrate Mass. In total, John Paul II travelled to 129 countries in all five inhabited continents. These journeys, Catholic thinkers came to realise, were not merely visits to his sprawling flock, but 'the forceful, global reassertion of Roman Catholic orthodoxy through a new sacramental exercise using jet planes, television and a remarkable stage presence'.

Karol Jozef Wojtyla was born in Poland in 1920, the younger son of a retired army captain. His mother, Emilia, died in childbirth when he was 9; a year later, his beloved older brother succumbed to scarlet fever. A star pupil at his grammar school, the young Wojtyla loved football, and had an intense interest in Polish literature: in his late teens, he wrote, produced, and acted in a series of experimental plays. In 1938, he moved with his father to Cracow, where he studied Polish language and literature at the Jagiellonian University. The Nazis invaded Poland the following year, and Wojtyla was conscripted to work in a stone quarry; it was backbreaking labour, often in temperatures of -30°C. Yet in the evenings, he continued to write and perform, at some risk to his life, with an underground theatre company. Later, there is evidence that he was blacklisted by the Nazis for smuggling Jews out of the country. In 1941, his father died, and he turned to the priesthood. He trained in secret, while working nights in a chemical plant, and was ordained in 1946. Soon after, he was sent to study in Rome. He returned three years later to a Poland run by a communist regime determined to stamp out 'religious superstitions'.

In 1958, Wojtyla was appointed Auxiliary Bishop of Cracow, and in 1964, the archbishop of the see. He was active in the Second Vatican Council (1962–1965), and in 1967, Pope Paul VI nominated him a cardinal. In 1978, Paul died, and was replaced by John Paul I whose pontificate lasted just 33 days. At the next conclave, the cardinals chose Wojtyla on the eighth ballot. Romans were stunned by the appointment of this obscure figure – their first non-Italian bishop for 450 years. Emerging on the central balcony of St Peter's Basilica, the new pontiff addressed a bemused, expectant crowd. 'I have come,' he said in Italian, 'from a faraway country – far away, but always so close in the communion of faith.' There were scattered cheers. 'I do not know whether I can express myself in your – in our – Italian language,' he said, pausing. The crowd roared. 'If I make mistakes,' he added, smiling suddenly, 'you will correct me.' Tumult erupted. The cheers went on and on: 'Viva il Papa! Viva il Papa! Viva il Papa!'

John Paul II did not come to the papacy with a plan to dismantle the communist bloc, said *The Times*. 'But by relentlessly focusing on human rights, particularly the primary right to religious freedom, he attacked the heart of the communist project – its claim to be the twentieth century's true humanism and true liberator.' In 1979, he became the first reigning Pope to set foot on Communist soil. 'I come as a pilgrim,' he said, as he arrived in his homeland. In Warsaw's Victory Square, he celebrated Mass in front of a million people. 'Christ cannot be kept out of the history of Man in any part of the globe,' warned the Pope in his homily. 'We want God,' chanted the crowd. As he travelled the country, 13 million people turned out to see him. In 1980, he encouraged Polish workers to hold out for legal recognition for their trade union, Solidarity. And when Soviet troops began massing on the border, he wrote to Leonid Brezhnev, asking him to recall his forces.

'The meaning of sexuality cannot be defined in terms of pleasure alone, as this would practically amount to abolishing all restrictions on sexual behaviour: if the principle of pleasure reigns supreme, anything goes'.

But the Pope's involvement in Polish politics went well beyond rhetoric, said John Cornwell in the *Sunday Times*: in 1981, General Wojciech Jaruzelski imposed martial law and arrested the Solidarity leadership; at this point, the Pope secretly gave the union $32m. (The gift was probably made via the Mafia banker, Roberto Calvi.) He was denied entry to Poland in 1982, but visited again in 1983 – 'looking sorrowful' at the continued persecution of the Solidarity leadership – and in 1986, when he addressed a million people near the Gdansk shipyard where Solidarity had been born. In 1989, Poland held free elections, 'setting in motion the loss of Soviet control of the satellites in eastern Europe'. It is undeniable that John Paul II was in part responsible for 'one of the most extraordinary paroxysms in modern history, the break-up of the Soviet empire' – although he always said that he 'merely gave the tree a good shake'.

The Pope followed up his first trip to Poland with visits to Ireland – where he begged the IRA to 'turn away from the path of violence' – and the USA. There, anyone who thought he was an unquestioning ally of the capitalist West was swiftly disabused, said the *Daily Telegraph*: in an address at the Yankee Stadium, he decried the West's selfishness in consuming such a large slice of the world's resources, and 'judging all human values in terms of personal satisfaction'. Following the attempt on his life of 1981, John Paul II became the first Pope to visit Great Britain. He arrived in the spring of 1982, as the Parachute Regiment took Goose Green, kissed the tarmac at Gatwick in his trademark fashion, and set about a tour of major cities in an armoured Popemobile. He drew spectacular crowds in this predominantly Protestant nation: a million people lined the streets in Liverpool, and in Glasgow, nearly half of Scotland's 800,000 Catholics filled Bellahouston Park (possibly the largest crowd of Scots ever assembled together in one place). By the time he left, the proportion of Britons who approved of his visit had risen from 39 per cent to two thirds. His next visit was to Argentina.

Although John Paul II opposed totalitarian regimes, he believed that democracies brought their own dangers, said *The Times*. In a 1991 encyclical, he argued that democratic societies had to respect the dignity of the human person; Communism had reduced human beings to economic units. 'Without fundamental values, capitalism would do the same.' He followed the long-held doctrine that life began at the point of conception, and abhorred the 'culture of death' prevalent in the decadent West. He was dismayed to find that, after the collapse of communism, similarly libertarian attitudes to abortion, pornography, and promiscuity began to take hold in the old eastern bloc.

On the question of contraception, John Paul II was immovable, said *The Independent*: he knew he could not expect wholehearted obedience even from loyal Catholics (Italy has one of the lowest birth rates in Europe). But he stood by the principle, apparently because he believed 'that the meaning of sexuality cannot be defined in terms of pleasure alone, as this would practically amount to abolishing all restrictions on sexual behaviour: if the principle of pleasure reigns supreme, anything goes'. Critics, particularly outside the church, argued that the Pope should adapt to changing social norms, but in his 1993 encyclical *Veritatis Splendor*, he made it clear that he was having no truck with moral relativism, said Cristina Odone in *The Observer*. It was not up to the individual to fashion his own morality. 'The twenty-first century, like the first, offers temptations that must be resisted and authority that must be obeyed.'

The Pope's stance provoked ridicule and disdain among the 'chattering classes', and outraged many Catholics – as did his attitude towards dissent. Frequently accused of 'centralising' power, he disciplined a number of theologians (including Hans Kung) for voicing contrary views; he was accused of parachuting in his own 'placemen' into difficult sees, and in 1979, he rebuked Latin American bishops for encouraging the new doctrine of liberation theology, which argued that the church should ally itself with the poor in a Marxist-inspired struggle for justice. The bishops were told, in no uncertain terms, to remember that they were pastors, not politicians. For John Paul II, unity among Catholics was not enough; he sought harmony among all religions. In May 2001, he became the first pontiff officially to visit a mosque (in Damascus); he was also the first to visit Rome's synagogue, where he asserted that the Jews were still God's 'chosen people'; in 1998, he apologised for 2,000 years of Catholic anti-Judaism, and in 2000, he visited the Holy Land. However, his instinctive support for Palestinians, and his beatification of Pius IX, the nineteenth-century Pope who described Jews as 'dogs', undid some of his good work.

> **He argued that democratic societies had to respect the dignity of the human person; Communism had reduced human beings to economic units. 'Without fundamental values, capitalism would do the same.'**

The Pope's almost superhuman workload took its toll on his health, said the *Daily Telegraph*; in his last decade, the man once known as 'God's athlete', for his love of swimming and skiing, suffered an intestinal tumour, Parkinson's disease, and a number of broken bones. He became such a frequent visitor to Rome's Gemelli's hospital that he dubbed it 'Vatican

Number 3' (after his main office, Vatican 1, and Vatican 2, his summer palace). Yet even when he was dying, the 'great communicator' refused to hide away in his private apartments, or disguise his suffering. Instead, he used 'the most powerful imagery – that of a dying man – to bear witness to the life and death of Christ'.

13 May 1981:
'It was as if someone guided this bullet'

On 13 May 1981, a Turkish gunman came within a fraction of an inch of changing the course of history, said John Follain in the *Sunday Times*. As the Pope toured St Peter's Square in Rome, Mehmet Ali Agca shot him from just nine feet away. The bullet broke the Pope's finger, before tearing through his abdomen, missing vital organs by millimetres. Later, John Paul II said that he was convinced that Mary, the Mother of God, had intervened to save him, as predicted in the third secret of Fatima (which he read after his recovery). 'Agca shot with confidence, with perfection,' he said. 'But it was just as if someone guided this bullet.'

Before reaching hospital, John Paul II told his secretary that he forgave his assailant. Two years later, he visited him in prison. Agca, a professional assassin, claimed at first that he had been hired by Bulgarians, leading to speculation that the KGB was behind the plot. Although he later recanted this statement, the theory was later given fresh credence by the release of Stasi files showing that Agca trained at a guerrilla camp run by Carlos the Jackal, known to have functioned partly at the behest of the Soviet and East German secret services.

The Bulgarians dismissed the renewed interest in the case as a crude attempt to derail their bid for membership of the EU. And Agca has never revealed any more details about the assassination attempt. When asked about the subject, he has shown only a nervous interest in the supernatural forces that helped his intended victim survive. On John Paul II's death, Agca applied – in vain – to be allowed to leave prison to attend his 'spiritual brother's' funeral in Rome.

Renowned artist who was one of the founders of Pop Art

SIR EDUARDO PAOLOZZI

1924-2005

Sir Eduardo Paolozzi was one of the most influential figures to emerge from the British art scene in the post-war years. A prolific sculptor, collagist, print-maker and collector of junk and ephemera, he won international renown as one of the fathers of Pop Art.

Paolozzi was born in Leith, Scotland, where his Italian immigrant parents ran an ice-cream parlour. His father, an admirer of Mussolini, sent him to a fascist youth camp in Italy every summer. It was there, said *The Independent*, that he starting making scrapbooks 'dense with images from magazines and comic books'. When war broke out, his father, grandfather and uncle were arrested as enemy aliens and put on a ship bound for Canada. The ship was torpedoed and they all drowned – a family tragedy that helped shape Paolozzi's often gloomy, combative personality. Conscripted in 1943, the young Paolozzi spent a year with the Pioneer Corps, aimlessly bivouacked on a soccer pitch in Slough. He eventually feigned insanity to secure his release, and enrolled at the Slade School of Art.

Paolozzi's traditionalist tutors disapproved of his fondness for modern artists such as Picasso, said the *Daily Telegraph*. But his cubist-inspired collages and primitivistic sculptures delighted the critics, and after a hit one-man exhibition in 1947, he decided to move to Paris without finishing his degree. He was befriended by Brancusi, Braque and Giacometti, but failed to make much impression on French dealers or critics. He returned, downcast, to London, where he shared a studio with Lucian Freud and made friends with Francis Bacon. It was around this time, said Frank Whitford in *The Guardian*, that Paolozzi really hit his stride. Somewhat simian in appearance, he could often be seen rummaging in skips near his home in Chelsea, looking for the cultural detritus that inspired much of his work. He produced roughly cast bronze figures 'thickly encrusted with nuts, bolts, bits of toys and junk collected from dustbins', as well as delicate screenprints of heads filled with fragmentary autoparts. For his collages, meanwhile, he plundered glossy magazines, scientific illustrations, lurid paperback covers and American film posters – showing an intellectual appreciation of mainstream culture which helped usher in the era of Pop Art.

Paolozzi was an energetic teacher as well as artist; among other posts, he taught ceramics at the Royal College of Art and sculpture at Munich University (where Stuart Sutcliffe, one of the original Beatles, was a pupil). He also took on numerous public commissions, designing an abstract monument for Euston Square in London, the mosaic interior of Tottenham Court Road tube station, and the huge bronze sculpture of Sir Isaac Newton in the courtyard of the new British Library.

Paolozzi was made a CBE in 1968 and a knight in 1989. Public recognition

> **'Sometimes I feel like a wizard in Toytown, transforming a bunch of carrots into pomegranates.'**

delighted him, said Whitford; he was particularly thrilled to be asked to appear on *Desert Island Discs*. In 1994, eager to leave behind some legacy of his vision, he made a large donation of his works to the Scottish National Gallery of Modern Art. Housed, at his request, separately from the rest of the museum, it also included his reference library and thousands of found objects. 'Our culture decides quite arbitrarily what is waste and rubbish,' he once explained. 'I like to make use of everything. Sometimes I feel like a wizard in Toytown, transforming a bunch of carrots into pomegranates.'

Oscar-winning actress and star of *The Graduate*

ANNE BANCROFT

1931-2005

'**D**avid Selznick rightly predicted that his death would be greeted everywhere by the headline, "Producer of *Gone with the Wind* Dies". By the same token, said Philip French in *The Observer*, Anne Bancroft knew her name would always be associated with one role: that of Mrs Robinson, the suburban housewife who coolly seduces her neighbours' son in *The Graduate*.

Born in 1931, Anna Maria Louisa Italiano grew up in the Bronx, the daughter of working-class Italian parents. Money was scarce, but Anna was so keen to perform that, by the the time she was 2, her parents were paying for singing and dancing lessons. Even so, when she left high school, she decided to find work as a lab technician; it was her mother who persuaded her to enrol in the New York Academy of Dramatic Arts. Within two years of graduating, she was performing regularly on TV as Ann Marno. Spotted by a 20th Century Fox talent scout, she was given a $20,000 a year contract, and told to change her name. She chose Bancroft because it sounded 'dignified'. In 1952 she made her big screen debut in *Don't Bother to Knock*, alongside Marilyn Monroe.

Bancroft's early days in Hollywood were not a success, said *The Times*.

She appeared in any number of films, many of which have been forgotten, as girlfriends, gangsters' relatives, and Indian squaws. 'In reality,' she said, 'every picture I did was worse than the last.' During that time, she married the heir to a Texas oil fortune, but began drinking heavily and, tiring of Hollywood, returned to New York. She divorced her husband, went into therapy, attended the Actors Studio, and worked with a voice coach, said *The Guardian*. 'Then came *Two for the Seesaw*, starring opposite Henry Fonda, and a triumphant return to acting.' This was swiftly followed by *The Miracle Worker*, playing Helen Keller's teacher Annie Sullivan, and, when the play was transferred to screen, Bancroft won an Oscar. In the words of one critic, 'she left Hollywood a failure and returned a star'. In 1964 she starred in *The Pumpkin Eater*, opposite James Mason, which won her a Bafta and the second of her five Oscar nominations.

Jeanne Moreau and Doris Day apparently both turned down the role of Mrs Robinson; and almost everyone discouraged Bancroft from taking the part too, because of its then controversial subject matter. But Bancroft was interested in Mrs Robinson not specifically as the sullen seducer of a younger man, but as a woman with unfulfilled dreams, stuck in a conventional life with a conventional husband. Starring opposite Dustin Hoffman, who was in fact only six years her junior, Bancroft successfully made the part her own. 'Film critics said I gave a voice to the fear we all have: that we'll reach a certain point in our lives, look around and realise that all the things we said we'd do and become will never come to be – and that we're ordinary.'

Despite – or perhaps because of – the success of *The Graduate*, Bancroft struggled to find good roles in the 1970s and 1980s, though there were more Oscar nominations for her performances as a ballet dancer in *The Turning Point*, and a nun in *Agnes of God*. She was also in *Young Winston*, as Churchill's mother, and *84 Charing Cross Road*. Anne Bancroft was married to the comedian Mel Brooks for more than 40 years. Told her son was going to marry an Italian Catholic, Brooks's mother had replied, 'Bring the girl over – I'll be in the kitchen, with my head in the oven'. Such comments notwithstanding, their relationship was known as one of the most stable in showbusiness.

Inspirational founder of the modern hospice movement

DAME CICELY SAUNDERS

1918-2005

Dame Cicely Saunders was the mother of the modern hospice movement, and widely regarded as a kind of 'secular saint', said the *Daily Telegraph*. A compassionate yet authoritative nurse-turned-doctor, she enabled millions of terminally ill people to die in relative comfort, surrounded by love. Her mission, she said, was to 'help the dying to live until they die and their families to live on'.

It all began in 1948, when Saunders, then a shy young lady almoner (medical social worker), was working at St Thomas' Hospital in London. On her first rounds, she met David Tasma, a Jewish waiter who, having escaped the Warsaw ghetto, was now dying of cancer. He was all but alone in London, said *The Times*, and there was no consolation for him, except for the friendship she was able to provide. They talked about the possibility of creating a place where terminally ill patients could receive both expert medical treatment and sympathetic care. When he died, he left her everything he had – £500 – saying, 'I'll be a window in your home.' Nineteen years later, Saunders founded her first hospice, St Christopher's in Sydenham, where Tasma's bequest is commemorated by a single sheet of plate glass.

Born in Barnet in 1918, Cicely Saunders was the daughter of a prosperous estate agent. The family had every material comfort, but her parents' marriage was a disaster. At the age of 10, Cicely was sent to boarding school – Roedean – where she was lonely and friendless. 'I was awkward and gawky and talked at the wrong time,' she said. 'It left me with compassion for the underdog.' When war broke out, she abandoned her studies at Oxford in order to train as a nurse. Shortly after qualifying, however, a severe back problem forced her to retrain as an almoner. It was during this period that she discovered her faith, while on holiday with a group of Christians. 'It was as though I suddenly felt the wind behind me rather than in my face,' she said. 'I thought to myself, "Please let this be real." I prayed to know how best to serve God. Then I met my Pole.'

After Tasma's death, Saunders realised that to make real changes, she would need to become a doctor. So, at the age of 33, she retrained once again, qualifying in 1957. At that time, doctors tended to look upon terminally ill patients as failures. They were largely abandoned, and only given pain relief when they cried out in agony. Saunders believed that such patients should be given constant relief from discomfort – 'constant pain needs constant control'. It made all the difference. 'They used to see how long I could go without an injection,' said one patient, recently transferred from a busy hospital ward. 'I used to be pouring

> **'I was awkward and gawky and talked at the wrong time,' she said. 'It left me with compassion for the underdog.'**

with sweat because of the pain. I couldn't speak to anyone and I was having crying fits… The biggest difference is feeling so calm.'

In 1960 Saunders fell in love with another dying Pole, Antoni Michniewicz. His death broke her heart, said Esther Rantzen in the *Daily Mail*, but the experience of loss was, yet again, to prove a resource. Confident that she now knew enough about the needs of the dying and their relatives, she began to devote herself to founding a hospice of her own. Between 1961 and 1964 she wrote 10,000 letters, and raised £300,000. The hospice, she said, should have the atmosphere of a friendly village with light, airy wards and plenty of space for visitors. Religion would play a part, but would not be forced on patients. The object, said *The Guardian*, 'would simply be to convince patients that they were not alone, that they still had value as human beings'.

Building started in 1965. Local children helped lay the garden, and firemen hung the curtains. The first patient was admitted in 1967. Throughout, Saunders had been supported in her work by her love for a third Pole, the painter Professor Marian Bohusz-Szyszko. They married in 1980, remaining together until his death in 1995.

Dame Cicely Saunders was the recipient of many honorary fellowships and doctorates, and the author of several books. St Christopher's has trained more than 50,000 students, spreading palliative care programmes to more than 120 countries. She died there herself, said Esther Rantzen, 'confident she would meet those she loved in Heaven'.

Irreverent politician who brought hope to Northern Ireland

MO MOWLAM

1949-2005

M o Mowlam was one of the most popular and charismatic figures in British politics, said *The Times*. Irreverent, fun-loving and honest, with an extraordinary gift for empathy, she routinely topped surveys of popular politicians, and in May 1997, scored an approval rating of 86 per cent – higher than the Prime Minister's. Diagnosed with a brain tumour in 1996, she was admired for the courage with which she coped with her illness, and proved an effective, strongwilled politician: as Northern Ireland Secretary, Mowlam refused to give up on the seemingly intractable problems of the province, and brought renewed hope to the peace process. She was one of the key players behind the Good Friday Agreement, and when Tony Blair paid tribute to 'our one and only Mo' during his speech at the 1998 party conference, she was rewarded with a standing ovation.

But paradoxically, the qualities that made Mowlam so popular would eventually count against her. There were those who did not wish to be hugged. Unionists in particular came to dislike her touchy-feely style and her coarseness (she once told Ian Paisley to 'f*** off'), while ministers and civil servants complained she could be too broad brush in her approach, and was 'impatient' when it came to detail. As her career unravelled, she claimed there was a whispering campaign against her, said Julia Langdon in *The Guardian*. But 'such an effort would not have been necessary'. Mo Mowlam had become her own worst enemy.

Marjorie Mowlam was born in Watford in 1949. Her father worked for the post office; a 'charming' but disappointed man, he descended into alcoholism, and was prone to violent rages. Mo – as she was always known – sought refuge in her schoolwork. She passed the 11-plus, and was briefly educated at Chiswick Girls' Grammar. When the family moved to Coventry, she enrolled at one of the earliest comprehensives, Coundon Court, where she was a star of the hockey pitch, obtained a Duke of Edinburgh Award, and became head girl. Afterwards, she went to Durham University, largely because it was so far away from home. She studied sociology and anthropology, rowed with her college's women's eight, and joined the Labour Party. 'Everyone says, "first woman Prime Minister"', noted her tutor. After graduating, Mowlam followed a boyfriend to the USA, where she studied for a PhD in political science at the University of Iowa. She later taught at Florida State University. In 1979 she returned to the UK to take a job at Newcastle University. At around that time, an American boyfriend she later described as the love of her life drowned while swimming in a lake in Florida. Mowlam had many relationships after that, said Langdon, but it would be another 16 years before she married Jon Norton, a merchant banker and Labour fundraiser.

Mowlam tried, and failed, to get a seat at the 1983 election, and seemed doomed to fail again in 1987, said the *Daily Telegraph*. But at the last minute, the longstanding MP for Redcar, James Tinn, suddenly announced his retirement, and Neil Kinnock put Mowlam's name forward as a suitable alternative. Three weeks later, she was in Parliament. Flirtatious, leggy and blonde, Mowlam immediately established a reputation for her foul language, dirty jokes, and disregard for convention. 'On the opposition front benches, she shocked Tory MPs by kicking off her shoes and tucking her legs underneath her as she listened to debates.' Nevertheless, Mowlam was placed on the fast track: ten months after joining the Commons, she was made deputy Northern Ireland spokesman, and 18 months after that, she joined Gordon Brown's Treasury team. Brown and Mowlam, however, were united in their dislike for one another, and after John Smith's death, she became the first shadow cabinet minister 'to opt decisively for Blair'. She hoped to manage Blair's leadership campaign, but – having established a somewhat 'dangerous' reputation, not least for her 'carefree attitude to sex' – he called on Jack Straw instead, and gave her Northern Ireland.

Mowlam was disappointed by the appointment, said Tam Dalyell in *The Independent*. But as the months went by, reluctance turned into fascination and enormous enthusiasm. 'When she became Northern Ireland Secretary in 1997, her warmth was an enormous plus as far as the republican side was concerned. But there was another side of the coin and her increasingly cryogenic relations with the Unionists were a minus.' They were irritated by the way she would tear off her wig halfway through meetings, and distrusted her informal style. (David Trimble cannot have appreciated being referred to as 'Trimble-Wimble', and it later emerged that she had addressed Martin McGuinness as 'babe'). But worse than that, they suspected that, at heart, she was an Irish nationalist – and planting kisses on strait-laced Unionist politicians who would normally only be kissed by their wives, and then in private, did nothing to reassure them. Mowlam was routinely 'praised for "cutting through political crap", but the "crap" was often very real objections in the latter days from the Unionists'. Yet at times, said David McKittrick in the same paper, Mowlam's unconventional approach worked wonders. For instance, when the peace process was endangered by restless loyalist inmates in the Maze Prison, Mowlam took the unprecedented step of going into the H-blocks herself and meeting them. 'The move was risky, but it worked: within hours of her visit they agreed to stick with the process, and the talks went on.' The US Senator George Mitchell described her thus: 'She is blunt and outspoken and she swears a lot. She is also intelligent, decisive, daring and unpretentious. The combination is irresistible. The people love her, though many politicians in Northern Ireland do not.'

In 1999 Blair replaced her with Peter Mandelson. Some said he felt threatened by her popularity with voters; the reality was more complicated, said the *Daily Telegraph*. Key figures in Northern Ireland were refusing to do business with her, and her earthy ways were becoming a political embarrassment: she insisted, for instance, on broadcasting the fact she had asked her security police to buy her tampons. In June 1999 Blair offered her the health ministry, but she held out for the post of Foreign Secretary, although it was never a serious possibility. She was eventually appointed Cabinet Office Minister – a post she had previously denounced as 'minister for the *Today* programme' – where she remained until standing down as an MP at the 2001 election.

The man who brought Nazi killers to justice

SIMON WIESENTHAL

1908-2005

Having survived the Holocaust, Simon Wiesenthal dedicated his life to tracking down Nazi war criminals. His motive was not revenge, but a desire to bring the perpetrators of evil to justice, so that neither their crimes nor their victims, would ever be forgotten. 'When history looks back,' he said, 'I want people to know the Nazis weren't able to kill millions of people and get away with it.'

Simon Wiesenthal was born in 1908 in Buczacz, a town in the province of Galicia – then part of the Austro-Hungarian Empire, today split between Ukraine and Poland. Anti-Jewish sentiment was growing across Europe, something the 9-year-old Simon experienced first-hand when a Cossack soldier slashed his thigh with his sabre, cutting it to the bone. After leaving school, he trained as an architectural engineer in Prague, and in 1936, married his childhood sweetheart.

Over the years, he and his family had become familiar with invasions. They had fled when Galicia was conquered by the Russians in 1914, and returned with the reconquering Austrians in 1917, only to see Galicia 'liberated' by Ukrainians, Poles, Bolsheviks, and then Poles again. 'To survive under such circumstances is a school,' Wiesenthal once said.

'Nobody could teach us anything new – until a couple of liberations later we got Hitler.'

Within weeks of the German invasion of 1941, 6,000 Jews had been slaughtered and in July of that year, Wiesenthal was one of several dozen Jewish professionals rounded up to be shot. One by one they were murdered; but before the executioners reached Wiesenthal, the bells of the local church began to peal, so the killers laid down their guns and went off to pray. He escaped death, but ended up in Janwska concentration camp near Lvov, where he and his wife were assigned to the forced labour camp serving the local railway works.

Then in 1942, the Nazis began implementing the Final Solution, and in August, Wiesenthal's mother was sent to Belzec death camp. ('I was left,' he said, 'with nothing to remember her by – not even a photograph.') By September, most of his relatives had been killed and Wiesenthal, still working on the railway, realised that the best chance his fair-haired wife had of survival was to pass herself off as a Pole. So he agreed to make technical drawings of railway junctions for the Polish underground who in return provided his wife with false papers and spirited her out of the camp. She spent the war working as a Polish forced labourer.

Thanks to his ability to provide technical drawings on request, Wiesenthal soon won the trust of the labour camp's vice-commandant, Adolf Kohlrautz. Yet for all that he found himself, in April 1943, being rounded up again for execution – along with 40 other Jews – this time to 'celebrate' Hitler's birthday. The men were marched to a burial pit and ordered to strip naked, but just as the guards prepared to fire, a corporal appeared and told them to let Wiesenthal go. Kohlrautz had demanded him back, saying he needed him to paint a birthday banner. Later, when the rail workers were about to be eliminated, Kohlrautz turned a blind eye as Wiesenthal escaped. Such gestures shored up Wiesenthal's belief that there was no such thing as collective guilt: people should be judged not by their ethnic group but by their individual deeds.

After eight months on the run, Wiesenthal was recaptured and sent to a concentration camp. All the inmates were due to be exterminated, but the Red Army was closing in and the commandant realised that if there were no Jews to guard he and his troops would be sent into combat. So the 34 prisoners provided insurance for 200 SS officers as they joined the retreat westwards.

Wiesenthal ended the war in Austria's notorious Mauthausen camp, weighing just seven stone. Every night, inmates died around him, but he clung on. He would live another 15 minutes, he kept saying to himself: he had to see the expressions on the guards' faces when the Americans finally arrived.

Almost as soon as he was liberated, Wiesenthal provided the American War Crimes Unit with details of 91 of the most savage SS officers and was soon compiling dossiers of Nazi crimes. Soon after, he was reunited with his wife – both had thought the other dead. In 1947, he set up his own war crimes investigation unit in Austria. One early success was stopping Eichmann's wife declaring herself a widow – a ruse to get Eichmann's name off the 'wanted' lists. Later, he heard that the architect of the Final Solution was living in Buenos Aires and passed the information to the Israelis. But the response to his tip-offs was disappointing (the world's attention was focused on the Cold War) and in 1954, he closed down his office. Six years later, however, when Eichmann was dramatically seized by Mossad, the world's interest was reawakened, and Wiesenthal reopened his office in Vienna.

> **He would live another 15 minutes, he kept saying to himself: he had to see the expressions on the guards' faces when the Americans finally arrived.**

Over the years, Wiesenthal helped locate up to 1,100 war criminals, said Henry Weinstein in the *Los Angeles Times*. These included Franz Stangl, commandant of Treblinka, who, in 1945, signed an inventory of goods destined for Berlin which included 25 freight cars full of women's hair for use as insulation and mattress stuffing, along with 100 freight cars of shoes and 145,000kg of wedding rings. Held responsible for the deaths of 900,000 people, Stangl was extradited from Brazil in 1967, and sentenced to life in prison. A third notable success was the discovery of the Gestapo officer who had arrested the Frank family. The man's admission that the event took place helped discredit neo-Nazi claims that Anne Frank had never existed.

Wiesenthal's work won him many enemies, said *The Guardian*, not only among neo-Nazis, who frequently tried to have him killed, but among Jews. His insistence that the Holocaust was not simply a Jewish tragedy caused a rift with Eli Wiesel (who insisted it was a 'Jewish tragedy with universal implications'). He also fell out with the World Jewish Congress by refusing to brand the Austrian politician Kurt Waldheim a war criminal – a move that may have cost him the Nobel Peace Prize. Once, at a dinner, he met another Mauthausen survivor who after the war had become a wealthy jeweller. Had Wiesenthal gone back to architecture, the man suggested, he too could have become a millionaire. 'When we come to the other world and meet the millions of Jews who died in the camps and they ask us, "What have you done?", there will be many answers,' came Wiesenthal's reply. 'You will say, "I became a jeweller." Another will say, "I built houses." But I will say, "I didn't forget you."'

Publicity-shy comedian who made millions laugh

RONNIE BARKER

1929-2005

Ronnie Barker 'entertained millions over four decades with his hilarious sketches and sitcoms', said the *Daily Mail*. Naturally shy and reclusive, Barker was not only a fine actor but also a sketchwriter of rare ability.

The son of a clerk in the oil business, Ronald William George Barker was born in Bedford in 1929. He was brought up in Oxford, where he attended the local high school, opening his chemistry textbook one day to find the name T.E. Lawrence inscribed on the flyleaf. Barker's interest in acting was sparked by Laurence Olivier's performance in *Henry V*, said the *Daily Telegraph*. He played truant to watch the film time and again at his local cinema, despite the fact that the entrance was located directly opposite the headmaster's study window. After school Barker enrolled at architectural college, but his grasp of maths and physics was poor and, reluctantly, he decided to take a job as a junior bank clerk. Yet he dreamed of becoming an actor, said *The Times*, and 'kept his fellow clerks amused with impersonations' while appearing in amateur theatrical productions in his spare time.

In 1948, Barker took the decision to become a professional actor, despite his father's warning that he would not support him if he failed. Taking the afternoon off work, he auditioned (using six different accents) for a part at the Aylesbury branch of the Manchester Repertory Players, appearing on stage that same night. For the next seven years he worked steadily in local theatre, said *The Guardian*, and discovered a gift for comedy. The effect of his first big laugh was intoxicating. 'My mission in life was now crystal clear,' he recalled. 'Forget *Hamlet*. Forget *Richard II*. Give me *Charley's Aunt*.' Even so, Barker established a reputation as a classical actor with several fine performances, particularly at the Oxford Playhouse. The company included the young Maggie Smith, with whom Barker was so unimpressed that he advised her to give up acting. Recognising Barker's talent, the Playhouse's 21-year-old director, Peter Hall, cast him in a production of *Mourning Becomes Electra* in London. Soon he was appearing regularly on radio in *The Navy Lark*, but his big break in television came in 1966 when he was cast in *The Frost Report* alongside John Cleese. The show's creator, David Frost, had also spotted a diminutive comic named Ronnie Corbett, with whom Barker struck up an instant rapport. The pair had met some years before while Corbett was working as a barman; they now stuck together, not least because they felt slightly intimidated as grammar school boys in the company of so many university graduates.

> **'Tonight, we'll be asking: Should all married couples be frank and earnest, or should one of them be a woman?'**

The Two Ronnies, the show that turned both men into household names, began in 1971. A mixture of comedy sketches, songs and parodies, it ran until 1986 and regularly attracted more than 18 million viewers. Barker himself wrote much of the material under the pseudonym Gerald Wiley (see below) and was particularly fond of jokes based on wordplays and double entendres ('Tonight, we'll be asking: Should all married couples be frank and earnest, or should one of them be a woman?').

The success of *The Two Ronnies* allowed Barker to branch out into other forms of acting. His most memorable comic role came in the BBC series *Porridge*, in which he played a charming, gum-chewing prisoner, Norman Stanley Fletcher. (Prison Doctor: 'I want you to fill one of these urine bottles for me.' Fletcher: 'What, from 'ere?') Barker, who received letters from convicts praising the show's authenticity, reprised his role in *Going Straight*, in which Fletcher returns home to find his wife has left him for a cardboard box millionaire. Barker's career continued with *Open All Hours* (1976), in which he played a stammering Yorkshire shopkeeper opposite the unknown David Jason.

However, worried by his health – he had been shocked by the deaths of Eric Morecambe, Tommy Cooper and Leonard Rossiter – Barker announced his retirement in 1987 via a message on his answering machine. In the last 18 years of his life he ran an antiques shop in Chipping Norton with his wife, Joy, and found a lucrative sideline producing books about saucy postcards, said *The Times*. He appeared only rarely on screen, but The *Two Ronnies Sketchbook*, a revival of the series broadcast in 2005, attracted 8 million viewers. 'We never had a cross word,' said Corbett of his partner. 'It was 40 years of harmonious joy, nothing but an absolute pleasure. I will miss him terribly.'

Ronnie Barker's alter ego: the mysterious Gerald Wiley

While working on *The Frost Report*, Barker became disillusioned with the quality of the scripts and decided to do something about it, said the *Daily Telegraph*. Rather than draw attention to himself, he began submitting sketches via his agent under the pseudonym Gerald Wiley. At one stage, up to 75 per cent of the material in the programme was penned by Barker, yet none of his fellow comics had any idea who 'Wiley' was.

Barker went to great lengths to protect his identity, said Bob McCabe in the *Sunday Times*. At one point, he instructed his agent to phone Frank Muir and arrange a meeting with Wiley, which he later cancelled at the last minute. Ronnie Corbett was also suspicious, not least because he wanted to buy the rights to some of Wiley's material. Barker told his agent to charge Corbett £250. 'He wants £250 for it,' the unsuspecting Corbett told Barker. 'Don't pay it,' Barker replied. 'It's not worth that.' Later, however, Barker arranged for the sketch to be given to Corbett free of charge. Corbett was delighted and ran in to tell Barker the news. 'He's given it to me,' he told his comic partner. 'That's so nice of him.' Some time later, Corbett sent Wiley half a dozen crystal glasses, inscribed with the initials 'GW', as a gesture of thanks.

By now the *Frost* crew had set up a book to try to guess who Wiley was, said McCabe. Tom Stoppard? Noel Coward? Keith Waterhouse? Eventually Wiley summoned them all to a Chinese restaurant. Frank Muir arrived late, prompting several crew members to applaud. 'It's not me,' he insisted. Then Barker stood up. 'Can I just say something before we start? I'm Gerald Wiley. It's me.'

The 'mother' of the American civil-rights movement

ROSA PARKS

1913-2005

Rosa Parks was the black seamstress whose refusal to give up her bus seat to a white passenger marked the true start of black America's struggle for racial equality. 'She sat down,' said Reverend Jesse Jackson, 'so that we might all stand up.' Although often portrayed as a random, 'almost chance act' of defiance by a weary middle-aged woman, it was, in fact, the defining moment in a life devoted to the civil-rights movement.

Born in Alabama in 1913, Rosa McCauley grew up in 'a land of lynchings and burnings and the white-robed night-riders of the Ku Klux Klan, an age when survival was the most to which blacks could aspire', said Rupert Cornwell in *The Independent*. Her mother, however, was determined that she should at least be educated, and sent her to a private school in Montgomery set up by a group of Northern liberals. Later, she attended Alabama State College. In those days, the only jobs open to educated black women were as clerks or seamstresses, said Sheila Rowbotham in *The Guardian*. Rosa became skilled in the latter trade. 'Years later, she recalled how racism permeated the details of everyday life. Black women were served last; when they tried on a hat in a store, the saleswoman would first put a bag inside it.'

In 1932, aged 19, she married Raymond Parks, a barber, with whom she became involved in the National Association for the Advancement of Colored People. The Montgomery chapter was keen to tackle the issue of segregation on buses – a long-standing battleground for black rights activists. (Parks was herself ejected from a bus in 1943 for refusing to enter by the back door.) On 1 December 1955 she boarded a bus outside the department store where she worked and sat down in the front row of the 'blacks only' section. But as the bus began to fill up, a white man was left standing, so the bus driver moved the sign back a row, and told Parks to vacate her seat. She refused. 'If you don't stand up, I am going to call the police.' 'You may do that,' came her reply.

Duly arrested, Parks was charged and bailed. That night, said the *Daily Telegraph*, she resolved to fight the case. The NAACP had been planning to test the law for some time, but previous contenders had proved unsuitable. (One was a teenager who turned out to be pregnant; another had a drink problem.) Parks – a respectable married woman with a quiet dignity – was a far more promising candidate. E.D. Nixon, president of the NAACP branch, called a meeting of black leaders. A group of female university professors distributed leaflets urging a bus boycott, and the Montgomery Improvement Association (MIA) was founded to organise it.

The following Monday, Parks was convicted, setting the stage for a federal appeal. That night, thousands of people gathered in a local church to see the then little-known Martin Luther King anointed as the leader of the MIA. 'We in Montgomery,' declared the young pastor, 'are determined to work and fight until justice runs down like water and righteousness like a mighty stream.' The boycott would last 381 days: on 20 December 1956 the federal court declared segregation on buses illegal.

For Parks, victory did not come cheap. She and her husband lost their jobs, and were harassed and threatened. Raymond suffered a nervous breakdown. In 1957 they moved to Detroit, where Parks worked as a

Black women were served last; when they tried on a hat in a store, the saleswoman would first put a bag inside it.

seamstress until 1965, when she was employed as a receptionist to the Democratic Congressman John Conyers. She remained active in civil-rights work but was unknown to the general public until the late 1970s, when historians began properly to investigate the movement's history. Featured in magazine articles and TV documentaries, Rosa Parks was hailed as an American hero. Streets were named after her, and, on her death, she became the first woman to lie in honour in the United States Capitol Rotunda. She, however, was always humble about her place in American history, insisting that she had done nothing especially heroic that December afternoon in 1955. 'I did not get on the bus to get arrested,' she once said. 'I got on the bus to get home.'

Photographer who snapped Bianca Jagger and Diana

THE EARL OF LICHFIELD

1939-2005

A t the peak of his fame, the Earl of Lichfield was 'arguably more glamorous and better known than most of his subjects', said Andrew Pierce in *The Times*. A cousin of the Queen, with a dandyish dress sense and bouffant hairdo, he took pictures of everyone from rock stars to royalty, and in the process became one of the most dashing denizens of Swinging London.

Born in 1939, Thomas Patrick John Anson was the son of Viscount Anson and his wife Anne (née Bowes-Lyon). He grew up at Shugborough Hall in Staffordshire, and was educated at Harrow, where he supplemented his pocket money by taking pictures of leavers for 9d a time. But from Harrow, he followed the conventional path to Sandhurst and thence into the Grenadier Guards. His father died in 1958, and when his grandfather also died in 1960, he became the fifth Earl of Lichfield. Two years later, said *The Times*, he resigned his commission, 'turned his back on the career of land management which had been proposed for him' and became a photographer's assistant. His family was appalled – they considered photography 'only marginally better than hairdressing' – and promptly cut off his allowance. Years later, Lichfield observed that although the 1960s were remembered for liberating working class talent, the 'toffs' had been liberated, too. 'The barriers were broken down for us as well and we came into contact with people we wouldn't normally have met. My son won't meet any parental opposition to what he wants to do.'

Throwing himself into his new career, Lichfield began taking pictures of debutantes and friends, and was soon a regular contributor to *Queen* magazine. His big break came when Diana Vreeland, editor of *American Vogue*, commissioned him to take some pictures of the Duke and Duchess of Windsor. The normally grim-faced royal exiles looked uncharacteristically cheerful; the photographer, it later emerged, had just fallen through his chair. By dint of extremely hard work, and aided by his

> **His family considered photography 'only marginally better than hairdressing'.**

illustrious contacts and legendary charm, the Earl steadily became one of London's foremost photographers alongside his arguably more talented friends David Bailey and Terence O'Neill. In 1971 he was the photographer at Mick and Bianca Jagger's wedding; ten years later he performed the same function for Diana, Princess of Wales. This time he brought a little levity to the group portraits by marshalling the guests with a referee's whistle.

A bon viveur, Lichfield wrote several books, was involved in a number of restaurants, including the Deals chain, and made a fortune by investing in the musicals *Oh! Calcutta!* and *Hair*. This funded his 'jet-set lifestyle', and enabled him to buy a house on Mustique, where he cemented a longstanding friendship with Princess Margaret. (There were rumours, unsubstantiated, of an affair.) In 1975, amid 'great fanfare' (2,500 guests attended the reception), Lichfield married Leonora Grosvenor, sister of the Duke of Westminster, said *The Independent*. They had three children, to whom he was devoted, but divorced after 11 years. The fact that Lichfield spent 200 nights a year away on assignment, surrounded by beautiful women, cannot have helped the marriage. Nor can the endless tabloid stories about his alleged affairs. Nevertheless, the split came as a terrible blow, and he 'forgot to eat' for a while. 'Until my marriage break-up I'd never had any form of emotional upset,' he said in 2004. 'I might have broken a few hearts but my own was pretty much intact. That shows how spoiled I was.'

Minister who lied to Parliament – and repented for 40 years

JOHN PROFUMO

1915-2006

John Profumo was the central figure in one of the biggest scandals in British political history. The Profumo Affair had everything – toffs, showgirls, orgies, Soviet spies, suicide – but Profumo himself is perhaps of most interest not for the lie he told about his fling with Christine Keeler, as for the way he atoned for it. Unlike politicians today, said the *Daily Telegraph*, he did not try to turn disgrace into a 'revolving door' resignation. He withdrew completely from public life, and dedicated the next 40 years to charitable work in London's East End. He never spoke of the affair that bore his name; he wrote no memoir, granted no interviews. 'No one judges Jack Profumo more harshly than he does himself,' said the late Jim Thompson, the Bishop of Bath and Wells. 'He says he has never known a day since it happened when he has not felt real shame.'

Born in 1915, John Profumo was the eldest son of a barrister of Italian descent who held the title Fourth Baron Profumo. Educated at Harrow and Oxford, he won a 1940 by-election to become, at 25, the youngest MP. And on 8 May that year, he was one of 40 Tories to vote against Neville Chamberlain over the Norway crisis, thus ensuring Churchill's succession. Profumo had a good war: he was mentioned in despatches during the

North Africa campaign, and was appointed OBE (Mil) during the Italian campaign. In 1959 Harold Macmillan appointed him Minister of State for Foreign Affairs. He became Secretary of State for War the following year. 'Aged 45, rich, elegantly dressed, highly regarded by colleagues, and with an attractive wife (the actress Valerie Hobson), Profumo had reason to feel pleased with life,' said *The Independent*. 'A cabinet seat was now a reasonable expectation.'

Then in 1961 he had his first, fateful encounter with the 19-year-old Christine Keeler. Profumo and his wife had been invited to Cliveden, Viscount Astor's Berkshire mansion, in whose grounds Stephen Ward, a society osteopath with a reputation for procuring beautiful young women, had rented a cottage. On the sultry night of 8 July, the minister and his host, both wearing dinner jackets, went for a walk, and came upon Keeler – Ward's guest – frolicking naked in the swimming pool. The minister was entranced, and Astor invited Ward and Keeler to join the party at the 'big 'ouse'. The next morning, a young Soviet naval attaché joined them, and was beaten by Profumo in a swimming race.

That night Keeler went home with Yevgeny Ivanov, but Profumo had asked for her telephone number, and within days the minister and the topless dancer were lovers. Their affair was not one of the great passions, said Dominic Sandbrook in *The Observer*. Profumo was a philanderer, but a happily married one. He probably saw the liaison as an exciting diversion. Keeler described it as a 'very, very well-mannered screw of convenience', for which she picked up small trinkets and some gifts of cash. In any case, the affair is believed to have lasted little more than a month: in August, Profumo was warned that British secret intelligence was using Ward to get to Ivanov. Immediately, Profumo scribbled Keeler an affectionate note, cancelling their next meeting – the so-called 'Darling' letter which more or less ended their relationship.

After that Profumo probably thought he could breathe easy, said *The Times*. But Keeler didn't just disappear. She took as her lovers two West Indians, one of whom, a Notting Hill drug dealer named John Edgecombe, became jealous of the other. On 14 December, Edgecombe called around at Keeler's flat and fired several shots. Edgecombe was arrested, and during the subsequent investigation Keeler told police about Profumo. Rumours began to swirl around Fleet Street and Westminster. Confident that no one would take the word of a 'whore' over a minister of state, Profumo, in private, repeatedly denied having an affair, and his enemies felt too constrained by their own sexual improprieties to challenge him. But when Labour MP George Wigg, who had a longstanding grudge against the minister, got hold of the Ivanov angle, he took advantage of parliamentary privilege to ask questions about the affair, and its security aspect, in the House.

At 2am the following morning, 22 March 1963, Profumo was awoken from a heavy sleep and summoned to a meeting of Tory grandees to draft a statement. The next day he told the House of Commons 'there was no impropriety whatsoever in my acquaintanceship with Miss Keeler'. But the story wouldn't die, not least because Stephen Ward's hedonistic activities were now coming under police investigation. Faced with the prospect of an inquiry, Profumo finally confessed all to his wife over lunch in Venice. 'Oh darling,' she said, 'we must go home as soon as we can and face up to it.' He resigned on 5 June – but when Ward was prosecuted for living off immoral earnings, the scandal only intensified.

Throughout the summer of 1963 – the summer of the Great Train Robbery and The Beatles' 'She Loves You' – the press had a field day, said *The Guardian*. Rumours circulated about upper-class orgies and S&M parties featuring a mysterious 'man in the mask' – a high-ranking politician, or a member of the royal family – who served guests naked and ate from a dog bowl. A weakened Macmillan resigned after being diagnosed with cancer. The Tory party, already perceived as out of touch, lost the 1964 election. Abandoned by his society friends, Ward committed suicide on the last day of his trial. Ivanov – who later said he'd only slept with Keeler because she was a 'bimbo', and had never even told his bosses about her, let alone used her to extract military secrets – fled back to Moscow, where he drank himself to death. Keeler never got over her notoriety, fell into penury, and is now living in London under an assumed name.

A few weeks after resigning, Profumo walked into Toynbee Hall, a welfare centre in the East End, and asked if there was anything he could do to help. The dapper aristocrat made tea, cleaned lavatories, danced with old ladies, and collected rents. Later, he was asked to take over the charity's fundraising campaigns, and became its chairman. He was made CBE in 1975. As his wife said, 'It isn't what happens to a man, it's what he does with it that matters.'

The Anglophile who spent $6bn a week on weapons

CASPAR WEINBERGER

1917-2006

As Ronald Reagan's Secretary of State for defence, Caspar Weinberger 'oversaw the biggest and costliest military build-up in the United States' peacetime history', said the *New York Times*. An 'implacable foe of the Soviet Union', Weinberger said his mission was to 're-arm America', and he did just that, at a cost of $2 trillion. His critics accused him of exaggerating the threat from Moscow, and wasting billions of dollars, but he remained convinced his hardline course had been the right one. 'Yes we used a worst-case analysis, but you should always use a worst-case analysis, because in this business you can't afford to be wrong,' he said. 'In the end, we won the Cold War, and if we won by too much, if it was overkill, so be it.'

Born in San Francisco in 1917, Caspar W. Weinberger was the son of a Jewish lawyer. His mother, English by origin, was Episcopalian, and he shared her faith, as well as her Anglophilia. His interest in politics developed at a young age: as a child, he read congressional reports at bedtime, and even then considered himself a Republican. In 1938 he graduated from Harvard summa cum laude, but his training to become a lawyer was interrupted when, a few months before Pearl Harbour, he joined the army as a private. After wartime service in the South Pacific, he returned to California and joined a law firm. In 1952 he was elected to the state legislature. He served under Ronald Reagan when the film star became governor, and in 1970 joined Nixon's White House.

In those days, Weinberger was known not for spending, but for slashing, said the *Daily Telegraph*. Indeed, he showed such zeal in dismantling Lyndon Johnson's Great Society programmes that he became known as 'Cap the Knife'. By contrast, as Reagan's defence secretary from 1981, he lavished money on military hardware, said *The Guardian*, 'raising the annual defence bill by 50 per cent in real terms, at a weekly cost to the American taxpayer of $6bn'. He met pretty much every demand made by the Services, and backed the Strategic Defence Initiative (Star Wars) as an alternative to MAD (mutually assured destruction). But in the words of one critic, the Pentagon was a 'swamp' of waste and inefficiency, and Weinberger was forced to admit that even under his watch, costs had run out of control. In 1982, for instance, the Pentagon was paying $17.59 for a simple metal bolt that, two years earlier, had cost just 80 cents.

The plan was partly to encourage the Soviets to bankrupt themselves. But the effect of all this spending – combined with Reagan's tax cuts – was felt all over the world, said *The Times*. As Reagan's policy adviser, Weinberger must bear some of the responsibility for the US's multibillion-dollar deficit, and its dire effect on the world economy.

In the late 1980s, Weinberger's distrust of the Soviets began to put him at odds with colleagues who felt deals could be made with Gorbachev's Kremlin. In 1987, not long before the stockmarket crash, he resigned, saying he wanted to spend more time with his wife who was seriously ill. The following year he was awarded an honourary knighthood, for persuading Ronald Reagan to give military assistance to Britain during the Falklands War. His reputation was marred, however, when it was revealed that he had become embroiled in the Iran Contra affair. He was indicted for lying to Congress, among other things, but spared trial when, in 1992, President Bush gave him an official pardon.

A pugilist in politics, Weinberger was 'softly spoken, almost courtly' in personal encounters, said the *New York Times*. This softer side was revealed in 1983, when the defence secretary – himself the owner of a collie – refused to allow dogs to be shot so that army doctors could use them to practise treating wounds.

Hollywood's
king of trash TV

AARON SPELLING

1923-2006

Aaron Spelling won a place in the *Guinness Book of Records* as television's most prolific producer. With a string of glossy, trashy but seemingly irresistible shows – *Charlie's Angels*; *Dynasty*; *Beverly Hills 90210* – he dominated American television in the 1970s and 1980s, turned Joan Collins into an international star, and made so much money he was able to build himself California's largest private residence, a 56,000sq ft, 123-room Bel Air mansion in the style of a French château. Spelling's daughter Tori complained it was so big she needed a golf buggy to get around.

Aaron Spelling specialised in shows about beautiful, rich people, often doing horrid things. His own beginnings, however, were distinctly humble. Born in a slum district of Dallas, Texas, in 1923, he was the son of an impoverished Jewish tailor. There weren't many Jews in Texas in those days (his grandfather had reportedly ended up there because 'cowboy' was one of only two English words he knew when he arrived from Poland) and at school, the 8-year-old Aaron was subjected to bullying so severe that he suffered a nervous breakdown and spent a year in bed, where he devoured books and developed an ambition to become a writer. During war-time service in the US airforce he wrote for *Stars and Stripes* magazine. Later he directed plays while completing college in Dallas. One of them was by a black author, which so enraged local worthies that Spelling was effectively forced out of town. By 1954 Spelling was making a living as a bit-part actor in Hollywood (with his strange hairstyle, large eyes and skinny frame, he was mostly cast as 'weirdos', as he put it, in low-budget TV shows) while hawking scripts around the studios. His first series was *Johnny Ringo*, which ran for a year in 1959.

In the 1960s, he moved into producing, and was so successful that he was granted an exclusive contract with the ABC network. Numerous hits followed: *Starsky & Hutch* made stars of David Soul and Paul Michael Glaser (catchphrase: 'Freeze') and their red 1974 Ford Torino; *Charlie's Angels* – featuring three female private detectives sent each week to infiltrate some criminal set-up, usually dressed as go-go dancers or ice skaters – was considerably less gritty but no less popular. *Dynasty* (set in Denver and launched as a rival to CBS's *Dallas*) struggled in the ratings until Joan Collins swept into the series as Alexis Carrington. Last seen in soft-porn flicks such as *The Stud*, 'she proved the perfect bitch', said *The Independent*. And through her battles with her ex-husband Blake (John Forsythe) and endless cat fights with his new wife Krystle (Linda Evans),

> **Although most of Spelling's shows were brainless trash (or 'mind candy', as he preferred to call it), he also produced some serious work.**

she helped give the show the high-octane drama and kitsch glamour (huge shoulder pads, big hair) it needed to win fans in 70 countries. Other Spelling hits included *Hart to Hart*, *TJ Hooker*, *Fantasy Island*, and *The Love Boat*.

When *Dynasty* was axed in 1989, Spelling's critics figured he was finished, said the *Daily Telegraph*. A year later, however, he bounced back with *Beverly Hills 90210*, set in a smart California high school, which ran for ten years. Although most of Spelling's shows were brainless trash (or 'mind candy', as he preferred to call it), he also produced some serious work. He was most proud of his Emmy award-winning TV movie *And the Band Played on*, which was one of the first mainstream dramas to tackle the Aids crisis.

Tales of Spelling's extravagance were legion: his house had an indoor ice rink, and an entire wing devoted to his wife's wardrobe; he travelled the country in a private train, and imported snow by the truckload, so his children could experience a white Christmas. Yet in person, Spelling was a shy, intensely private, mild-mannered figure. Writing in the *Independent on Sunday*, the British actress Emma Samms, who starred as *Dynasty*'s Fallon, recalled a courteous, 'exceptionally generous', and thoughtful man, who – unusually for an LA producer – was devoted to his family and had absolutely no interest in exploiting his own (vast) casting couch.

'The greatest bloody fast bowler that ever drew breath'

FRED TRUEMAN

1931-2006

Fred Trueman was a cricketer of exceptional skill, strength, speed and stamina, said the *Daily Telegraph*, with a stormy temperament to match. Modesty was not among his virtues. (He once described himself, only half-jokingly, as the 'greatest bloody fast bowler that ever drew breath'.) But 'who could argue with his record'? Not only was the combative Yorkshireman the first player to take 300 wickets in Tests, at an average of 21.57; in a first-class career lasting from 1949 to 1968, he claimed 2,304 wickets at only 18.29 apiece, a better record than any other genuinely fast bowler.

The son of a miner, Frederick Sewards Trueman was born in 1931 in the village of Stainton, near Rotherham, weighing an impressive 14lbs 1oz. His father encouraged him to play cricket and, at the age of 16, he joined his local club side at Sheffield. He was summoned for indoor winter training sessions at Headingley the following year, and made his Yorkshire debut against Cambridge University in 1949. All the while, he was working as a tally hand at the Maltby Main pit. He made his Test debut against India at Headingley in 1952, while on leave of absence from National Service in the RAF, and caused a sensation by taking three of the first four wickets in the match, leaving India with a score of none for four. However, his bad language and unruly behaviour in the West Indies in 1953–1954 meant that over the next four and a half years he played only seven more Test matches. That rankled with Trueman for the rest of his days, said *The Times*, and 'understandably so'.

Trueman's England heyday was between 1957 and 1963, when he and Brian Statham proved a lethal combination, 'Statham quiet and undeviating, Trueman as fiery as he was versatile. Trueman played to the crowds; they loved his flamboyance, the histrionics, the sight of his running in to bowl, dark hair flowing, power and rhythm building, his left arm pointing as he came into the delivery stride'. He memorised the weaknesses of every batsman, and wound up the opposition with his notorious dressing room visits, said David Close in the *Mail on Sunday*. Trueman would sweep in, cast his eye over the players, and announce which of them he expected to bowl out that day. As they left the pavilion for the crease, he'd shout: 'Don't close t'gate, you won't be long out 'ere.' Trueman 'loved to spread fear in opposing ranks', said *The Guardian*: 'a Roy Ulyett cartoon – in which a West Indian mother urges her children to go to sleep "or that Fred Trueman will come and get you" – gave him great delight'.

Trueman retired from first-class cricket in 1968, after captaining Yorkshire to victory against the Australians. In the 1970s, he became a successful after-dinner speaker, known for his wit, and also a regular presenter on *Test Match Special*; his often-heard complaint about the modern game – 'I just don't know what's going off out there' – became his catchphrase. He remained on the Yorkshire committee until 1984, when he was voted out by supporters of Geoffrey Boycott. Prime Minister Harold Wilson had described Fred Trueman as the 'greatest living Yorkshireman', but it wasn't until 1989 that he was appointed OBE, for his charity work.

> **As they left the pavilion for the crease, he'd shout: 'Don't close t'gate, you won't be long out 'ere.'**

Former pacifist who led resistance efforts in southern France

FRANCIS CAMMAERTS

1916-2006

Francis Cammaerts began the War as a conscientious objector, and ended it as one of the most highly regarded members of the Special Operations Executive. During 15 months working with the Maquis, 'le grand diable Anglais' created from scratch a network of 10,000 resistance fighters who helped pave the way for the Riviera landings and the liberation of south-eastern France in the summer of 1944.

Francis Cammaerts was born in London in 1916, the son of Emile Cammaerts, a Belgian poet who had moved to England after marrying the Shakespearean actress Tita Brand. Educated at Mill Hill school and Cambridge, Cammaerts began his career as a teacher, first in Belfast and later at Penge Grammar School. On the outbreak of war, he registered as a conscientious objector, and was sent to work as a farm labourer in Lincolnshire, where he met his wife, Nan. However, the death of his brother, an RAF pilot, caused him to reconsider his pacifism, and in 1942 he was recruited to the SOE. Cammaert's instructors did not rate him very highly (one described him as a 'plodder').

Nevertheless in March 1943 he was flown into northern France. He was due to join the Carte network but mistrusted its security arrangements, and made his way to the Riviera. (His instinct was correct: Carte had been infiltrated by German military intelligence.) Over the next few months he set up his own circuit (codenamed Jockey), formed reception committees, co-ordinated arms drops, secured a wireless operator and, in the spring of 1944, began work on sabotage operations. Although he kept tabs on all his fighters, they never knew where he was, as he never stayed more than one or two nights in the same place. At 6ft 4ins tall, he stood out in a crowd, and there were several near misses. Once, he was stopped getting off a train in Avignon. While the Germans were leafing through his papers, Cammaerts bit his lip and spat blood on the platform. Terrified of contracting TB, the Nazis handed back the papers and sent him on his way.

A few weeks after the Normandy landings, Cammaerts was caught by a German road patrol, and sentenced to death. His life was spared thanks to the bravery of his courier, a Polish countess known as Christine Granville, who persuaded his captors to let him go. After the War, he returned to teaching, working in England, Kenya and Botswana. For

Cammaert's Special Operations Executive instructors did not rate him very highly (one described him as a 'plodder').

his wartime gallantry, Cammaerts was awarded the DSO, and the French Croix de Guerre, among other honours. However, he always said the real credit belonged to the French fighters, and the ordinary French people who risked everything to help the resistance effort. 'The most important element was the French housewife who fed us, clothed us and kept us cheerful.'

The Jehovah's Witness who created Mike Hammer

MICKEY SPILLANE

1918-2006

Mickey Spillane was one of the best-selling authors of the twentieth century, and the creator of Mike Hammer, a hardboiled, 'unreconstructed' private investigator who cruised the streets of New York, 'fending off impossibly pneumatic women, fighting dirty and blowing away assorted hoodlums with his trusty .45 automatic'. The critics detested Spillane's violent, sexually explicit fiction, said the *Daily Telegraph* – churchmen, community leaders and politicians despised it too. In fact, as *Life* magazine once put it: 'No one likes [his books] – except the public.' Said to have sold more than 180 million, Spillane was the most translated author in the world apart from Lenin, Tolstoy, Gorky and Jules Verne: 'and they're all dead,' he liked to say.

Frank Morrison Spillane was born in 1918, the son of an Irish-American bartender, and brought up in a rough district of New Jersey. Baptised a Catholic, he was given the saint's name Michael, and was thereafter known as 'Mickey'. Spillane began submitting stories to magazines such as *Dime Detective* at the age of 14 and, after drifting through a series of odd jobs, he found work at a Manhattan-based comic books publisher called Funnies Inc. While there, he developed a reputation for churning out copy at remarkable speed. He enlisted in the Air Force the day after Pearl Harbour, and claimed to have fought combat missions over Europe, although in reality, he was largely confined to a base in Mississippi.

In 1947 he produced his first novel, *I, the Jury*. Written in just nine days on a Smith-Corona manual typewriter, it introduced the world to Mike Hammer, a war veteran out to avenge a friend's murder. The book contains the most famous last lines in pulp-fiction history. Discovering that the killer is the woman he's fallen for, Hammer shoots her at point-blank range through her naked belly. "'How c-could you?" she gasped. I only had a moment before talking to a corpse, but I got it in. "It was easy," I said.'

I, the Jury was panned by critics, said the *Los Angeles Times*. One called it a 'vicious ... glorification of force, cruelty and extra-legal methods'. Another denounced its 'lurid action, lurid characters, lurid plot, lurid finish'. Spillane 'let the critical barbs roll off him like Jack Daniels over ice'. 'I don't give a hoot about reading reviews,' he declared. In any case, his 'customers', as he referred to them, lapped it up: *I, the Jury* sold two million copies as a 25 cent paperback in just two years – and subsequent books sold in similarly vast numbers. Once, 'some New York literary guy' approached him at a party and said, 'I think it's disgraceful that of the ten best-selling books of all time, seven were written by you.' 'You're lucky I've only written seven books,' came Spillane's reply.

In the 1950s, Spillane bought a mansion on the coast of South Carolina. He divorced his first wife ('my wife-type wife') in 1962, and two years later married a 23-year-old who'd posed on the front cover of one of his books. 'I told them to send a good-looking, leggy blonde,' he liked to say, 'and I didn't send her back.' In fact, they lived relatively separate lives, and the marriage ended in a messy divorce. His third wife was a former Miss South Carolina. For much of the 1970s and 1980s, Spillane gave up writing novels, but his profile remained high, not least because of his self-parodic appearances, dressed in a trench coat and fedora, in a series of adverts for Miller Lite beer. (He also appeared on the front cover of his own books, and starred as Mike Hammer in a film version of one of his books.)

Contrary to his hardboiled image, Spillane, who had four children, was a Jehovah's Witness, whom friends described as affable and softly spoken. He played golf, drank modestly, remained on good terms with his family, and was so fond of animals that he refused to allow hunting on his land. 'I'm actually a softie,' he said in 2004, aged 86. 'Tough guys get killed too early.'

The former socialite who, at 82, set up an orphanage in Rwanda

ROSAMOND CARR

1912-2006

Rosamond Carr abandoned her life as a socialite in Manhattan in order to settle in Africa with her adventurer husband, said the *Daily Telegraph*. She made her home in rural Rwanda, where she remained until forced out by the genocide of 1994. Four months later, aged 82, she returned to the country to run an orphanage dedicated to the care of its victims.

The daughter of a Wall Street trader, Rosamond Halsey was born in 1912, and enjoyed a life of privilege until the Depression narrowed her options. Forced to work, she became a fashion illustrator by day, and socialite by night. In 1941 she was invited to a showing of films by the British-born big-game hunter Kenneth Carr. Instantly captivated by this 'dashing, exotic figure', she agreed to marry him, only later discovering that he was broke, 'painfully inhibited', and did not want children.

In 1949, in a last-ditch attempt to save their marriage, they moved to Rwanda; initially appalled by the conditions, Rosamond soon fell in love with the region, and decided to stay on there, even after divorcing her husband in 1955. For the next 40 years, she eked out a living growing and selling flowers; for a long time her best friend in the area was Dian Fossey, the zoologist murdered in 1985.

When militant Hutus went on the rampage, Carr took in several refugees, but was unable to save them from a club-wielding mob. Having initially intended to stay, she was persuaded it was too risky, and was evacuated, wearing just a nightdress. But surveying the horror from the comfort of the USA, she felt, she said, 'like a traitor'. So in August 1994 she returned home to Rwanda, to turn what remained of her flower-growing shed into an orphanage; she called it Imbabazi, meaning 'a place where you will receive all the love and care a mother would give'. It became home to 120 children, Hutu and Tutsi.

Initially appalled by the conditions, Rosamond soon fell in love with Rwanda.

First Lady
of the LSE

ELISABETH RIVERS-BULKELEY

1924-2006

Elisabeth Rivers-Bulkeley was a pioneering female stockbroker, columnist, broadcaster and socialite. A stylish and original figure, she first made the headlines with her campaign to let women be elected to the Stock Exchange.

Elisabeth (Liesl) Charlotte Marie Neustadtl was born in Vienna, anglicising her name when she moved to Britain in 1939. She and her second husband, Major Robert Rivers-Bulkeley, spent five years breeding prize-winning pigs in the Scottish Borders – alas, unprofitably. So in 1957 she turned her attentions to the City, becoming an attaché to the firm of Hedderwick, Borthwick & Co. She also wrote a successful column about investment from a woman's point of view for the *Daily Telegraph*. In the 1960s and 1970s she tried and failed several times to be elected to the Stock Exchange, which was then a private club, with applications to trade being vetted by a panel of senior members. For a while her name 'struck fear into the hearts of every London broker determined to keep Throgmorton Street an all-male province', said the *Financial Times*. Finally, in a blaze of publicity in March 1973, Rivers-Bulkeley, by then a partner at Capel-Cure, Garden & Co, was one of 14 women grudgingly permitted to trade.

Rivers-Bulkeley combined her business achievements with a hectic social life. A founder member of Annabel's nightclub, she was admired for her ability to mix Chanel clothes with M&S. On learning she had cancer, she decided, characteristically, to take control of her death. She took her own life at the Swiss assisted-suicide clinic Dignitas.

Brilliant actor behind the ruthless Urquhart

IAN RICHARDSON

1934-2007

Ian Richardson was a founder member of the Royal Shakespeare Company with a distinguished 50-year stage career. But he will be most remembered for a single TV role, as the ruthless politician Francis Urquhart in the 1990 TV mini-series *House of Cards* and its two sequels, *To Play the King* and *The Final Cut*. The trilogy, adapted by Andrew Davies from the novels by former Tory MP Michael Dobbs, was a massive hit, catching the nation's mood at a time of growing disillusion with politics. But a large part of its success, said *The Independent*, was due to Richardson's portrait of the scheming politician who would stop at nothing, even murder, to get to No. 10. Ever the Shakespearean, he modelled the character on Richard III, and delivered Urquhart's signature phrase – 'You might think that, I couldn't possibly comment' – with such charismatic evil that it entered the national lexicon.

Ian William Richardson was born into a Scottish working-class family. His strict Presbyterian father, John, who drove a horse and cart for a biscuit factory, opposed his son's theatrical ambitions. But while his father was serving abroad in the Second World War, his mother encouraged him to join a local amateur dramatic society. After doing his National Service,

Richardson successfully auditioned for Glasgow's College of Dramatic Art. Asked why he wanted to become an actor, he replied, 'Because I can conceive of no other career I could possibly exist in.' As one of the RSC's earliest contract players, recruited by Peter Hall, Richardson was immediately tipped for greatness. An acclaimed Hamlet at 24, he played a succession of leading roles for the RSC before deciding, aged 39, that it was time for a change.

At first, said the *Daily Telegraph*, his foray into popular culture did not go well. TV and film directors were underwhelmed by his Shakespearean CV. He was obliged to go on the dole, and was once spotted picking up discarded vegetables in Covent Garden. He suffered a breakdown, recovering at a nursing home run by nuns in Regent's Park.

Then in 1979 he scored the first in a string of late-career TV successes, bringing unsympathetic characters to life, said *The Guardian*. He gave a mesmerising performance as Soviet mole Bill Haydon in *Tinker, Tailor, Soldier, Spy*, and as the spoil-sport head of a Cambridge college in *Porterhouse Blue*, before *House of Cards* made him a household name. The role won him a Bafta Best Actor Award in 1991, among other accolades, but he grew tired of the association, complaining that all the subsequent roles he was offered were 'a relation of Francis Urquhart'.

> **Asked why he wanted to become an actor, he replied, 'Because I can conceive of no other career I could possibly exist in.'**

The richest
woman in Asia

NINA WANG

1937-2007

Nina Wang gained control of her husband's massive Hong Kong-based business empire following his kidnapping and disappearance in 1990. 'Her personal style was as bizarre as her life story,' said the *Daily Telegraph*. Wang liked to be known by her Cantonese nickname Siu Tim-Tim ('Little Sweetie'), after a girl in a Japanese comic book; even in late middle age she wore pigtails, leather microskirts, ankle socks, platform shoes and white PVC macs.

Kung Yu Sum (she later adopted the name Nina) was born into a Shanghai business family in 1937. She and her husband-to-be, Teddy Wang, were childhood sweethearts. Like many of Hong Kong's oligarchs, he fled Shanghai during the Revolution; later he sent for her, and they married in 1955. Wang made his fortune buying up large areas of Hong Kong's New Territories from farmers. As mainland refugees flooded into the colony and demand for housing soared, so did the value of his company, Chinachem.

Teddy Wang, a hard businessman who rarely paid contractors on time or in full, made many enemies as he built up his property empire, said *The Times*. He also refused to hire bodyguards, and in 1983 was kidnapped by a Taiwanese gang. Released after Nina paid a ransom of around HK$11m,

Teddy berated her for paying so much so soon. But after he was kidnapped for the second time in 1990, he was never seen again. It was not until 1998 that one of the kidnappers confessed that Teddy had been thrown into the South China Sea as a naval vessel approached their boat.

In his absence, Nina took control of Chinachem. But her standing came under threat in 1999 when her late husband's father, Wang Dinshin, claimed that the will bequeathing her the company was a forgery, and that his son had cut her out of his real will, after discovering that she had had an affair with a warehouseman in 1968. In response, Nina accused her father-in-law of smoking opium and keeping a concubine. In 2002 a Hong Kong court ruled that the will benefiting her was a fake, and that she had probably forged part of it. Only last year, in the court of final appeal, did Nina manage to overturn this decision, winning the legacy and becoming the richest woman in Asia: *Forbes* magazine estimated her fortune at

She was known to shop at cheap outlet stores, eat fast food and 'rarely leave a dinner party without a doggie bag'.

$4.2bn. Even so, she was 'breathtakingly frugal', said the *New York Times*. She was known to shop at cheap outlet stores, eat fast food and 'rarely leave a dinner party without a doggie bag'.

The practical joker who turned business green

ANITA RODDICK

1942-2007

Dame Anita Roddick was founder of the cosmetics chain the Body Shop, and one of the country's most successful entrepreneurs, said *The Independent*. By adopting an 'ethical approach to cosmetics', she pioneered a new industry and 'made saving the planet fashionable'. At its height, the Body Shop empire had more than 2,100 branches in 55 countries, making Roddick one of the richest women in Britain. Yet despite her financial success, she continued to consider herself more an activist than a businesswoman, and campaigned for a diverse number of causes from children's charities to Greenpeace.

Anita Lucia Perilli was born in 1942 in Littlehampton, Sussex, the daughter of Jewish-Italian immigrants who ran a café. After a brief dalliance with both acting and teaching, she set off to work in a Kibbutz in Israel, only to be thrown out for being a practical joker. She spent the next 18 months travelling the world – stopping briefly in 1970 to marry Gordon Roddick, son of a well-heeled Scottish grain broker – before resuming the hippie trail with her husband in tow. She returned to run a b&b in Littlehampton, but it was only when Gordon disappeared for two years – to 'fulfil a lifelong dream' of riding a horse from Buenos Aires to New

York – that the Body Shop came to fruition. The first shop opened in 1976 in Brighton, selling 25 ethically sourced skin and hair care products, based partly on Bedouin recipes gathered on Roddick's travels, and partly on her mother's beauty habits. The trademark green branding was established by accident, she later said, being the only colour that could cover the mould on the walls of her shop.

From modest beginnings, the enterprise soon proved so popular that she opened a second outlet and, by the mid-1980s, the Body Shop had become a leading retailer, with a presence on almost every high street. 'Principled, outspoken and opportunistic,' blessed with Latin looks and a 'fondness for laddered tights and Doc Marten boots', Roddick proved to be a shrewd self-publicist, said the *Financial Times*, winning free editorial space for the Body Shop worth millions of pounds. The company's flotation in 1985 was a huge success, and by 1990, when shares hit 35p, the Roddicks' 30 per cent stake made her the fourth-richest woman in the country.

Green was the only colour that could cover the mould on the walls of her shop.

But the flotation also proved to be her 'greatest mistake', said *The Times*. 'The Body Shop was being measured only by profit and loss, and her vision of a company that brought honestly paid work in decent conditions to deprived communities was floundering.' Two decades later, in 2006, her values were further compromised when the Body Shop was bought by French cosmetics giant L'Oreal, a company with a record of animal testing. The transfer, worth £652m, prompted critics to accuse Roddick of selling out to an industry she had previously described as 'a monster selling unobtainable dreams, one that lies cheats and exploits women'. Roddick argued that the Body Shop would act as a 'Trojan Horse', subverting the industry's unethical practices from the inside.

Roddick made almost £130m from the sale, £30m of which was channelled straight into her foundation. Having always described it as a disgrace to die rich, she dedicated her remaining time, money and energy to various charitable commitments. But Roddick's lasting legacy will be her blending of activism and business, said John Sauven, director of Greenpeace. 'She was the one to put green and environmental issues on the business agenda. Thanks to her, this idea is now mainstream.'

Presenter of *Loose Ends* who changed the face of television

NED SHERRIN

1931-2007

Ned Sherrin was not a singer, actor or entertainer in the conventional sense, said Philip Hoare in *The Independent*. Nevertheless, this 'consummate and extraordinary man of the theatre' was, for more than four decades, one of the best-loved and most influential figures in British entertainment.

The son of a Somerset farmer, Sherrin never took to the great outdoors, said the *Daily Telegraph*. As a child he was 'a mystery to the rest of his family', dressing up, making model theatres out of old Shredded Wheat packets and never getting his hands dirty. 'What use is that boy?' asked his father as he watched the young Sherrin collecting wild flowers, writing short stories and 'thumping out show tunes' on the family piano. At the age of 11, he was sent to Sexey's School in Bruton – where he was seduced by the head prefect in the back of a car during a school trip to Stratford-upon-Avon. Following National Service, at his father's insistence, he went to Exeter College, Oxford, to study law. Called to the Bar in 1955, he had no intention of pursuing a career as a barrister, instead, taking up a position with the regional television station ATV. 'In a long career of happy accidents,' he later wrote, 'perhaps the most useful was to have been born in

1931 and to complete the National Service, Oxford and Bar exams precisely in time for the opening of commercial television.'

Sherrin made his first 'distinctive mark' on British broadcasting in 1962 as the co-creator of *That Was The Week That Was*. A subversive, satirical news programme, TW3 – as it became known – 'cast an unsparing gaze on the hidden corners of British political life', said *The Times*. Transmitted by the BBC late on Saturday evenings, TW3 was 'like nothing seen on television before'. Inspired by the success of the satirical revue *Beyond the Fringe*, 'it attacked politicians, trade unions, the press and organised religion. It is scarcely too much to say that the standing of politicians and the business of governing have never been quite the same since.' Sherrin's 'hand-picked performers' included Willie Rushton, Roy Kinnear, Bernard Levin and, as presenter, 'a little-known cabaret performer' named David Frost. All were condemned as 'pedlars of smut and destroyers of all that Britain holds dear' by a predictably outraged Fourth Estate, said the *Daily Telegraph*. But the show was watched by more than ten million people, including Princess Margaret, who encouraged Sherrin to write a sketch about 'the absurdly reverential way the press reports us'. The following week, the TW3 team did a skit about the Queen's barge sinking in the Thames.

> **'What use is that boy?' asked his father.**

In an extraordinarily wide-ranging career Sherrin worked as a movie producer for Columbia Pictures and wrote songs, novels, short stories, memoirs and musicals, as well as numerous plays for the stage, radio and television. He also directed several West End hits, including *Jeffrey Bernard Is Unwell* (1989). Yet he was rarely off the airwaves. 'Every time I think Ned Sherrin is dead,' complained one journalist, 'he crops up on TV with some programme in appallingly bad taste which proves only too conclusively that he is still alive.' He was perhaps best known as the host of Radio 4's *Loose Ends*, unfairly described by one critic as 'mostly Ned droning on about Binkie Beaumont with the three or four other people left in Britain who know who he is'. Openly gay, Sherrin admitted that he had difficulty forming relationships and had used male prostitutes throughout his life. He was a 'big, generous, funny, clever, irreverent and fearless character,' said Alistair Beaton in *The Guardian*. 'And I wish he'd had the good sense to live till he was at least 100.'

The first woman to be elected PM of a Muslim country

BENAZIR BHUTTO

1953-2007

Benazir Bhutto, assassinated at the age of 54, was the first woman to be elected prime minister of a Muslim country. Her landslide victory in Pakistan in 1988 was followed by a 'sustained love affair with Western politicians and journalists', said the *Daily Telegraph*. In this she was aided by her impeccable English, undoubted charm, and the glamorous good looks that led *People* magazine to name her as one of the world's 50 most beautiful people. In her home country, however, Bhutto was never quite as popular as the foreign press coverage made out, and her two periods as PM were seen as ones of promises unfulfilled, tainted by the aura of corruption. Twice ousted from office, she went into prolonged exile in 1999, returning to Pakistan in October 2006, just two months before her tragic death.

Born into a wealthy landowning family in Karachi, she was brought up in an atmosphere of cosmopolitan luxury. Her father, Zulfikar Ali Bhutto, was a lawyer turned politician who became PM in 1970. By then, Benazir was studying PPE at Oxford, a time she would remember as 'the best years of my life'. Known to her friends as Bibi or Pinky, she revelled in the freedoms of a Western university, going about with her head unveiled and driving a yellow convertible sports car. She also developed a taste for slushy romance novels, shopped at Harrods, and, in times of stress, consoled herself with large helpings of ice cream (in later years, Ben & Jerry's caramel fudge became her particular favourite). The first sign of the ambition that would characterise her political career came when she stayed at Oxford for an extra year to be president of the Union. But the real turning point was the death of her father. Deposed by General Zia ul-Haq in 1977, he was imprisoned on a trumped-up charge, and hanged. Benazir, who saw him just before his execution, said he had made her promise to continue his work (overlooking his two sons, with whom he had never been close).

A decade passed before she got the chance to fulfil her pledge. In 1988 Zia was killed in a mysterious plane accident, and the 35-year-old Bhutto, by then leader of her father's party, was swept to power by an electorate tired of austere military rule. But although many may have admired Bhutto's style and determination, said *The Times*, 'few could praise her for effective government'. No major piece of legislation was passed during her first period in office; those who expected her to push for greater freedom and openness in Pakistan found her surprisingly autocratic, and her leadership was undermined by her association with her husband, Asif Zardari, a former playboy who became known as 'Mr Ten Percent' for his dodgy business dealings. (Ironically, Bhutto had agreed to an arranged marriage on the grounds that it would make her more electable.) Dismissed as PM in 1990 amid allegations of corruption and incompetence, she returned to power three years later. But her second stint was barely more successful and ended in the same way as the first. There followed years of exile in Dubai and London, and her political career seemed all but finished.

But Bhutto was far from idle during this period, said *The Guardian*. She gave frequent interviews and lectures, and journalists who referred to the corruption allegations against her received 'polite emails reminding them that the charges had never been proven and were politically motivated'. As the political climate in Pakistan changed during 2006 – with the president, General Pervez Musharraf, making a series of disastrous tactical errors – Bhutto saw the chance for a glorious homecoming. Her return that October was marred by an assassination attempt that missed its target, but killed some 140 of her supporters. But the courage she demonstrated in the face of this threat, and the rousing speeches she made across the country calling for an end to militancy and invoking the legacy of her father, were 'vintage Bhutto'.

The Hollywood icon with a face from another century

CHARLTON HESTON

1923-2008

Charlton Heston was a Hollywood icon who, in his prime, represented qualities of courage and decency that Americans claimed as their own. He was often cast in sword-and-sandals epics such as *The Ten Commandments* – the result, he said, of having 'a face that belongs in another century'. In his later years, however, 'many felt it was not just Heston's face and acting that were suited to another century, but also his politics', said *The Herald* (Glasgow). As president of the National Rifle Association (NRA), he defended what he saw as the inalienable right of an American to bear arms, famously declaring that his gun would only be prised from his 'cold, dead hands'.

Born Charles Carter, he was brought up in a village in Illinois, where his father owned a mill. As a child he loved to shoot, but acting was his passion (the reason, he once explained, was because he was painfully shy, and welcomed the chance to be someone other than himself) and before the outbreak of the Second World War he attended drama school. After an uneventful war stationed in the Northern Pacific, he took the name Charlton Heston – a composite of his mother's maiden name and his stepfather's surname – and began auditioning for parts. His big break came in 1951 when he was spotted by the legendary director of biblical spectaculars, Cecil B. de Mille. De Mille thought he saw a similarity between the actor's profile, with its rugged jawline and broken nose (acquired playing football at college), and Michelangelo's sculpture of Moses. A few years later, he cast this non-Jew as the man who led the Jews out of slavery.

In this, as in other roles, Heston showed rare dedication, said *The Times*, poring over the Bible and period histories. Critically slated, *The Ten Commandments* was adored by the public, and turned its lead actor into a star. There followed the noir classic *Touch of Evil* and *The Big Country* with Gregory Peck. But his greatest triumph came in 1959 when he was cast in William Wyler's remake of *Ben-Hur: A Tale of the Christ*. Heston spent a month learning to ride a four-horse chariot for the climactic race against Messala, played by Stephen Boyd (during which, Heston said, his arms were 'nearly pulled right out of their sockets'). The role of Judah Ben-Hur, matching brawny physicality with a Christian gentleness, proved perfect for him, and won him an Oscar.

Heston was no reactionary in those days, said *The Independent*. On the contrary, he marched with Martin Luther King in 1963 (later saying, 'in a long life of activism in support of some good causes, I'm proudest of having stood in the sun behind that man, that morning'). But in the mid-1960s he experienced a conversion to Republicanism – just as his career took a dip with stodgier epics such as *The Agony and the Ecstasy* (dismissed

He defended the inalienable right of an American to bear arms, famously declaring that his gun would only be prised from his 'cold, dead hands'.

by one critic as 'all agony, no ecstasy'). Overall, Heston's work shows 'an actor of limited range', said the *Daily Telegraph*. Later successes included *Planet of the Apes* (1968), but more typical fare was big-budget disaster dross like *Earthquake* (1974). His nadir came in the 1980s when, sporting a hairpiece, he played Jason Colby in the *Dynasty* spin-off, *The Colbys*, which folded after two series.

In later life, the actor became something of a target for liberals. Gore Vidal gleefully revealed in 1996 that, while working on the script for *Ben-Hur*, he had envisaged the hero and Messala as having once been gay lovers – and that, unbeknown to Heston, Boyd had agreed to play it that way. Two years later, Heston became NRA president, and was singled out for opprobrium by Michael Moore's anti-gun documentary *Bowling for Columbine*. But in the eyes of many, this had the opposite to the desired effect, since Heston was by then suffering from Alzheimer's disease, and no longer fair game. Similar bad taste was shown by the actor George Clooney at a ceremony in 2003, when he quipped: 'Charlton Heston announced again today that he is suffering from Alzheimer's.' Heston responded, saying: 'I don't know the man, never met him, never even spoken to him, but I feel sorry for George Clooney: one day he may get Alzheimer's disease. I served my country in World War Two. I survived that. I guess I can survive some bad words from this fellow.' He spent his last years at his home in Beverly Hills, surrounded by his dogs and his books (he was a particular fan of Patrick O'Brian novels) and looked after by Lydia, his wife of 64 years.

Glamorous pilot who broke the women's air speed record

DIANA BARNATO WALKER

1918-2008

Diana Barnato Walker was 'the original fast lady', said Tony Rennell in the *Daily Mail*. As wealthy as she was beautiful, she spent the Second World War flying Spitfires – even though in those days, as she said herself, 'it was assumed war was men's business. But we had a duty to back them up. We could hardly sit about looking pretty and doing nothing, could we?' As if this weren't enough, Barnato Walker later became the first British woman to break the sound barrier.

Diana Barnato was born in London, the daughter of the millionaire racing driver Woolf 'Babe' Barnato. He gave her a dove-grey 4.25 litre Bentley for her 21st birthday, but by then Diana was in love with flying, said *The Independent*. She obtained her licence after just six hours training and in 1939 enlisted in the Air Transport Auxiliary (ATA). Women weren't then allowed to be fighter pilots, but they were allowed to fly planes from factories to air fields. This was dangerous work: 'Ata-girls' were targeted by passing Messerschmitts and had to fly a vast range of unfamiliar aircraft. 'I strapped an extraordinary assortment of aeroplanes to my backside,' Barnato once said, a feat made all the more impressive by the fact she was just 5 foot tall, and often had to sit on a cushion to reach the controls.

She had several close shaves – her silver powder compact once fell from her pocket while she was performing illegal acrobatics, and covered her face in white powder. Nevertheless, she succeeded in landing all her planes without a scratch, and made many friends. A fellow Atagirl remembered her as 'fine-boned, clear-cut, and, with all her money, strangely unspoilt'.

When it came to romance, however, Barnato's luck deserted her, said Rennell. In 1942 she fell for a dashing Battle of Britain ace, but a few days after they became engaged he died in the wreck of his Spitfire. It later emerged he'd had another girlfriend from the base on his knee at the time, which must have made the plane harder to control. Two years later, she married Wing Commander Derek Walker. For their honeymoon they flew Spitfires side-by-side to Brussels without permission, and were docked three months' wages for their pains. He was killed the day after they moved in together.

When the ATA disbanded, Barnato Walker devoted herself to the Women's Junior Air Corps, instructing its young members. In 1963 she flew a Lightning T4 at 1,262mph (Mach 1.65), breaking not only the sound barrier but also the women's air speed record. She was later awarded an MBE. For three decades

> **'It was assumed war was men's business. But we had a duty to back them up. We could hardly sit about looking pretty and doing nothing, could we?'**

Barnato Walker was the mistress of the American racing driver Whitney Straight, but she never asked him to leave his wife. 'I was perfectly content,' she explained. 'I had my own identity.'

The unsung heroine of the Warsaw Ghetto

IRENA SENDLER

1910-2008

Irena Sendler is credited with having saved the lives of some 2,500 children from the Warsaw Ghetto during the Second World War. She risked her own neck to do so, said *The Independent*, but never considered herself a heroine. 'That term irritates me greatly,' she reflected in 2005. 'The opposite is true – I continue to have qualms of conscience that I did so little.'

Born in Warsaw, the daughter of a Roman Catholic doctor, she was brought up to help the needy. 'If you see someone drowning,' her father used to say, 'you must jump into the water to save them, whether you can swim or not.' When the Nazis herded the city's 500,000 Jews into an area of barely four square kilometres, to await transportation to the death camps, Irena joined Zegota, the secret Council for Aid to Jews. She and her colleagues visited the ghetto disguised as nurses, purportedly to treat the inhabitants for disease. In reality, however, they were spiriting the children to safety in sacks, in baskets, even in coffins, before hiding them in convents or with sympathetic Gentile families. They told the Nazis that the infants in question had died of typhoid.

Late in 1943, Sendler's home was raided by the Gestapo after a tip-off. She just had time to give her list of the identities of the rescued children to a friend (who hid it in her underwear) before being taken away. She was tortured, her broken legs and feet leaving her permanently disabled, but she told her captors nothing. Finally she was sentenced to death, but Zegota managed to bribe her guard to release her. After the war, she became a social worker and director of vocational schools. For decades, Sendler's wartime bravery went unrecognised, said the *Daily Telegraph* – the communist authorities were more concerned with rewarding the deeds of party members. It wasn't until 2003 that she received Poland's highest honour, the Order of the White Eagle, and in 2007 she was nominated for the Nobel Peace Prize (it

> **'I continue to have qualms of conscience that I did so little.'**

went to Al Gore). She spent her last years in a nursing home being looked after by one Elzbieta Ficowska, whom, in July 1942, Sendler had smuggled from the ghetto in a carpenter's toolbox.

The man who almost killed Hitler

PHILIPP VON BOESELAGER

1917-2008

Philipp von Boeselager spent much of his life 'haunted' by the knowledge he could have shot Adolf Hitler, said *The Independent*. His chance came in March 1943, when he and a group of fellow army officers planned to unload their pistols into the Führer during a military dinner. But the plot was called off at the last moment, and Von Boeselager spent the rest of his days ruing the missed opportunity. 'I see Hitler passing in front of me,' he said, 'and I think: "If only you'd shot him after all."'

The fourth of eight children, Von Boeselager was born into a wealthy aristocratic family near Bonn. He joined the army at 19 and was swiftly promoted. However, he turned against the Nazi regime in 1942 on learning of the 'special treatment' being meted out to Jews and Gypsies. Von Boeselager fell in with a group of conspirators headed by his commander, Field Marshal Günther von Kluge, and after initial reluctance ('I had not become an officer to shoot a head of state'), agreed to kill Hitler. The aim was to dispose of Heinrich Himmler at the same time, but the SS leader failed to show on the chosen day, and Kluge cancelled the plan, fearing that if Himmler became Führer he might prove worse than his predecessor. So the conspirators formed a new plan using explosives. Here again Von

Boeselager could help, as he had experience testing munitions, said the *Daily Telegraph*. It was he who chose and delivered the materials for the bomb with which Colonel Claus von Stauffenberg attempted to kill Hitler at his Wolf's Lair in East Prussia. On 20 July, Von Boeselager was on his way to take control of Berlin with 1,000 cavalrymen, when he received the coded message: 'Everyone back in the old holes.' The plot had failed. (Someone had chanced to move the briefcase containing the bomb, and Hitler had been protected from the blast by the leg of a heavy oak table.) Kluge took poison. Stauffenberg was shot. Somehow Von Boeselager managed to escape, though for the next two years he carried cyanide in case the Gestapo should catch up with him.

'I had not become an officer to shoot a head of state.'

Von Boeselager was just 28 at the end of the Second World War. He went on to study economics and manage his family estates. As his bravery in the two plots gradually became recognised, he also began giving interviews, in which he urged his fellow Germans to 'show more civil courage, which we always lack'. In this, he was impelled by nightmares about Hitler and a sense of duty to the conspirators who had not survived. 'I feel they are watching me,' he once said.

Outlandish explorer and lover of pigs

LYALL WATSON

1939-2008

Lyall Watson might have 'sprung fully formed from a Victorian adventure by Jules Verne or H. Rider Haggard', said the *Daily Telegraph*. He led scientific expeditions to the Arctic, the Amazon, and the Kalahari, and organised sumo wrestling events in Britain. But he achieved his greatest fame as a writer exploring 'the soft edges of science'. Some of his more outlandish theories – that plants react with dismay if you drop a live shrimp in boiling water, for example – were derided by critics, but Watson stuck to his guns. 'I find the cavils of self-appointed committees for the suppression of curiosity very tedious,' he once stated.

Malcolm Lyall-Watson was born in 1938 in Johannesburg, the son of a farmer. As a child he learnt bush lore from a former Zulu chief, who gave him a pet warthog. He studied ethology in London and then worked on *Tomorrow's World* (abandoning his given name of Malcolm). But it was the publication of *Supernature* in 1973 that really propelled him into the limelight, said *The Times*. The book's New Age theories (e.g. that if you leave razor blades under a cardboard model of the Pyramid of Cheops, they will be sharper in the morning) struck a chord with students, and it became an international bestseller.

He began writing a book a year, but ran into controversy with his sixth, in which he outlined his 'hundredth-monkey' theory. According to Watson, when a hundred monkeys perform a task such as washing potatoes, a shift in consciousness takes place, and other monkeys nearby start performing the same task. The scientific pretensions of this were instantly debunked, but Watson was unrepentant, insisting the theory had merely been 'a metaphor'. He continued writing, later scoring a hit with *The Whole Hog: Exploring the Extraordinary Potential of Pigs*, which was a tribute to his childhood pet.

'I find the cavils of self-appointed committees for the suppression of curiosity very tedious.'

Gulag novelist who exposed the horrors of Stalinism

ALEXANDER SOLZHENITSYN

1918-2008

For much of the twentieth century, vast swathes of the Russian populace were held in virtual slavery in Soviet labour camps. Millions died from starvation or exhaustion, yet few in the West knew anything about it, said Mark Le Fanu in *The Independent* – until the publication, in 1962, of *One Day in the Life of Ivan Denisovich* by Alexander Solzhenitsyn. It would be hard to overestimate the impact of this short book, about a typical 24 hours in the gulag; it could even be argued that, in revealing the Communist regime's blend of brutality and crass inefficiency, it contributed to the downfall of the Soviet Union. The novel was simply written, in clear, stark prose, but as its author put it, quoting a Russian proverb, in 1970: 'One word of truth shall outweigh the whole world.'

Alexander Isayevich Solzhenitsyn was born in 1918 in the Caucasus town of Kislovodsk, the son of an artillery officer. As a child he shone academically, showing particular aptitude in mathematics. And although various of his relatives had fallen victim to Soviet brutality, he also grew up a dedicated Marxist, so much so that on his honeymoon in 1940 he is said to have spent more time poring over his copy of *Das Kapital* than attending to his wife, Natalya. Then in February 1945, his life was turned upside down, said the *New York Times*. He was arrested by Smersh, the Soviet army's counter-intelligence agency, and put on trial as an enemy of the people. Their only evidence was a letter he had written while serving his country in the Second World War, in which he referred to Stalin – disrespectfully, Smersh said – as 'the man with the moustache'. Solzhenitsyn was sentenced to eight years in the labour camps, during which time his wife divorced him, and he developed cancer (which he survived).

After being incarcerated in various transit camps, in 1950 he was transferred to Ekibastuz in Kazakhstan, a penal camp where he was put to work as a bricklayer. It was here that Solzhenitsyn began writing, on tiny notes of paper which he would then destroy, having first committed the lines to memory. He used a variant on the Catholic rosary, with beads made from pellets of bread, as an aide memoir. During this time, he produced around 100,000 words, which formed the basis of several of his later works. Foremost among them was *One Day in the Life of Ivan Denisovich*, a fictionalised account of his experiences in Ekibastuz.

Freed on the day of Stalin's death in 1953, Solzhenitsyn worked as a teacher, while pouring out his thoughts, in secret, on paper. He wrote on the assumption that he would never be published (he kept at it, he said, because 'when you've been pitched headfirst into hell, you just write about it'). But the rise to power of Nikita Khrushchev created, briefly, a gentler political climate. He returned to Moscow, where he was reconciled with Natalya, and in 1961, was finally emboldened to submit his first book. 'Its publication in 1962 was a major event in the Soviet Union, and made its writer famous overnight,' said the *Daily Telegraph*. 'He was admitted to the Union of Soviet Writers and hailed in *Pravda* as a "true helper of the party" in the "sacred and vital cause" of de-Stalinisation. Within a year the book had been translated into all the major European languages, and it was met with almost universal praise.'

But after Khrushchev was ousted from power in 1964, the period of 'de-Stalinisation' came to an abrupt halt, and Solzhenitsyn fell out of favour with the authorities. His manuscript for his next novel, *The First Circle*, was confiscated by the police, while *Cancer Ward*, which used the disease as a metaphor for Russia's decline, was banned. It was a turbulent time for the writer, in private as well as public, said the *Daily Telegraph*. Thanks in part to his ascetic manner, stern demeanour and Old Testament beard, Solzhenitsyn was perceived by many as a great moral arbiter. Yet it transpired that while demanding absolute submission from his wife, he had felt himself at liberty to have affairs. Then, to his surprise – he thought cancer treatment had left him infertile – he fathered a son by his mistress, also called Natalya. When he divorced his wife in order to marry Natalya, she attempted suicide.

Although Solzhenitsyn's novels were criticised for being wordy and rambling, his reputation in the West continued to grow, both as a writer and as a dissident. In 1970 he was awarded the Nobel Prize for Literature, which further aggravated the Soviet authorities. Three years later, when *The Gulag Archipelago* – a massive history of the labour camps, regarded by many as his greatest achievement – was published abroad, they decided that Solzhenitsyn should be expelled. (He was, by now, too high-profile a figure to silence by other means.)

Banished from his homeland in 1974, he eventually settled in Vermont, but he did not take to the USA. He built a high fence around his house, topped with barbed wire, and made no attempt to integrate, regarding Western culture as inferior to the traditions of pre-Soviet Russia (he took particular exception to pop music, which he described as 'intolerable'). Yet when he finally returned to Russia in 1994, after the fall of Communism, he found a nation in thrall to soap operas and quiz shows. In his last years, Solzhenitsyn's political views became increasingly nationalistic, and he was seen as a somewhat embarrassing figure by fellow writers. (He described Nato as 'no different from Hitler' for its bombing of Serbia, and applauded President Putin's attempts to restore national pride.) Most disastrously, his later literary efforts, such as the historical-novel cycle *The Red Wheel*, were judged virtually unreadable.

There was a backlash against his once towering reputation: some pointed out that even his early works had been backward-looking, standing on the shoulders of Tolstoy and Dostoevsky; others simply felt that his time was past. The author of *One Day in the Life of Ivan Denisovich* and *The Gulag Archipelago* will always have his disciples, said Mark Le Fanu. Yet it is probable that Solzhenitsyn's lasting significance will be as a 'moral rather than a literary phenomenon'. His courage in standing up to the Soviet authorities throughout his life, and telling the truth while so many were attempting to conceal it, will ensure his status as a hero in Russia's history.

Literary agent who knew the art of silence

PAT KAVANAGH

1940-2008

Pat Kavanagh was 'a rare combination of disconcerting wide-eyed beauty, honeyed voice and incisive literary acumen', said *The Times*. As literary agent to countless household names – including Dirk Bogarde, Wendy Cope, Clive James, Nicci French, and her husband, Julian Barnes – she was adept at squeezing money from publishers, partly thanks to tricks learnt from her mentor, A.D. Peters. 'The great secret of negotiation,' he once told her, 'is silence.' It was a lesson that Kavanagh, who was laconic by nature, took to heart, often persuading editors to increase their offer by coolly saying nothing until they did.

Patricia Kavanagh was born in Durban in 1940, the daughter of a journalist and sometime ostrich farmer. Strikingly beautiful, with a petite figure, green eyes and rich auburn hair, she at first harboured ambitions to be an actress. But after she moved to London, her career failed to ignite, although she does make a brief appearance in the film version of *Under Milk Wood* (1972). 'I never got paid,' she later recalled, 'but I did get to snog Richard Burton.' By then, however, Kavanagh had all but given up acting, and was working for the doyen of literary agents, A.D. Peters. She slowly built up one of the best client lists in the business, early captures including Arthur Koestler and S.J. Perelman. Authors appreciated her blend of taste, discretion and unswerving dedication, said Hermione Lee in *The Independent*. Pat's services were not easily won ('I'm always wary of taking on a writer on the basis of a first novel,' she said once, 'in case that's all there is in him.') but they were rarely withdrawn.

Many were attracted to more than Kavanagh's professional abilities, said the *Daily Telegraph*. Koestler dubbed her 'my little shark', and J.B. Priestley begged her to wear fishnets to work. She met Barnes, then unpublished, at an office party in 1978. When he proposed 18 months later during a trip to Romania, her first response was: 'That's brave.' Their marriage had its rough patches. Kavanagh left Barnes briefly in the mid-1980s to live with the novelist Jeanette Winterson. Nevertheless, he remained devoted to her. When one of his oldest friends, Martin Amis, ditched Kavanagh as his agent in 1995 because he could get more money with Andrew 'the Jackal' Wylie, Barnes wrote to him ending their friendship. Asked what the letter said, Amis replied that it contained a well known colloquialism, consisting 'of seven letters. Three of them are Fs.'

When Julian Barnes proposed, her first response was: 'That's brave.'

Kavanagh liked to dance; Barnes didn't. She tuned in to *The Archers*; he would leave the room with a groan. Yet mostly they worked as 'a complete team', said Lee, whether on walking tours in France and Italy, or attending plays and concerts. When she led a breakaway from her firm in 2007, all her big-name clients stayed with her. Kavanagh died of a brain tumour five weeks after it was diagnosed.

Pulitzer-winning broadcaster who listened to ordinary people

STUDS TERKEL

1912-2008

S tuds Terkel was a writer and broadcaster in the same way as Louis Armstrong was 'a trumpeter' and the Empire State Building is 'an office block', said *The Guardian*. For an hour every weekday, for nearly fifty years, his tough Chicago accent and rasping laugh could be heard on his WFMT radio show, as he spun his favourite blues and jazz records and chatted with celebrities. But his greater claim to fame lies in his thousands of interviews with ordinary Americans – pensioners and prostitutes, busboys, barbers and blue-collar workers – which make up 'not only the most complete American history of the last century, but also the most compassionate'. For Terkel believed everyone had a story to tell, and was brilliant at persuading them to tell it. His secret, he said, was simple: 'it's listening.'

Born in New York in 1912, Louis Terkel moved to Chicago at the age of 11, where his mother ran a boarding house. It was here he developed a taste for the stories of ordinary people as he stayed up late listening to the drifters, truck drivers and travelling salesmen who passed through town. After studying law at university (where he was 'miserable'), he began working as a DJ, borrowing the name 'Studs' from the hero of a series of crime novels. His career branched out into television in the 1940s with

Studs' Place, in which he hobnobbed with singers such as Billie Holiday and Woody Guthrie. But the show was axed during the McCarthy era on account of its host's left-wing politics. For a while, Terkel struggled to make ends meet, and was supported by his wife, Ida. ('She earned a lot more money than I did,' he later recalled. 'It was like dating a CEO. I borrowed twenty bucks from her for our first date. I never paid her back.') Then in 1952, he began hosting *The Studs Terkel Programme* on WFMT, which ran for the next 45 years.

In his mid-fifties, Terkel added a new string to his bow, said the *Chicago Tribune*. Impressed by his ability to coax honest replies from celebrities, a publisher suggested a series of interviews with Chicago residents, focusing on race. The result was *Division Street: America*, which became a huge bestseller, and was followed by such self-explanatory titles as *Hard Times: An Oral History of the Great Depression* (1970) and *Working: People Talk About What They Do All Day and How They Feel About What They Do* (1974). In 1984, Terkel won a Pulitzer Prize for *The Good War* (collected memories of the Second World War), prompting some to mutter that he was not really a writer, since all he did was record what people said. His defence was to compare what he did to prospecting. 'What first comes out of an interview are

> **Terkel believed everyone had a story to tell, and was brilliant at persuading them to tell it.**

tons of ore; you have to get that gold dust in your hands,' he said. 'Now, how does it become a necklace or a ring or a gold watch? You have to get the form; you have to mould the gold dust.'

Whether or not his talent should be called literary, Terkel had a rare ability to coax the best from people, said *The Times*. At 5ft 5in, he was a small man, invariably clad in a scruffy red check shirt (he had a blue check shirt, his wife said, but rarely wore it), and clumsy with the tape recorder, often wiping his interviews by mistake. Yet these homely qualities put people at ease, whether it was the woman whose mother-in-law was born into slavery, or the fireman whose friend 'committed suicide by Blockbuster' (after the loss of his wife, he watched videos and drank Scotch until he died). Terkel's favourite interview, he used to say, was of one Hobart Foote, who had to cross so many railway lines to get to work (and couldn't afford to sit idly at level crossings while long freight trains trundled past) that his morning car journey was a daily adventure involving any number of different routes, depending on the train schedule. This served to illustrate Terkel's general principle, which was that ordinary people live extraordinary, uninventable lives.

He suffered a blow in 1997 with the death of his wife of almost 60 years. ('Who's going to laugh at my jokes?' he lamented.) For a time, many thought Studs was 'a goner', said the *Chicago Tribune*. Yet despite increasing infirmity, he never let up the work rate. His last book, *P.S. Further Thoughts from a Lifetime of Listening*, was published a month after his death. For his epitaph he suggested: 'Curiosity never killed this cat.' He also asked that his ashes be mixed with Ida's and scattered in their local park. 'It's against the law,' he said gleefully. 'Let 'em sue us!'

The cheery-faced driver from *On the Buses*

REG VARNEY

1916-2008

Reg Varney was a stage and TV actor best known for his portrayal of the irrepressible Stan Butler in the sitcom *On the Buses*. Although critics derided the ITV show, the public loved it, said *The Independent*. At the height of its success in the 1970s, it commanded audiences of 15 million: figures that stand testament to the appeal of its star. Week after week, the public rejoiced as Varney's cheery-faced, 5ft 5in bus driver outwitted the taller, toothbrush-moustached inspector, Blakey (Stephen Lewis), who was left twitching in pop-eyed rage, while intoning his catchphrase: 'I 'ate you, Butler!'

Reginald Alfred Varney was born in Canning Town in 1916, the son of a tyre-factory worker. When he was 15, his parents bought him an accordion, and Varney soon developed a routine of jokes and songs for the music-hall circuit. But it wasn't easy supporting a family (he married his girlfriend, Lily, in 1943) at a time when variety was yielding to TV in the public's affections. And when Varney saw the success of Benny Hill (who had once played straight man to Varney in the stage show *Gaytime*), he considered packing it all in and opening a pub.

Yet TV ultimately proved the making of Varney, said *The Guardian*.

Sitcoms such as *The Rag Trade* (1961–1963) and *Beggar My Neighbour* (1966–1968) turned him into a household name. (His fame led him to be chosen as the first person ever to withdraw money from an ATM, when he performed the opening ceremony at the Enfield branch of Barclays in 1967.)

His biggest success, however, was *On the Buses*. Varney took the job seriously, said *The Times*, insisting on gaining a licence so he could drive the bus himself. The trick to comedy, he once said, was to 'play it straight', and remove even good jokes 'if they interfered with the truth of the situation'. The show ran from 1969 to 1973, and spawned three feature-length films, the first of which (simply titled *On the Buses*) was the most successful British film of 1971, outperforming *Diamonds Are Forever*. However, Varney's next sitcom, *Down the Gate*, about the fortunes of a Billingsgate fish porter, failed to ignite the popular imagination. In his later career, he took his variety routine to Australia and New Zealand, where *On the Buses* retained a particularly loyal following. In retirement, Varney painted and spent time at his villa in Malta.

> **When Varney saw the success of Benny Hill, he considered packing it all in and opening a pub.**

'A beacon of enlightenment in the South African murk'

HELEN SUZMAN

1917-2009

Helen Suzman was a South African politician who devoted her career to opposing the injustices of apartheid. In her 13 years as the only Progressive member of parliament, she was a lone voice amid the din of the Nationalist majority, as it pushed for the racial segregation or 'apartness' of blacks and whites. For six of those years, she was also South Africa's only female MP, leaving her exposed to the chauvinist jibes of her peers. Prime Minister John Vorster mocked her for beating her 'pretty little pink hands' against apartheid; his successor, P.W. Botha, called her 'a vicious little cat'. Yet Suzman refused to be cowed by this bullying, said *The Independent*, and frequently gave as good as she got. Asked by one Nationalist MP why she never said hello to him, she replied simply: 'Because I don't like you.' Told by another that she was asking questions that were embarrassing to her country, Suzman shot back: 'It is not my questions that embarrass South Africa. It is your answers.'

She was born Helen Gavronsky in the town of Germiston outside Johannesburg on 7 November 1917 (on the same day as the Russian Revolution, as she liked to remark), the daughter of Lithuanian immigrants. While reading economics at university, she met Moses Suzman, a doctor

14 years her senior, whom she married. It was also around this time that she became aware of the systemic nature of the racism in South Africa, said the *New York Times*. She was particularly incensed to learn of the so-called Pass Laws, which placed restrictions on the areas where blacks could live and work. When the opportunity arose in 1952, Suzman ran for parliament as a member of the Unionists, and was voted in. But she and some of her colleagues felt their party was not offering a convincing opposition to the ruling Nationalists, and in 1959 eleven of them broke away to form the Progressive party. They didn't then call for universal suffrage; they merely suggested extending the right to vote to anyone with seven years of schooling, or four years of schooling and two years of employment. Nevertheless, these proposals caused outrage. Suzman was the only member of the new party to retain her seat at the next general election, and from then on most of the opprobrium from those who wanted to preserve the status quo fell on her.

Fortunately, she was well equipped to handle it, said *The Guardian*. A petite, attractive woman, Suzman 'seemed to have more energy than anyone else', a quality she attributed to the fact she never drank wine – only whisky. She was also 'completely fearless' in circumstances in which others would have quailed. When the PM Hendrik Verwoerd was killed by a schizophrenic parliamentary messenger in the House of Assembly in 1966, Botha pointed his finger at Suzman, and yelled: 'It's you who did this. It's all you liberals. You incite people. We will get you.' He later apologised for the outburst, but for many years death threats were a routine feature of Suzman's life.

Undaunted, she continued to stand up for what she believed in. (She was, for example, the only MP to oppose the legalisation of detention without trial for 90 days, which was later extended indefinitely.) Suzman's resistance had 'virtually no success', said *The Independent*, but Nelson Mandela would later cherish the memory of her as 'the first and only

> **Told that she was asking questions that were embarrassing to her country, Suzman shot back: 'It is not my questions that embarrass South Africa. It is your answers.'**

woman' to visit him in his cell on Robben Island, and she was admired internationally as 'a beacon of enlightenment in the South African murk'. In 1974, the Progressive party scored a success when five of her colleagues were voted in as MPs. Yet, somehow, their opposition en masse lacked the intensity of Suzman's solitary stand. As the years went by, she found herself criticised for not being sufficiently extreme. Some decried, for instance, her opposition to economic sanctions against South Africa (on the ground, as she put it, that it wasn't clear 'how wrecking the economy of the country will ensure a more stable and just society'). Suzman retired in 1989 when the fall of the Nationalists was all but inevitable. She lived the rest of her life garlanded with awards, which included an honorary DBE, and 27 honorary doctorates from universities around the world.

The first man to climb 'the savage mountain'

ACHILLE COMPAGNONI

1914-2009

A chille Compagnoni was (along with team-mate Lino Lacedelli) the first man to climb K2, the world's second-highest mountain. Achieved in 1954, this feat should have helped restore Italy's pride after the disaster of the Second World War. But in the event, it quickly became 'soured' by controversy, said *The Guardian*. Compagnoni accused a younger team-mate, Walter Bonatti, of having siphoned off some of the oxygen from his canisters, which almost scuppered his attempt. Bonatti – who went on to become one of the greatest mountaineers of all time – responded that, on the contrary, it was the 39-year-old Compagnoni who had almost killed him. He alleged that the older man, jealous of his youth and fitness for the summit, had deliberately changed a meeting place, leaving Bonatti and his Pakistani porter exposed on the mountain for the night. The porter lost fingers and toes to frostbite as a consequence.

Compagnoni was born in the village of Santa Caterina di Valfurva in northern Italy in 1914. As a young man he joined the elite mountain corps the Alpini, and later worked as a ski guide and rescuer. He was picked for the 1954 expedition, not for his skills as a climber, but for his strength and powers of endurance, which would prove invaluable on K2. Dubbed the 'savage mountain', it has taken one life for every four men who have scaled it – and, according to Compagnoni, it almost took his, said the *Daily Telegraph*. As he and Lacedelli neared the 28,251ft summit, their oxygen ran out, he later claimed. Nevertheless they struggled on, reaching the top at 6pm on 31 July. They planted Italian and Pakistani flags, as well as a small standard from Compagnoni's village.

On their return, he sued the Italian Alpine Club for the frostbite he contracted while taking photographs on the summit. Yet these same pictures were later used as evidence to undermine his charges against Bonatti, since they showed Compagnoni wearing his oxygen mask and both men still carrying their heavy canisters, said *The Times*. After his triumph of 1954, he did not attempt many other climbs, but instead opened a small guest house in the resort of Cervinia.

K2 has taken one life for every four men who have scaled it – and, according to Compagnoni, it almost took his.

For the rest of his life, Compagnoni remained proud of his conduct on the slopes of the savage mountain. According to his wife, he kept a little museum in his home filled with souvenirs from the expedition. He and Bonatti were never reconciled. When the 50th anniversary of the climb was celebrated at the K2 base camp, neither man attended.

Stick-thin German who pioneered dance theatre

PINA BAUSCH

1940-2009

Pina Bausch has often been hailed as the outstanding choreographer working in European contemporary dance over the past 30 years. Yet 'choreographer' isn't quite the right term to describe her, said Alastair Macaulay in the *New York Times*. Bausch's works of *tanztheater* (dance theatre), as it became known, often relied on the spoken word, and most strikingly, elaborate scenic effects. In her version of Stravinsky's *The Rite of Spring* (1975), the semi-clad participants performed on a thick layer of soil, so they became gradually filthier as the performance progressed. In *Palermo, Palermo* (1989), the evening began with the toppling of an immense wall, to the alarm of the audience. The dancers themselves were occasionally clumsy, apparently lacking in classical training. That, however, was part of the point. 'I'm not interested in how people move,' Bausch once explained, 'but in what moves them.'

Born in the German town of Solingen in 1940, Bausch grew up watching her father's clients, wide-eyed, from under the tables of the restaurant he owned. Shy of speech, she found it easier to dance for their entertainment, said *The Times*, and realised this was her vocation. In 1958 a scholarship took her to New York to study under Antony Tudor. A fellow dancer at the time remembers Bausch as one of the thinnest human beings he had ever seen; on-stage, she moved 'sharply, though a bit unevenly, like calipers on paper'. Bausch returned to Germany in 1962 and created her first work six years later. From the outset she was determined to reject inherited wisdom, or as she put it herself, 'Any movement I knew, I didn't want to use.' In 1972 she was appointed artistic director at the Wuppertal Ballet, a role she never left.

The style she developed over the years that followed continues to divide critics, said *The Guardian*. To some, her work was wilfully bleak, revelling in what one called 'the pornography of pain'. (Her 1976 version of Brecht's *The Seven Deadly Sins* featured a graphic scene of gang rape.) Yet her supporters, above all her dancers, were fanatic in their loyalty. As Sylvie Guillem once observed, 'You work for Bausch – I think it's like joining a cult.' 'Even if you objected, as I did, to much of Bausch's work, you couldn't deny its impact,' said Macaulay. 'She deserves, like George Balanchine before her, to be recognised not only for her achievements in dance, but also as one of the great dramatists of her generation.'

> **'I'm not interested in how people move,' Bausch once explained, 'but in what moves them.'**

The fighting Tommy who hated war

HARRY PATCH

1898-2009

Harry Patch was the last British soldier to have fought in the trenches during the First World War. He was also the veteran who, in his later years, retained the fiercest indignation at that conflict, said the *Daily Telegraph*. A pacifist with strong religious beliefs, Patch recalled his terror at going over the top (if any man claimed to have viewed that prospect without fear, he used to say, he was a 'damned liar') and his shame at having left wounded men to die in no man's land. 'We weren't like the Good Samaritan in the Bible,' he once confessed to an interviewer. 'We were the robbers who passed them by.' But above all, Patch grieved for the loss of the three friends who died at his side when a shell burst on 22 September 1917. Dismissing Remembrance Sunday as 'showbusiness', he instead observed a personal ritual on that date each year, in memory of his fallen comrades.

The son of a stonemason, Henry John Patch was born in Somerset in 1898 and educated at the local Church of England school. By his own account, he would never have volunteered to fight, said *The Times*, but at 18 he was called up and assigned to a machine-gun crew in the Duke of Cornwall's Light Infantry. A few months later, they arrived near a little village named Passchendaele. The camaraderie – he and his crew members shared all their packages from home – made for close friendships, but Patch was sickened by the slaughter, as he saw countless men on both sides mown down by machine-gun fire. Then it was their turn to go over the top. Almost a century later, Patch remembered coming across a soldier disembowelled by a shell. 'Shoot me,' the man begged, but before they could do so, he had died, the word 'mother' on his lips. Shortly afterwards, an enemy soldier ran forward from a trench, his bayonet lowered. Mindful of the Lord's commandment not to kill, Patch, who was a crack shot, aimed his revolver at the man's leg. 'I brought him down. He called something out to me in German. I don't suppose it was complimentary.'

Somehow he and the rest of his crew emerged from that day unscathed. It was while returning to the support trenches, after being relieved, that a shell got them, obliterating one of his comrades completely, and killing two others. As for Patch himself, a sliver of shrapnel lodged itself in his groin. Afterwards, four men had to hold him down while this was extracted by a doctor who had run out of anaesthetic. 'I could have killed that doctor,' Patch later remarked. He was invalided back to Blighty, where he met his future wife, Ada, literally colliding with her on his way to a bus stop in Sutton Coldfield, said *The Guardian*. And by the time he was well enough to return to the war, it was over.

> **'The politicians should have been given the guns and told to settle their differences themselves, instead of organising nothing better than legalised mass murder.'**

Patch then worked as a plumber, setting up his own firm in Bristol. He was too old to fight in the Second World War, but served as a fireman. Ada predeceased him in 1976, as did his second wife, Jean, in 1984, and his two sons by his first marriage. And throughout all those years, Patch never even watched a war film, let alone spoke about his experiences in the trenches. It wasn't until he was approached by a documentary maker in 1998, when he was 100 years old, that he began to reminisce. The memories that came spilling out were vivid, laced with humour, but also full of anger, said the *Daily Telegraph*. The politicians who took us to war, Patch wrote in his autobiography, *The Last Fighting Tommy*, 'should have been given the guns and told to settle their differences themselves, instead of organising nothing better than legalised mass murder'. In the nursing home where he spent his final years, the light outside his room prompted nightmares about the moment when his friends were killed. 'I can still see that damned explosion now,' he used to say. In 2004, the BBC took Patch back to Ypres to meet Charles Kuentz, a 107-year-old German veteran. 'I was a bit doubtful before meeting a German soldier,' he admitted later. 'Herr Kuentz is a very nice gentleman, however. He is all for a united Europe and peace, and so am I.' Kuentz gave Patch some Alsatian biscuits, in exchange for a bottle of Somerset cider.

The best England football manager since Alf Ramsey

SIR BOBBY ROBSON

1933-2009

Anyone re-reading a tabloid from the late 1980s would be amazed to learn that Sir Bobby Robson was one of the most likeable and successful football managers of the past half-century, said *The Times*. A dishevelled, mildly eccentric figure, he was vilified by the red-top press for his perceived failings while managing the national side. Popular epithets to describe him were 'plonker' and 'prat', and after one disappointing game, a headline even exclaimed, 'In the Name of God, Go!' (Then, when England drew with Saudi Arabia, the same paper urged, 'In the Name of Allah, Go!') Yet when Robson's record is examined – he took his team to the quarter-finals of the World Cup in 1986, and the semis in 1990 – it's clear that he was, in fact, the most effective manager England has had since Sir Alf Ramsey.

Robert William Robson was born in the village of Sacriston, Co. Durham in 1933. His father, a miner, instilled in him a love of football in general, and Newcastle Utd in particular. He never played for his local side, but was snapped up by Fulham as a promising inside-forward in 1950. Robson went on to represent West Bromwich Albion and later England as a wing-half, appearing 20 times for his country. And if, by his own account, his playing career 'fizzled out', he more than made up for it in his second incarnation as a manager. Robson won his spurs during 13 glorious years at Ipswich, during which time he guided that team to a renaissance, with highlights including triumphs in the FA Cup in 1978 and the Uefa Cup in 1981. The following year, he was invited to take on the England side.

No one could call Robson 'a master tactician', said the *Daily Telegraph*. Indeed he often seemed inept, forgetting players' names and coming out with malapropisms and muddled statements. ('We didn't underestimate them,' he insisted after a near-defeat against Cameroon. 'They were a lot better than we thought.') Yet he had a paternal air that made players want to do their best for him. And they did. In both his World Cup campaigns England did well, and were only beaten by the eventual winners. The first saw hopes dashed by Diego Maradona's infamous 'Hand of God' goal, the second by a penalty shoot-out at the end of a game many thought England had deserved to win. And throughout all this, Robson put up with the scorn of the tabloids, which overlooked his achievements and the fact that no one was more tormented by a defeat than he was. Of the 1990 World Cup, he once remarked, 'Not a day goes by when I don't think about the semi-final, and other choices I might have made.'

If there were any doubts about the abilities of this 'sensitive and decent man', they were laid to rest in his later career, said *The Independent*. In the 1990s, he enjoyed successes with PSV Eindhoven and Porto, before winning the European Manager of the Year Award in 1997 for his work with Barcelona. One of the pivotal decisions he made for that team was the $19.5m signing of the Brazilian genius, Ronaldo, although in general it was thought that Robson's old-school approach was at odds with the increasingly commercial spirit of the game. (When he signed to West Bromwich Albion in 1956, it had been for a measly £25,000 – yet that had been a record for Albion at the time.) His final stint as manager was with his beloved Newcastle Utd, during which time he took them to the Champions League. Bobby Robson devoted his entire life to a single pursuit, said *The Times*. Even in the last stages of his battle with cancer, he could be seen supporting his team from the stands, 'hoping despite all the disappointments to escape the darker demands of existence through the thrill of football'.

The founder of the Special Olympics

EUNICE SHRIVER

1921–2009

Eunice Shriver was the sister of Jack and Robert Kennedy, and the mother-in-law of Arnold Schwarzenegger. Yet her legacy as the founder of the Special Olympics and campaigner for the rights of the disabled will arguably prove greater than that of any other member of her family, said the *New York Times*. As her son Robert put it, 'My mom never ran for office and she changed history. Period. End of story.'

Eunice Mary Kennedy was born in 1921 in Boston into 'one of the most extraordinary families in US history', said *The Independent*. Her father Joseph urged his nine children to 'win, win, win', and though Eunice's character was imbued with this spirit, she was also devout (becoming known as 'the conscience of the Kennedys'). In the year Eunice went up to Stanford to study sociology, Joseph sent her older sister Rosemary, who had mental problems such as mood swings and depression, for a prefrontal lobotomy, then thought to be a cutting-edge cure. In fact, it left her severely brain-damaged. Eunice was aghast, and determined to devote her life to helping those she called the world's 'most scorned and hidden citizens'.

In 1962 she and her husband, the politician Sargent Shriver, set up a summer camp for young people with intellectual disabilities. The activities at the camp, based at their Maryland home, grew into the Special Olympics, which (unlike the Paralympics) emphasise participation over victory. More than a million people around the world now take part in these events each year. Shriver was awarded the Presidential Medal of Honour in 1984 and in 1995 became the first living woman to appear on a US coin.

Veteran correspondent who spent 30 years at the BBC

BRIAN BARRON

1940-2009

B rian Barron was a distinguished BBC foreign correspondent, said *The Independent*, who 'had the reporter's good fortune to be on hand to witness some of the most far-reaching and tragic events of his era' – from the fall of Saigon to the overthrow of Idi Amin, the Northern Ireland Troubles to the protests at Tiananmen Square. Ruggedly handsome, ruthless in pursuit of a story and seemingly fearless, he was held in awe by other journalists. But while he became a familiar face on TV, he did not achieve the celebrity of some of his contemporaries. This was because Barron never made the move into newsreading or presenting, preferring to remain in the field throughout his career: 'the last major story he covered was the 2003 Gulf War, three years after his official retirement'.

Born in 1940, Brian Barron left Bristol Grammar School aged 16 in order to work for a local newspaper, said *The Guardian*. He quickly made his name as a reporter, and by 1965 was working for the World Service. His first job as a radio correspondent took him to Aden, where he witnessed the end of 130 years of British rule. 'Among the half-dozen or so end-of-empire sagas I have witnessed,' he later told the BBC's *From Our Own Correspondent*, 'this was the saddest, the most abject. Whoever chose "Things Ain't What They Used To Be" for the military band bidding farewell to the last governor evoked the right note of seediness and frayed national self belief.' But Barron's big break came in 1969, when he was sent to report on the Vietnam War – 'the first television war' – for radio and TV. It was a 'huge learning experience for him', in which he discovered the US army's capacity for dispensing misinformation, and the consequent need to rely on his own journalistic instinct. After US troops had left Saigon, he stayed on with his cameraman, Eric Thirer, to witness the North Vietnamese troops march in in 1975, said *The Times*. As shell-fire rattled the windows, the BBC ordered him to evacuate – but Barron refused. 'What foreign correspondent would walk away from the biggest story yet?' he later explained.

The following year he became the BBC's chief correspondent in Africa,

> **The Vietnam War was a 'huge learning experience for him', in which he discovered the US army's capacity for dispensing misinformation.**

where he reported on the war in Rhodesia and the overthrow of Idi Amin in Uganda. In the presidential palace, Barron ransacked the fridges, mindful of 'persistent reports' that Amin was wont to keep his victims' heads on ice. 'With relief,' he recalled, 'we found no evidence to back this up.' In 1980, he achieved a significant coup when he tracked Amin down in Saudi Arabia and persuaded him to agree to an interview. He went on to spend three years in the rather more staid environs of Washington, but was back in the thick of things in 1989 when, after the violence at Tiananmen Square, he and his crew were rounded up by secret police, kicked and cuffed, and ordered to kneel at gunpoint. Later, he was forced to sign a document confessing to 'rumour-mongering'. In 2007, Brian Barron was awarded an MBE for services to broadcasting.

Brave memoirist of
the Cultural Revolution

NIEN CHENG

1915–2009

Several years before Jung Chang's *Wild Swans*, the memoir of another of China's victims, Nien Cheng, became a bestseller in the West, said *The Guardian*. Cheng was jailed for six years on trumped-up charges, and *Life and Death in Shanghai* is a moving account of her ordeal. Even under torture, she refused to confess, instead citing quotations from Mao's *Little Red Book* to foil her tormentors. When the political tide finally turned and Nien was allowed to go, she insisted she wouldn't leave jail until the government admitted she was innocent. 'In all the years of the detention house,' the prison guards said as they threw her out, 'we've never had a prisoner like you, so truculent and argumentative.'

Yao Nien Yuan was born in Beijing in 1915. Her father, an anglophile, sent her to study at the London School of Economics. There she met her husband, Kang-chi Cheng, whose Nationalist sympathies left her at risk after his early death. In 1966, Red Guards broke into her house in Shanghai, trashed the place and arrested her and her daughter, Meiping. Nien was put in solitary confinement in the infamous No.1 Detention House, where interrogators tried in vain to get her to admit to espionage. Her ordeal was horrific, said *The Times*. She succumbed to pneumonia and haemorrhages;

all her teeth fell out. What kept her going, she said, was sheer rage at the way she was treated.

On her release, she was told Meiping had killed herself, but she later found out that her daughter had been beaten to death for refusing to denounce her. Nien then moved to the USA, where, after her memoir came out in 1987, she was hailed as a hero. Her later life was a happy one, marred only, she admitted in a *Time* interview, by a sense of depression that sometimes set in at dusk. 'But next morning, I invariably wake up with renewed optimism to welcome the day as another God-given opportunity for enlightenment and experience. My only regret is that Meiping is not here with me.'

What kept her going, she said, was sheer rage at the way she was treated.

The PM who cooked curry for the troops

SAMAK SUNDARAVEJ

1935-2009

Samak Sundaravej achieved the rare distinction of becoming prime minister of his country while also carrying on a lucrative career as a TV chef. In the latter capacity, he was notorious for the foulness of his language, said *The Times*. Sundaravej's show, *Tasting and Ranting*, provided an amusing blend of his peculiar recipes (e.g. pork leg stewed in Coca-Cola) with profane diatribes in which the right-wing pundit would sound off about whatever happened to be annoying him in Thailand at the time. This same mixture of the political and the nutritional was seen in his brief career as PM. With his popularity waning, Sundaravej tried – without success – to win over the army by serving chicken curry to the troops.

He was born in Bangkok and studied law at university. In his thirties he entered politics, holding a variety of cabinet posts over the next few decades. It would be a mistake to view Sundaravej as a purely comic figure, said *The Guardian*. On the contrary, he was involved in two of the darkest episodes in Thai history. It was his rhetoric that prompted riots in 1976 and the deaths of dozens of left-wing students. ('It's no sin to kill Communists,' he remarked at the time.)

Then, in 1992, as deputy PM, he defended another massacre, saying that for the army to open fire on protesters was no worse than the US invasion of Iraq in the first Gulf war.

Sundaravej's political clout earned him a TV career. This in turn was the key to his surprise emergence as the new PM in December 2007. Many members of the public, especially in rural areas, identified with his earthy language (for which he was nicknamed Dog Mouth by his critics). But this didn't help Sundaravej bring order to a country in turmoil. After just nine months, he was ousted again, officially because his TV work constituted a conflict of interest as prime minister.

His TV show provided an amusing blend of his peculiar recipes with profane diatribes.

Oscar-winning actress and wife of David O. Selznick

JENNIFER JONES

1919-2009

In 1943, the actress Jennifer Jones won an Oscar for her sweet, wide-eyed performance in *The Song of Bernadette* as the young girl at Lourdes who had visions of the Virgin Mary. The day after the award ceremony – in a move not entirely in keeping with the nature of the part for which she had just been honoured – she served divorce papers on her husband, the actor Robert Walker. For by then Jones had embarked on an affair with the movie mogul David O. Selznick. He exercised a Svengali-like grip on her career, though after early successes his choice of films for her to star in became 'increasingly erratic', and she floundered in numerous turkeys. In any case, though Jones was undoubtedly pretty, said *The Times*, she lacked the magnetism of a true star. Her nadir was perhaps her turn as a fading porn star in *Angel, Angel, Down We Go* (1969), which required her to deliver the less than immortal line, 'I have made 30 stag films and never faked an orgasm.'

Born Phylis Lee Isley, she caught the acting bug from her parents, who toured their native Oklahoma with a tent show. In her teens she won a place in the American Academy of Dramatic Arts in New York, and it was there she met Walker. The pair married and moved to Hollywood, determined to become stars – which they both did, up to a point. (Walker is now best remembered for his role as the villain in Hitchcock's *Strangers on a Train*.) But success didn't come overnight. Even after Isley had caught the eye of Selznick, it was four years before she appeared in *The Song of Bernadette* – billed, at Selznick's suggestion, as Jennifer Jones. She went on to marry her mentor, and star opposite big names such as Gregory Peck and Humphrey Bogart. But she also had to cope with an increasing rate of failure, and Walker's untimely death at 32.

Selznick died in 1965 leaving Jones with heavy debts, said *The Guardian*. Already prone to depression, the ageing actress – who hadn't shone in a film since *Love Is a Many-Splendored Thing* a decade earlier – tried to kill herself with sleeping pills and was found lying in the surf on a Miami beach. But she found renewed happiness with her third marriage, to the multi-millionaire art patron, Norton Simon. At their wedding (which, like her second marriage, took place on a yacht), Simon presented her with a £1.2m still life by the 17th-century Spanish master Zurbarán. 'I own many works of art,' he remarked, 'but Jennifer is better than any of them.'

> **Her nadir was *Angel, Angel, Down We Go*, which required her to deliver the less than immortal line, 'I have made 30 stag films and never faked an orgasm.'**

The foul-mouthed
enfant terrible
of British fashion

ALEXANDER McQUEEN
1969-2010

Alexander McQueen was the Damien Hirst of fashion, said *The Independent*. Regarded as a genius by some, by others as a brash self-publicist, he held his position at the top of a notoriously fickle industry for over a decade, before taking his own life at the age of 40. Like Hirst's, his success relied partly on shock tactics. A McQueen show might involve models bathed in blood, or an obese woman in a glass box, naked save for a gas mask. And if this distracted from his tailoring skill ('Sometimes the show steals the show,' as he put it), that was in keeping with his ambivalent attitude to his job. Throughout his life, the foul-mouthed McQueen slated other designers, but he was just as likely to describe his own work as 'crap'. His 2009 Paris fall collection involved hats made from bin-liners and a catwalk strewn with discarded items from his previous work, suggesting either that he regarded the fashion world as garbage, or else that he wanted to hint at the ruin of his talent, or both.

Born in South London, Lee Alexander McQueen had a difficult childhood. His father, a cabby, regarded him as effeminate, said the *Daily Telegraph*, and at school he was called 'McQueer'. (The designer later claimed to have known he was gay from an early age, and called himself 'the pink sheep of the family'.) He left with one O level and one A level, both in Art. Soon after, he took a job as an apprentice at Anderson & Sheppard, the Savile Row tailors who taught him his craft. But even then McQueen couldn't contain his rebellious streak. According to a story he sometimes denied, he once wrote the words 'I am a c*nt' on the lining of a jacket being made for the Prince of Wales. He went on to study at Central Saint Martin's College of Art and Design, and it was here, in 1994, he was discovered by Isabella Blow, the eccentric, aristocratic former fashion editor of *Vogue*.

As he became successful, McQueen didn't cease to bite the hand that fed him.

With Blow's support, McQueen's label thrived, and he became the *enfant terrible* of British fashion, said the *New York Times*. His 1995 'Highland Rape' show, which included tartan-clad, ravaged-looking models, was an attack on English colonialism; his low-slung 'bumster' trousers were derided by critics, but somehow caught on, and arguably lowered the waistline of trousers across the world. As he became successful, McQueen didn't cease to bite the hand that fed him. When he was taken on as head designer by Givenchy in 1996, Blow expected he would offer her a role. He didn't, and their friendship never fully recovered. Nor, it turned out, was the move to Paris a success. The French were unimpressed by his offerings, and he felt homesick. However, his new financial security did enable him to fulfil one lifelong ambition: to buy a house for his mother, Joyce, whom he always adored.

The McQueen brand has continued to do well. In 2001 he was presented with his third British Designer of the Year Award by none other than Prince Charles (not wearing, it is to be hoped, his doctored Anderson & Sheppard jacket). Yet the couturier was increasingly plagued by the demons so often suggested in his work, said *The Guardian*. A long-term relationship ended, there was talk of drug abuse, and then his mother died after a long illness; he took his own life later the same month. In an interview in *The Guardian* a few years earlier, conducted by Joyce herself, she had asked her son what his greatest fear was. 'Dying before you,' came the reply.

Much-loved maverick who always fought for his beliefs

MICHAEL FOOT

1913-2010

At the peak of his career, Michael Foot was one of the most derided figures in British politics, said *The Times*. As leader of the Labour Party in the early 1980s, he was mocked as an ineffectual, wild-haired old relic – cruelly dubbed Worzel Gummidge by the press – and the reputation seemed borne out when he presided over the worst election defeat suffered by the Left in half a century. Yet when he died, at the age of 96, a more balanced picture of the man emerged. For all his weaknesses of management and self-presentation, Foot was lamented as the last of a breed of statesmen who fought for what they believed in. He was remembered for the force of his oratory in public, and his unfailing courtesy in private. Above all, in an age when the very word politician has become synonymous with duplicity, he was praised for his honesty. Another Labour leader, John Smith, liked to tell how he once asked Foot's advice on the best way to get a difficult bill through parliament. Foot replied, only half-jokingly, 'In politics you should never neglect the possibility that you might have to fall back on the truth.'

Michael Mackintosh Foot was born in Plymouth in 1913 into a family of unusual talent. His father, the Liberal MP Isaac Foot, a strict Methodist and temperance preacher, was such a bibliophile that when his library became too big he bought another house. Michael, too, was throughout his life a great lover of books – and wrote many himself, including a highly regarded study of Jonathan Swift, one of his heroes. Like two of his brothers before him, he became president of the Oxford Union, and on leaving university was employed by a shipping firm in Liverpool, where the appalling conditions persuaded him to join the Labour Party. He then embarked on a journalistic career, first working at the left-wing weekly *Tribune*, and later for the *Evening Standard*, where to the dismay of left-wing associates he befriended the paper's proprietor, Lord Beaverbrook – a left-wing hate figure. But that was typical of the man, said the *Daily Telegraph*. All his life he was attracted to mavericks, regardless of their political leanings. His heroes included Tory figures like Swift and Disraeli. He even wrote a book, *The Politics of Paradise*, claiming that another of his heroes, the mad, bad poet Byron, was really a radical libertarian.

In 1945 Foot was swept into parliament in the Labour landslide as MP for Plymouth Devonport. He lost the seat ten years later, but when his friend Aneurin Bevan (another glamorous rebel) died in 1960, he replaced him as MP for Ebbw Vale, and represented the constituency until his retirement. Early on he won a reputation as a powerful speaker, yet he never sought a front-bench role: often he seemed to disagree as much with his own party (e.g. on unilateral nuclear disarmament, which he supported) as with the Tories (e.g. on Britain's entry to the Common Market, which he opposed). In truth, Foot was a natural backbencher, 'far better suited to criticism than construction', said the *Telegraph*, and to a literary rather than a political career. (The depth of Foot's erudition was startling. When Enoch Powell – another maverick he got on well with – chided him for using the neologism 'remuneration' in a speech, Foot quoted its occurrence in *Love's Labour's Lost*.) Many were therefore shocked when Foot accepted a ministerial role in 1974. 'It was as if Mary Whitehouse had turned up in the cast of *Oh! Calcutta!*' as one journalist put it. Yet he proved an effective Secretary of State for Employment, said *The Guardian*: he restored trade-union rights lost in the Tory Industrial Relations Act of 1971, legitimised the closed shop despite Fleet Street opposition, and created the Health and Safety Executive.

That he went on to become Labour leader in 1980 was largely due to his being seen as the best man to hold his party together, the internal divisions between Labour moderates and extremists having come to a head with the return of the Tories to power in 1979. But within a year Foot had failed: the Gang of Four, led by Roy Jenkins, broke away to form the Social Democratic Party. Foot's position was further weakened by his perceived lack of resolve over the Falklands conflict. Yet perhaps an even bigger problem was his image, said *The Independent*. Almost 70, unkempt, shortsighted and reliant on a walking stick (following a car crash in the 1960s), he just did not look the part. And when he appeared at the Cenotaph on Armistice Day, wearing what looked like a donkey jacket, the press savaged him. In vain did Foot plead that it was actually a stylish dark-green car coat – the Queen Mother had even complimented him for wearing 'a smart, sensible coat for a day like this': it still made him look like 'an out-of-work navvy', as one of his own MPs put it, and seemed disrespectful.

When Enoch Powell chided him for using the neologism 'remuneration' in a speech, Foot quoted its occurrence in *Love's Labour's Lost*.

The last nail in his coffin was Labour's hard-line election manifesto of 1983 – advocating unilateral disarmament, higher taxation and a more interventionist industrial policy. 'The longest suicide note in history,' Labour MP Gerald Kaufman called it. That year, the party took just 27.6 per cent of the vote, and almost came third to the Liberal-SDP alliance. Foot resigned as leader, to be replaced by Neil Kinnock. Some argue that Foot did at least preserve the Labour Party in those difficult years, said Philip Webster in *The Times*, but in truth his real legacy was to make it so unelectable it had to change to survive. The result, albeit unintended, was the rise of New Labour and Tony Blair. Foot stayed on as an MP until 1992, but increasingly focused his energies on his writing. He was predeceased in 1999 by his wife, the documentary film maker Jill Craigie.

A man of literary concerns

'The men who do not read are unfit for power.' So wrote Michael Foot in the most famous of his bon mots. Yet he himself was proof that the reverse is not necessarily true, said Roy Hattersley in *The Times*:

'The first time I realised that, for all his erudition, Foot wasn't really suited to high office was when the Gang of Four split from the Party in 1981 to form the SDP. It was then rumoured – falsely – that I was planning to join them. So when I arrived at work on the morning after the Brixton Riots, and found a letter from Foot which began "Some offences may be overlooked…" and ended "I expected your resignation to be awaiting me…" I naturally assumed he thought I was jumping ship.

'Not a bit of it. What had offended Foot was an article I'd written in *The Guardian* in which I had described the American humourist Dorothy Parker as a "superficial" and "meretricious" writer. As the morning unfolded, Foot sent me increasingly urgent messages in defence of Parker's integrity, citing passages from short stories she had written while in Spain. I was impressed, of course, by his literary knowledge, but couldn't help feeling that, as opposition leader, he should have been thinking more about the Riots than about Parker.'

Classics professor with a passion for sexual honesty

SIR KENNETH DOVER

1920–2010

Sir Kenneth Dover was one of the pre-eminent classical scholars of the twentieth century. His most famous work, though not necessarily his best, was *Greek Homosexuality*, which brought an unprecedented candour to a subject that had been shrouded in euphemism or denial. According to Victorian tradition, relations between men in Ancient Greece could sometimes be passionate, but it was a romantic passion, not a physical one. Dover overturned this notion, said the *New York Times*, while also demonstrating a cheery willingness to analyse the gritty facts of homosexual activity. Those who blanched at such openness were even more taken aback when the distinguished don, by then Chancellor of St Andrew's University, published a memoir that was no less explicit about his own sexual habits. At the age of 64, he revealed, he and his wife, Lady Audrey, enjoyed 'some of the best f***s of our life'.

Born in London, the son of a civil servant, Dover went to St Paul's School and then read classics at Balliol College, Oxford, where he also began his academic career as a tutor. Highlights among the books he went on to publish were *Greek Word Order* – 'no easy read', said *The Times* – and his own personal favourite, *Greek Popular Morality in the Time of Plato and*

Aristotle. When it appeared in 1974, he had served as Professor of Greek at St Andrew's University for almost two decades. Shortly afterwards, he returned to Oxford as President of Corpus Christi College.

But the book that really brought him to public attention was his memoir, *Marginal Comment*, published in 1994. In it Dover was not only explicit about his love life, said *The Scotsman*: he even revealed that he'd come close to murdering a fellow Oxford don, the manic depressive Trevor Aston. Aston's behaviour had been so disruptive, Dover explained, he'd seriously thought about killing him, and after the memoir came out, there was some debate as to whether he was in some way responsible for Aston's eventual suicide. Readers of the memoir will know, said the *Daily Telegraph*, that Dover in fact behaved 'impeccably' towards Aston, but one is still left wondering whether his reckless candour stemmed from an 'adolescent desire to shock' or was symptomatic of his lifelong passion for honesty. In later years, he and his wife were much-loved figures at St Andrew's, where Dover served as Chancellor.

One is still left wondering whether his reckless candour stemmed from an 'adolescent desire to shock' or was symptomatic of his lifelong passion for honesty.

Brilliant, mordant novelist whose eccentricity was a mask

BERYL BAINBRIDGE

1932-2010

Dishevelled clothes, high cheekbones, startled eyes; a cigarette in one hand and a drink in the other (she preferred whisky to wine, she used to say, because it didn't take one so long to get drunk) – Dame Beryl Bainbridge was a familiar and much-loved figure at London literary parties. Her house in Camden was famously crammed with bric-a-brac: there was a stuffed water buffalo in the hall, for instance, and a life-size dummy of Neville Chamberlain in her bedroom. All of which may have led some to dismiss her as 'a character', said *The Guardian*, yet in reality her eccentricity was a carefully cultivated act designed to keep the world at bay and free her for the serious business of writing. Author of 18 novels, most of them slim, mordant and highly entertaining, she was shortlisted for the Booker Prize five times, but never actually won. She did, however, win the Whitbread Prize (twice), the prestigious David Cohen Prize, and the *Guardian* Fiction Award, and was made a Dame of the British Empire. 'What they don't realise,' she once observed, 'when they say I'm a bit eccentric – and it's the only time I get hot under the collar – is the discipline needed to get something done, and get it done properly.'

Bainbridge was born in Liverpool in 1932. Her father was a bankrupt, her mother disdained him, and there was an air of violence about the house. Beryl, known as 'Basher Bainbridge' at school, was a pugnacious child, said *The Independent*. Expelled after being caught copying out dirty limericks, she did a stint at drama school, then acted at the Liverpool Playhouse (in 1961 she appeared in one episode of *Coronation Street* as an anti-nuclear protester), where she met a scene painter called Austin Davies. The pair married and had two children, but Bainbridge divorced him after discovering he'd been having an affair, and not long after tried to kill herself by putting her head in the oven. 'When one is young, one has these ups and downs,' she later remarked. In short, her formative years were wretched – but 'ideal' from a writer's point of view. Her early novels were semi-autobiographical, short – for every 12 pages she wrote, only one appeared in her final draft – and therapeutic. After completing ten of them, she 'felt better', she said.

By then the author had twice been shortlisted for the Booker Prize: for *The Dressmaker* (1973) and *The Bottle Factory Outing* (1974), a darkly humorous tale drawn from her own experience of factory work, which some consider her best novel. But she still wasn't financially secure. The blame for this, said A.N. Wilson in *The Observer*, should be laid at the door of her 'snooty' publisher at Duckworth, Colin Haycraft. He paid her a pittance, yet she remained with him out of a misplaced sense of loyalty. 'Don't press Colin too hard,' she'd murmur, when her agent suggested asking for higher royalties. But then again, Haycraft was also her mentor, said *The Guardian*, and it was he who wisely steered her towards historical fiction, after she had run out of things to say about herself.

Even when concerned with great events of the past – the Crimean War in *Master Georgie*, for instance – her books remained invitingly slim, and she liked to quote the aphorism attributed to Pascal, that they were only as long as they were because 'I didn't have time to make them shorter'. But even the historical novels were, on some level, about her own life. Her flawed father was the model for a number of her male protagonists, including Captain Scott in *The Birthday Boys* (1991) – even though 'Scott went to the South Pole, and my father never went further than the corner shop'. At the age of 60, she claimed to have given up sex ('I was just getting too old – you'd have to do it in pitch blackness') and for much of her life lived alone. Yet she was adored by her three children and seven grandchildren and loved and respected by everyone who knew her on the literary circuit.

The Devil Commander: 'Italy's Lawrence of Arabia'

AMEDEO GUILLET

1909–2010

A medeo Guillet 'crammed rather a lot into his 101 years', said the *Financial Times*. An Olympic-standard equestrian, the dashing, aristocratic Italian is best remembered for having led the last ever cavalry charge against British forces. On 21 January 1941, the advancing Allies were brewing up tea for breakfast in their camp at Keru Gorge in Eritrea when, to their astonishment, there emerged from the mist a mustachioed Italian astride a white stallion. He was clad in Arab dress and making straight for their 25-pounder artillery guns, screaming, 'Savoia!' (a reference to the home province of the Italian royal family, and Guillet's birthplace). Galloping beside and behind him were 250 Yemeni and Eritrean desperadoes, waving scimitars, firing antique carbines and scattering home-made grenades. Roughly half of them were killed. Yet the escapade – which earned the gallant lieutenant the nicknames 'Comandante Diavolo' (Devil Commander) and 'Italy's Lawrence of Arabia' – unnerved the Allies, and provided a distraction that saved some 9,000 Italian troops from almost certain capture.

Born into a family of minor nobility in the northern town of Piacenza, Guillet originally wanted to become a monk, but he was talked out of the idea. Instead he joined the Royal Military Academy at Modena and then the cavalry school in Pinerolo, where he was selected to join the Italian eventing team for the 1936 Olympic Games in Berlin. But when Mussolini sent his army to win him an empire in Africa, Guillet (pronounced Gee-yay) ditched his Olympic aspirations to join the invasion of Abyssinia. He later fought in the Spanish Civil War with Italy's Fiamme Nere (Black Flames) volunteer force. The atrocities he witnessed caused him to lose faith in fascism, though his loyalty to country, he said, remained intact.

There emerged from the mist a mustachioed Italian astride a white stallion.

Next he was posted to Eritrea, where he hoped to be joined by his beautiful Neapolitan cousin and fiancée, Beatrice. Mussolini's decision to join the War on Hitler's side 'ended these dreams', said the *Daily Telegraph*. With Eritrea surrounded by Italy's enemies, a reunion with Beatrice was out of the question. About this time he met Khadija, the wildly pretty 16-year-old daughter of a local chieftain, and asked her, flirtatiously, if she was married. 'Many men want to marry me,' she replied. 'It is I who will not marry them.' Yet within two hours she had fallen for the handsome lieutenant. Riding and shooting as well as any man, she went on to fight at his side in many skirmishes with the enemy.

By March 1941 the British had taken the Eritrean capital, Asmara, and most Italian soldiers had surrendered. Not Guillet, said *The Times*. He took to the hills and for nine months waged guerrilla war before finally making it back to Italy. After Italy switched sides, Guillet – always more a fan of the British than the Germans – found himself working undercover for his former enemies. Yet the chaos in the land of his birth sickened him, as did what he saw as the lack of patriotism of his fellow citizens. He married Beatrice (there is no record of what she thought of his liaison with the fiery Khadija) and pursued a diplomatic career as a means of escaping from Italy. Speaking fluent Arabic, Guillet was his country's ambassador to Egypt, Yemen, Jordan, Morocco and India. In his latter years he moved with his wife to County Meath, Ireland, where he spent much of his time fox-hunting. In 2002 he was presented with the Knight Grand Cross of the Military Order of Italy, his country's highest military award. Beatrice predeceased him. The fate of Khadija is not known.

The self-destructive genius who made snooker fascinating

ALEX HIGGINS

1949-2010

No one would ever have called Alex 'Hurricane' Higgins a calming presence, said *The Guardian*. The redoubtable snooker player once headbutted an official who had asked him for a urine sample, and another time filled the bottle and then hurled it at a nearby wall. And though he sometimes spoke of the importance of grace in defeat, he was not very gracious when he turned on Stephen Hendry, after being beaten by him in the 1991 UK Championship, and growled: 'Up your a***, you c***.' Yet for all his faults, the world of snooker owes Higgins an enormous debt, said *The Guardian*. The tension between his mercurial talent – as he prowled round the baize, pulling off seemingly impossible shots with a nervous, booze-fuelled energy – and the constant danger that he would wreck his chances by taking unnecessary risks, made for fascinating viewing, and helped transform the game from one played in smoke-filled backrooms for negligible prize money into a crowd-commanding TV extravaganza. Higgins regarded himself as the best of the best. The statistics tell a different story. In his 20 clashes with the great Steve Davis, for example, he triumphed a mere four times. Yet countless players say they only began their careers because of the allure of Higgins's bad-boy play-making. And

Davis himself summed up the reverence in which his rival was held by many when he called him 'the only true genius I have encountered in the game'.

Alexander Gordon Higgins was born in Belfast, the son of a wheel tapper. His childhood was secure and loving – he himself referred to it as 'the good old days' – giving little sign of the tormented talent it would produce, said the *Daily Telegraph*. When young, he wanted to be a jockey, but the ambition was gradually replaced by snooker. He first came across the game in the Jampot, a club where he pitted his skills against men twice his age, while surviving on a diet of fizzy drinks and chocolate. As his gifts grew, he moved on to Guinness and the odd banana – plus 80 Marlboros a day. At 18, Higgins won the Northern Ireland Amateur Championship. He was soon playing exhibition games in England, where he lived hand-to-mouth – in Blackburn he lived in a series of squats along a street, moving from one to the next – 9, 11, 13 – as each was demolished by the wrecking ball.

The tension between his mercurial talent and the constant danger that he would wreck his chances by taking unnecessary risks, made for fascinating viewing.

His talent soared, and in 1972 Higgins turned professional. In that same year he became, at 22, the youngest man to win the World Championship. He went on to win the Canadian Open (twice), the Masters (twice) and the Irish Professional Snooker Championships (five times). Yet he never dominated the game in the manner of Davis, say, or Hendry. His talent was too volatile, flourishing most *in extremis*. The classic instance was in the semi-finals of the 1983 World Championship: 59-0 down against Jimmy White, Higgins came back with a magnificent, daredevil break to win 69-59, a sequence that became the most reprised piece of snooker footage on TV. He went on to win his second world title and the images of the 'Hurricane' weeping as he called for 'my baby' – 18-month old Lauren, duly brought to him by his wife Lynn – are among the most moving in sport. Yet despite this winsome streak, he was far from a perfect husband, said *The Independent*. A ladies man, he could be as aggressive towards the women in his life as he was to the snooker officials he assumed were out to get him. After his second divorce he took up with Siobhan Kidd, a psychology graduate. In 1988 she pronounced him 'the gentlest man I've ever met'; two years later he broke her cheekbone with a hairdryer.

The former champion's latter years were dominated by disaster and self-delusion, said the *Daily Telegraph*. On one occasion he punched a press officer; on another, a 14-year-old boy. Then there was the time he told fellow player Dennis Taylor he'd have him shot. Meanwhile, he drank more, ate less, and the titles dried up. Yet as his life fell apart, Higgins persisted in the belief that he was the best in the world. In the twilight of his days, he became a haunting shadow of his former self. Treatment for throat cancer wrecked his teeth and reduced him to eating baby food. Painfully thin, he frittered away the millions he'd won and ended his life in sheltered accommodation. Through all this, there was little sign of repentance or doubt of his own worth. 'I think I was the most natural, charismatic player who ever lifted a cue,' he croaked in what was left of his ravaged voice. 'I'm not telling you this to bolster my own ego. It's what people tell me.'

The would-be priest who became a pornographer

BOB GUCCIONE

1930-2010

One of the great turkeys of movie history, the shockingly pornographic and artistically absurd 1979 film *Caligula*, opened with a line from the Bible: 'What shall it profit a man, if he shall gain the whole world, and lose his own soul?' The words could stand as an epitaph for the man who bankrolled that fiasco, the magazine publisher Bob Guccione, said *The Independent*. For much of his life, thanks to the success of *Penthouse*, the soft-porn magazine he founded, the one-time artist lived in the largest house in Manhattan. As well as a ballroom, a Roman-style swimming pool and a permanent string of Penthouse 'pets' (as his models were known), the house contained a world-class art collection. Chagall, Degas, Picasso – paintings by all these masters graced the walls. Yet by the time he died at the age of 79, Guccione had been forced to sell the lot, replacing them with works by his own hand. Free online porn had devastated the sales of his flagship magazine, while a series of disastrous commercial ventures (*Caligula* among them) had driven him to ruin. Guccione lived on in his home even when he no longer owned it, surrounded by a pack of Ridgeback hounds, checking the position of his hairpiece, and telling interviewers of the 'serious contribution' *Penthouse* had made to world culture. 'Everything new in men's magazines – everything! – was started by us,' he claimed in 2004.

Robert Charles Joseph Edward Sabatini Guccione was born in Brooklyn, the son of an accountant. The family was Catholic, of Sicilian descent, and at one stage Bob planned to enter the priesthood. Yet he also had artistic leanings, and with his wife Lilyann (they married when he was 18) he set sail for Europe with the aim of becoming a painter. Instead of studying, however, he wandered around the Med, sketching tourists. Then he took up with an English singer named Muriel, who became his second wife. The pair settled in London, and he ran a chain of dry-cleaning shops. But his ambitions stretched further than that. (Friends at the time called him 'J.C.' because of his Messianic self-belief.) In 1965, noticing how well Hugh Hefner's magazine *Playboy* was selling, he decided to set up an English rival. Early success came partly through luck. He sent out promotional material to addresses on a mailing list. The list was out of date, and the brochures landed on the doorsteps of clergymen and MPs. The ensuing scandal gave the magazine the boost it needed. From the start, *Penthouse* was entirely

> **Guccione lived on in his home even when he no longer owned it, checking the position of his hairpiece, and telling interviewers of the 'serious contribution' *Penthouse* had made to world culture.**

Guccione's creation, said *The Times*. He took many of the pictures himself, recreating pictures by his favourite artists. Misting the air with hair spray lent an Impressionist softness to the light. For greater intimacy, he worked with models one-on-one, telling them not to look at the camera to make it look as if they didn't know they were being photographed. 'That was the sexy part,' he noted. 'That was what none of our competition understood.' He was clearly on to something. By 1969, Guccione was financially strong enough to go head-to-head with *Playboy*. He bought offices in New York and took out an ad showing a *Playboy* 'bunny' in the crosshairs of a rifle. Caption: 'We're going rabbit-hunting.'

Thus began the copycat competition between the two publications that was dubbed 'the pubic wars'. After *Penthouse* ran the first picture showing pubic hair, *Playboy* followed suit. It did the same when the arriviste magazine pioneered girl-on-girl shots. ('Lesbianism was something of interest to me,' Guccione once revealed, 'and I recognised that I wasn't alone.') With his silk shirts and medallions, he seemed like a pornographer from central casting, said the *Daily Telegraph*. Yet he didn't drink or take drugs – on the contrary, he was obsessed with his health, spending millions on researching ways of extending his life. He even looked into having himself and his third wife Kathy cryogenically frozen and blasted into space. When once, at a meeting, he let slip the phrase 'if I die', his colleagues suspected he might be losing touch with reality. So it proved, said Andy McSmith in *The Independent*. The man who once knew instinctively what the public wanted began to misread the market. *Caligula*, with its scenes of depravity, bombed at the box office (though it proved popular on video). In the 1990s, with the advent of the internet, *Penthouse* became increasingly hardcore. Sales plummeted. His company, General Media, filed for bankruptcy in 2003. Guccione, convinced he was right about everything, fell out with his children. In his twilight years, as his empire crumbled around him, he found solace in painting.

The king of the film soundtrack

JOHN BARRY

1933-2011

No British man or woman has won more Oscars than the composer John Barry. He was awarded two for his music for *Born Free*, and one apiece for *The Lion in Winter*, *Out of Africa* and *Dances with Wolves*. Yet Barry will be best remembered for the lush, dramatic scores he wrote for 11 James Bond movies, said *The Guardian*. There was a dispute over who created the main Bond theme, first heard at the start of *Dr No* in 1962. Finally it went to court, where the judge ruled that the theme had been written by Monty Norman, while Barry had merely arranged it. But there is no disagreement over the authorship of other tracks, such as the magisterial theme song for *Goldfinger*, or the classic 'We Have All The Time In The World'. A later Bond composer, David Arnold, may have overstated it when he said: 'The success of the Bond series was 50 per cent Sean Connery and 50 per cent John Barry.' But certainly it's hard to imagine the films without Barry's contribution.

He was born John Barry Prendergast in York in 1933. His father owned a chain of cinemas and as a boy John would work the projector. Yet music was his first love, and he began learning the piano at 9 and the trumpet at 16. His big break came in 1959 when he was asked to write the music for an Adam Faith movie, *Beat Girl*. The film was nothing special, but the score was the first movie soundtrack ever to be released as an album in the UK, and its success led to his being drafted in to work with Monty Norman on *Dr No*. For the second Bond film, *From Russia with Love* (1963), Barry was sole composer. He is generally thought to have perfected the overblown, unmistakable Bond sound with 1964's *Goldfinger*, whose soundtrack knocked the Beatles off the No. 1 spot in the US charts.

> **'The success of the Bond series was 50 per cent Sean Connery and 50 per cent John Barry.'**

On the back of his work for the Bond movies, Barry became a major figure in the Swinging Sixties, said *The Independent*. He hung out with Terence Stamp and Michael Caine ('He looks as if he hasn't got a note of music in him,' Caine remarked of his friend's louche appearance) and at the age of 32 married the actress Jane Birkin, then just 17. ('I was besotted with John,' she later recalled.) That union didn't last – Barry had three further marriages – but his music went from strength to strength. *The Ipcress File*, *Midnight Cowboy*, *The Tamarind Seed*, *Body Heat*: all benefited from scores by Barry. He ceased involvement with the Bond franchise after *The Living Daylights* in 1987, on the grounds that 'all the good [Ian Fleming] books had been done'. Barry was awarded an OBE in 1999.

The Nazi hunter known as the Merciless One

TUVIAH FRIEDMAN

1922-2011

Tuviah Friedman devoted his life to hunting Nazis responsible for the Holocaust and bringing them to justice. In this pursuit, he was indefatigable – and in the eyes of some, intemperate, said the *Washington Post*. Friedman, who lost his parents and two siblings in death camps, revelled in the nickname of the Merciless One. He boasted of having whipped captive Nazis towards the end of the Second World War, as he had been whipped himself; of torturing some; and of putting others to death. But his proudest achievement was the role he played in the hunt for Adolf Eichmann, who was implicated in the deaths of millions of Jews.

Friedman was born in the town of Radom in central Poland. After the Nazis invaded, his father (who owned a printing business) was interned with his family in a labour camp, but young Tuviah managed to escape through the sewers. He joined the semi-official Polish militia, which, once the tide of war had turned, began scouring the country in search of Nazis. Later, working with Nazi hunter Simon Wiesenthal in Vienna, he tracked down some 250 Nazis linked to war crimes. He continued this work in Haifa, Israel, where he moved in 1952 – setting up the one-man Institute for the Documentation of Nazi War Crimes.

His most significant target was Eichmann, who organised the mass deportation of Jews to extermination camps, said the *Daily Telegraph*. No one knew what he looked like, so Friedman travelled to Linz, where Eichmann's father ran an electrical store. While buying a light bulb, he scrutinised the old man, but once outside, he smashed the bulb on the ground and spat on the shards. I have 'seen Satan's father', is how he described the encounter.

'All these years, I was a beaten man,' he remarked, 'but I had patience.'

His was a lonely obsession, said the *Washington Post*. His wife Anna, an eye surgeon, forced to bring up their child on her salary alone, begged him to abandon it. Many Jews preferred not to think about the Holocaust, and Friedman's insistence on bringing it to the forefront of attention was often resented: some would even address him mockingly as Herr Eichmann. Then, in 1959, a letter arrived from a Dachau survivor in Argentina, claiming (truthfully, as it turned out) to have news of Eichmann's whereabouts. Friedman passed it to the Israeli authorities, and the next year the former Nazi was kidnapped by Mossad and taken to Israel, where he stood trial and was hanged. Although Mossad later claimed that they tracked down Eichmann without Friedman's help, the Israeli justice department made a point of saying that if it hadn't been for 'people like Friedman', Eichmann might still be at large. And as far as Friedman was concerned, his struggle had been worth it. 'All these years, I was a beaten man,' he remarked, 'but I had patience.'

The man who crossed the Atlantic on a raft made of junk

POPPA NEUTRINO

1933-2011

Poppa Neutrino was an itinerant eccentric, who never stayed in one place for more than a year at a time. At various points, he was a seminarian, a gambler, a busker and an aspirant politician. He seldom had more than a few pennies to his name – yet that, he used to say, was how he wanted it. 'When I'm absolutely broke,' he declared, 'I feel liberated.' Temperamentally opposed to conventional morality, he set up his own religion, which he named the First Church of Fulfillment – 'the only church in the history of the world that didn't know the way', as he liked to joke. But despite the extraordinary variety of his life, Neutrino, who has died aged 77, will be best remembered as the first person to cross the Atlantic in a raft made out of junk, said the *Boston Globe*. In 1998 he set out from Newfoundland with his wife, two friends and three dogs. The expedition almost came to grief mid-ocean when the ramshackle craft was struck by a gale lasting 15 hours. 'At that point, I thought, "I really am sick in the head,"' Neutrino later confessed. Yet somehow they survived and washed up on the coast of Ireland hungry, battered, but unbeaten, 60 days after they had embarked.

Neutrino's life, as his biographer complained, was one that 'does not easily compress'. He was born William Pearlman in San Francisco, the son of a sailor. Soon after, his father vanished, and young William grew up with his mother, who made money as a gambler. Aged 12, he saw a documentary about Aborigines who periodically burned their clothes, possessions and homes, and walked away naked to start new lives. 'That's the way I want to live,' he remembered thinking as he left the theatre. 'I never want anything more.' It was a resolution he stuck to pretty closely over the next six decades.

Through the troughs and the peaks, Neutrino somehow always managed to stay afloat, said the *Daily Telegraph*. After his church burned down, he set up a group calling itself the Salvation Navy, which explored America's waterways on improvised boats. After suffering a two-year illness, he took a new name – Poppa Neutrino, after sub-atomic particles that travel at the speed of light – and formed a jazz band with his various children, The Flying Neutrinos. For a while, he lived on a cobbled-together houseboat known as Town Hall on the Manhattan waterfront, until the authorities dismantled it. Undaunted, Neutrino built another boat, Son of Town Hall, and set out on his epic trans-Atlantic voyage. In more recent years he started the Owl Party – so-named because its foreign policy was halfway between that of the doves and the hawks – and ran for president. His promises were threefold: eye contact, courtesy and due process. The frontrunners were not unduly alarmed.

> **He set up his own religion, the First Church of Fulfillment – 'the only church in the history of the world that didn't know the way'.**

The only intellectual in the English royal family

THE EARL OF HAREWOOD

1923-2011

'Our Royal Family, God bless it, is not noted either for its intellectual stature or for its artistic sophistication,' said Rupert Christiansen in the *Daily Telegraph*. The exception was the Queen's first cousin George Lascelles, the seventh Earl of Harewood, who 'changed the face of post-war British culture'. The achievements of which he was proudest, he once revealed, were as director of the Edinburgh Festival from 1961 to 1965. But he will best be remembered for his work with English National Opera (ENO) in the 1970s and 1980s. As its managing director and later its chairman, he demonstrated an instinct and panache (promoting lesser-known composers and putting on radical productions of popular works) that didn't always pay off – but his successes helped transform the company into a serious rival to the Royal Opera House. Or as Harewood himself once put it: 'If you want the flowers in your garden to be glorious and to smell good, you must risk an occasional stink.'

George Henry Hubert Lascelles, who has died aged 88, was born in Mayfair, the son of Viscount Lascelles and heir to the earldom of Harewood. His mother, Princess Mary, was the only daughter of George V. Young George became passionate about music at Eton and Cambridge, but it was only in the war that he had a chance to read up on the subject, said *The Independent*. While fighting in Italy, he was shot in the chest – a 'curiously disagreeable' sensation, as he later recalled – and captured. He eked out his time as a PoW at Colditz by reading and digesting *Grove's Dictionary of Music and Musicians* as far as the letter T. This was the origin of the encyclopaedic knowledge that would help to make his name. After the war he set up *Opera* magazine and penned a scathing review of *The Complete Opera Book* by Gustav Kobbé (1919). The publishers invited him to revise the next edition – Harewood accepted, and over the years the reference book came to include more entries by the editor than by Kobbé.

In person, the handsome Harewood was rather Bohemian, said *The Times*. He caused a scandal when he left his first wife, the pianist Marion Stein, for his second, the violinist Patricia Tuckwell, and for a time he was *persona non grata* at Buckingham Palace. At ENO opening nights he would sometimes appear in a flowing kaftan. There was some surprise when in 1985 he became the cinema-going public's moral guardian as chairman of the British Board of Film Classification. He devoted his latter years to the upkeep of the magnificent family seat of Harewood House in Yorkshire.

> **While fighting in Italy, he was shot in the chest – a 'curiously disagreeable' sensation, as he later recalled.**

Talented singer whose troubles became tabloid fodder

AMY WINEHOUSE

1983-2011

Amy Winehouse was one of the outstanding musicians of her generation, said *The Times*. When she burst onto the music scene in 2003, pop music was dominated by wholesome singers such as Dido and Katie Melua. 'It was immediately evident that Winehouse came from a very different tradition.' With her 'nicotine-stained bad-girl attitude', and powerful lived-in voice, the 20-year-old north Londoner revived the spirit of troubled divas of earlier eras such as Janis Joplin and Billie Holiday. The image could have been contrived. Alas, it was not. Even early on, it was clear that Winehouse had a self-destructive streak; but by 2007, following the release of her phenomenally successful second album, *Back To Black*, it was apparent that she was in the grip of full-blown addiction. Journalists reported finding the star – previously feisty, friendly and funny – glassy-eyed and incoherent; her record company waited in vain for a follow-up album; gigs were abandoned or cancelled; and the tabloid press, scenting celebrity meltdown, was perpetually on her trail. *Heat* magazine began a feature called 'Where's Wino?'; *The Sun* dubbed her Amy Declinehouse. Many were deeply shocked by her death, aged 27; few, however, can have been surprised.

Amy Winehouse was born into a Jewish family from north London, yet sounded as though she'd grown up in the speakeasies of Prohibition-era Chicago, said Neil McCormick in the *Daily Telegraph*. Her taxi driver father Mitch adored Frank Sinatra; her grandmother had once been engaged to Ronnie Scott. Smoky jazz clubs seemed to run in Amy's blood. Her entry into the music business, however, was fairly conventional, said *The Guardian*. Having caught the performing bug, she was attending stage school by the age of 8, but was later expelled from the Sylvia Young School for 'not applying herself', and having her nose pierced. By 16, she was regularly smoking cannabis. 'My parents pretty much realised that I would do whatever I wanted, and that was it, really,' she said later. By 18, she had signed a deal with Island Records, and moved out of her mother's house, and into her own flat in Camden.

Winehouse's first album, *Frank*, came out in 2003; jazzy, with a touch of hip-hop, it was nominated for several awards, but did not catch the public's fancy, and peaked at No. 13 in the charts. (Winehouse professed herself unhappy with it, and claimed not even to own a copy.) It was when she began work on her second one that a 'remarkable transformation took place'. In 2005, she met Blake Fielder-Civil, a junkie (according to *The Sun*) who worked on the periphery of the music business. Though he was already in a relationship, they embarked on an affair, said the *Daily Telegraph*. She had his name tattooed over her heart, he had hers tattooed behind his ear; and they bore matching scars on their arms (from his 'self-harming parties', it was said).

Winehouse was already a boozer; but from then on, her behaviour became increasingly erratic. During one performance, she ran off stage to vomit; and at the Q Awards in 2006, she heckled Bono during his acceptance speech with: 'Shut up! I don't give a f**k!' She 'wasn't the first person in history to be gripped by an uncontrollable urge to tell the U2 frontman to put a sock in it', said Alex Petridis in *The Guardian*, 'but the latter part of her heckle seemed to pertain less to his acceptance speech than herself, and to have a slightly troubling ring of truth about it.' When Fielder-Civil ended the relationship after about a year, she sank into a depression. 'I had never felt the way I feel about him about anyone in my whole life,' she said. 'I thought we'd never see each other again. I wanted to die.' She poured her misery into the songs that would make up *Back To Black*.

By the time the album came out, Winehouse was almost unrecognisable;

her voluptuous figure was gone; her newly emaciated body was covered in tattoos; and she had piled her dark hair into a 'vast, chaotic' beehive that, she said, rose and fell according to the bleakness of her mood. 'If nothing else, her visual overhaul told you she was still not an artist in thrall to the usual record company machinations.' The look – instantly and strikingly recognisable – was soon copied by Karl Lagerfeld on the catwalk, but it wasn't the kind of thing any stylist would have suggested. Her music was different, too: under the influence of producer Mark Ronson, she had produced a jazzy, soulful album that would 'change pop music in its wake'. The songs, including the defiant chart-topper 'Rehab', were so good, you might think they'd be a hit for any singer. But it was Winehouse's voice that made them phenomenal. Her heartfelt performances 'made you think of Tony Wilson's assessment of Joy Division: "Every other band was onstage because they wanted to be rock stars, this band was onstage because they had no f**king choice."'

> A UN drugs tsar was moved to describe Winehouse as a 'poster girl for drug abuse'. It was unfair. Gaunt, bruised and grubby, Winehouse was only a poster girl for her own misery.

Back To Black was a hit on both sides of the Atlantic, and swept the board at the Grammies. But its success seemed only to feed Winehouse's demons. Then, in early 2007, she was reunited with Fielder-Civil; they married a few weeks later. Her hopes for their life together were touchingly simple. 'I've always been a little homemaker,' she said. 'I know I'm talented, but I wasn't put here to sing. I was put here to be a wife and a mum and to look after my family. I love what I do, but it's not where it begins and ends.' Marriage, however, did neither of them any good. Her performances became increasingly shambolic; in August 2007 she had to have her stomach pumped, after she and her husband went on a bender fuelled by heroin, ecstasy, cocaine and ketamine. Under pressure from her parents, they checked into rehab, but lasted only three days. Then they were photographed fighting outside a hotel in Soho. Her face was cut and her feet were seeping blood through her ballet shoes. The implication was that she'd been injecting heroin between her toes. In early 2008, a UN drugs tsar was moved to describe Winehouse as a 'poster girl for drug abuse'. It was unfair, said McCormick. Gaunt, bruised and grubby, Winehouse was only a poster girl for her own misery.

The couple's relationship ended in July 2008, when Civil-Fielder was jailed for attacking a pub landlord and attempting to pervert the course of justice by offering him £200,000 to keep quiet about it. They divorced the following year, and Winehouse moved to St Lucia, to escape the drugs crowd in Camden, said *The Guardian*. There were reports that she had successfully weaned herself off narcotics, but she admitted that she was still struggling with alcohol addiction. In June 2011, she was booed off the stage during a concert in Belgrade. Her final public appearance came three days before her death, at the Roundhouse in Camden, where her goddaughter was performing. 'Winehouse danced in dreamy circles, then disappeared without singing a note.'

Child star who reinvented himself as a director of TV comedy

JOHN HOWARD DAVIES

1939-2011

'The fate of child stars is not always a happy one,' said *The Times*. Too often they seek and fail to recapture their erstwhile appeal. And so it might have been for John Howard Davies, who rose to fame aged 8, playing the lead in David Lean's brilliant film of *Oliver Twist*. His pale features and trembling lips were perfect for the innocent at large in a world of thugs and pickpockets, yet by his own account he was neither gifted nor handsome enough for a sustained career as an actor. Instead he went on to become the producer and director of some of TV's best-loved comedy shows: *Steptoe & Son*, *Monty Python's Flying Circus*, *The Goodies* and *The Good Life* all benefited from his sure hand. But many viewers will be most grateful for his input into the immortal *Fawlty Towers*. It was Davies who cast Prunella Scales as the grating Sybil Fawlty, and Davies who came up with the moment when Basil (John Cleese) hits Manuel (Andrew Sachs) on the forehead with a spoon. And it was Davies who suggested that the letters of the hotel sign should be in constant flux, spelling out 'Farty Towels' in one episode, 'Flowery Twats' in another.

Davies came from a showbusiness background. His great-grandfather was Lily Langtry's manager; his father, Jack Davies, wrote screenplays –

most notably for Norman Wisdom. It was at a party at his parents' home that young John was spotted by Lean's casting director. His turn as Oliver Twist was followed by a few other juvenile roles, after which he returned to the ordinary life of a schoolboy at Haileybury, and avoided acting altogether.

As an adult, he worked in the City, before taking a job as a BBC production assistant. His personal style was often at odds with that of the talents he worked with. The chaotic Graham Chapman of the Monty Python team remembered Davies as 'not a very human person', liable to tick you off like a schoolmaster if you made the slightest mistake. Yet he was, in Cleese's view, an excellent judge of what was and wasn't funny – a gift that led to his being appointed as the BBC's head of comedy in 1978.

> **Graham Chapman remembered Davies as 'not a very human person', liable to tick you off like a schoolmaster if you made the slightest mistake.**

Nevertheless, his touch rather deserted him in the 1980s, said the *Daily Telegraph*. Few now lament the passing of *All in Good Faith* (1985–1988), which cast Richard Briers as a well-intentioned vicar, or *Executive Stress* (1986–1988) with Geoffrey Palmer. There was an outcry from some quarters when, as controller of light entertainment at Thames, Davies axed *The Benny Hill Show* in 1988. Yet he soon found a worthy replacement in the form of another childlike, accident-prone figure – *Mr Bean*.

Brilliant, mercurial founding father of the modern computer era

STEVE JOBS

1955-2011

His admirers compared him to Christ. To his detractors, he was an egomaniac with a knack for gadgetry. But whatever you think of Steve Jobs there is no denying that he was 'one of the founding fathers of the modern computing and electronic era', said *The Independent*. Several of the gizmos created by Apple, the company he co-founded back in 1976, revolutionised their industries, whether it was the iPod, which enables people to carry their music collections in their pockets; the sleek, palm-friendly iPhone, with its touchscreen and myriad apps; the iPad, poised to transform the way people read literature; or the original Macintosh – a machine Jobs himself referred to as the most 'insanely great' computer in the world. He didn't invent these products. He was a designer and a salesman, not an engineer. But he had a phenomenal ability to intuit what people wanted, and to persuade them that by buying Apple they were buying into a life philosophy. 'Think different' was his company's slogan, which meant 'Think different and buy Apple.' It was a command the general public obeyed in droves.

'In the annals of modern American entrepreneur-heroes, few careers traced a more mythic sweep', said the *LA Times*. Adopted at birth, Jobs, whose natural father is from Syria, was brought up in California by a machinist and his accountant wife. He dropped out of Reed College after six months, to pursue electronics. A job with the games manufacturer Atari earned him the money to travel in India, where he joined an ashram and embraced drug-taking and Zen Buddhism. (Dropping LSD, he once said, was among the most important things he ever did.) Yet balanced with this New Age thinking was the will to succeed, and with the help of a computer wiz named Steve Wozniak he did so. The pair set up a company to market a user-friendly computer Wozniak had created.

Employees were afraid of getting stuck in the lift with him, in case they were unemployed by the time they got out.

They considered calling the firm Executek or Matrix Electronics, but opted for the jollier Apple Computers, inspired by Jobs's fruitarian diet at the time. There followed the release of a series of increasingly successful computers: Apples I, II and III, and finally the original Macintosh, which hit the high streets in 1984. By their late 20s, Wozniak and Jobs were multi-millionaires. However, the latter's Messianic self-belief (he once attended a party dressed as Jesus Christ) put people's backs up. He fell out with his CEO, the former president of PepsiCo – whom Jobs had lured to Apple by asking him: 'Do you want to spend the rest of your life selling sugar water, or do you want to come with me and change the world?' – and found himself ousted from his own company. 'At 30, I was out, and very publicly out,' he later recalled. 'What had been the focus of my entire adult life was gone, and it was devastating.' Yet instead of collapsing in defeat, Jobs pulled off one of the greatest comebacks in the history of business.

He not only founded NeXT, a manufacturer of business computers, but also purchased the computer graphics arm of George Lucas's production company, renamed it Pixar, and in 1995 broke box office records with the release of *Toy Story*. A year later Jobs's 'second coming' was complete when Apple Computers, by then in serious financial straits, acquired NeXT, thereby reinstating Jobs on the board of directors of his former firm. And under his guidance, Apple enjoyed a renaissance. Thanks to the huge success of the iPod, iPhone and the rest, in 2010 it overtook oil giant Exxon

– momentarily, at least – to become the most valuable company on the planet.

Word was that Jobs's management 'owed less to Zen Buddhism than to George Orwell', said the *Daily Telegraph*. He was controlling in all areas of his business, and volatile. Employees were afraid of getting stuck in the lift with him, in case they were unemployed by the time they got out. Yet Jobs also inspired people, said the *Wall Street Journal*, not only with his own success story, but with his 'gospel of self-fulfilment', which he preached at the elegantly produced launch events for his products. Clad in his habitual jeans and black turtleneck, the über-cool Jobs articulated his message of hope. 'Don't settle,' he would advise his cheering audience. 'Stay hungry. Find what you love.' His earnest optimism was all the more affecting in his last years, as he struggled with the pancreatic cancer that was slowly killing him.

For this, as for everything, Jobs had an answer. 'Remembering that you're going to die,' he once declared in an acclaimed speech at Stanford University, 'is the best way I know to avoid the trap of thinking you have something to lose. You are already naked. There is no reason not to follow your heart.'

Singer who pulled pints at the Rovers Return

BETTY DRIVER

1920-2011

For more than 40 years, Betty Driver was the 'nation's favourite barmaid', said *The Times*. As *Coronation Street*'s 'kindly' Betty Turpin, the actress appeared in some 2,800 episodes, dispensing wisdom and pints of ale from behind the bar of the Rovers Return. True to the genre, she had her ups and downs – an illegitimate son, the loss of a husband – but through it all, remained as dependable as the hotpot that was her culinary speciality. Yet her role in *Corrie* was actually Driver's second high-profile career. In an earlier incarnation, she had been a successful singer and forces sweetheart, with a Spitfire named after her by the RAF.

The daughter of a policeman, Betty Driver was born in 1920 and brought up in Manchester. She once remarked that if she could change anything about her life, she would have liked 'a bit more happiness'. She and her sister Freda had, she said, been robbed of their childhoods by their domineering mother, Nellie, who pushed Betty onto the stage at the age of 6; forced her to sing in a register that was too high for comfort (which eventually destroyed her voice); and spent the money that Betty earned, performing in variety shows, twice nightly, six days a week. In later life, Betty would recall that she and Freda (who would become her lifelong companion) received no birthday or Christmas presents, and no affection from their parents. 'We never got a kiss, only on New Year's Eve. That was the love for the year,' she said. 'It was a very sad little life, me and my sister.'

In her 20s, after suffering a nervous breakdown, Betty got away from her mother and made the transition to adult performer. For seven years she was the regular singer on the radio show *Henry Hall's Guest Night*; she entertained the troops with ENSA during the war; and had her own show, *A Date with Betty*. In the 1950s, she was briefly married to a womanising South African singer. He stole her money, and at around the same time, her voice collapsed. She turned to acting, and in 1964, auditioned for Hilda Ogden in *Coronation Street*, but was rejected for being too large. It was not until five years later – by which time she'd retired to run a pub with Freda – that she was offered the role of Betty, said the *Manchester Evening News*. Fellow cast members in the soap became firm friends – she was especially close to Julie Goodyear (Bet Lynch) – and provided her with the love she'd never known. The consequence, she once told an interviewer, was that for the last few years of life she was 'the happiest person in the world'.

> **She once remarked that if she could change anything about her life, she would have liked 'a bit more happiness'.**

The man
from Lipton tea

NOBLE FLEMING

1919-2012

Noble Fleming held one of the most powerful positions in the tea industry, said the *New York Times*. For nearly five decades, he visited plantations across the world – notably India, Sri Lanka and East Africa. There, impeccably dressed in a bespoke suit, he would carry out initial assessments of tea quality on behalf of the Thomas J. Lipton Company. Later, back at their tasting room in New Jersey, he would carry out a second test, sipping from a row of white bone-china tea cups, before spitting decorously into a chromium-plated cuspidor.

Born in Wales in 1919, Noble Fearnley Hutchinson Fleming grew up with a longing for travel intensified by reading the works of Rudyard Kipling. By hook or by crook he was determined to get out of 'rainy old London'. As luck would have it, the then-chief taster for Lipton was a family friend, who was able to secure an apprenticeship for the 19-year-old. After serving in the Royal Indian Navy during the Second World War, Noble was sent to the USA, where he quickly learnt that judging tea requires the same sort of expertise as judging wine. You had to know how the quality of leaves varied with such factors as the elevation of the plantation, its soil and its rainfall. At the tasting, you had to be aware of the importance of munching on an apple to cleanse the palate before each sip, of gauging the exact amount of purified water and skimmed milk that must be added to each cup, and much else besides.

Fleming retired in 1983, but not before passing on his secrets to apprentices: at Lipton, his legacy still lives on.

The most dangerous man in publishing

BARNEY ROSSET

1922-2012

Barney Rosset was once described as 'the most dangerous man in publishing'. He earned this accolade, said the *Daily Telegraph*, by being the first to introduce the US public to such controversial works of literature as William S. Burroughs's *Naked Lunch* (1962) and Henry Miller's *Tropic of Cancer* (1964). These visionary books, with their graphic descriptions of sex, were previously banned as 'obscene'. But Rosset, who made it his mission to test the limits of bourgeois morality, went to court again and again to defend his right to make them available to readers.

Born in Chicago, the son of a banker, Rosset had the kind of indulgent upbringing that allowed him to develop his alternative literary tastes. In 1951 he drew on his family's considerable wealth to buy a failing publishing imprint called Grove Press. Under this banner, and via its magazine offshoot, *Evergreen Review*, he introduced American readers to 'difficult' European authors, starting with Samuel Beckett, whose *Waiting for Godot* he purchased in 1953.

Publishing milestones over the years that followed included *Lady Chatterley's Lover* in 1959, *Last Exit to Brooklyn* in 1964, and *The Autobiography of Malcolm X* in 1965. A venture into movies (of the soft-porn variety) proved disastrous, however, and Rosset was forced to sell Grove Press in 1986. Although Beckett remained loyal, continuing to give him works to publish, his career was all but over. Nevertheless, said *The Guardian*, Rosset could take comfort in the thought that he had been 'the most influential avant-garde publisher of the twentieth century'.

The woman
who made even
Norman Tebbit quail

BERYL GOLDSMITH

1927-2012

In the 1980s, Tory MPs were said 'to be even more afraid of Beryl Goldsmith than they were of Mrs Thatcher', said the *Daily Telegraph*. For more than 30 years, she worked as Norman Tebbit's private secretary, 'yet she was far more than a parliamentary factotum'. A formidably hard worker, Goldsmith organised Tebbit's diary with terrifying efficiency, zealously guarded access to her boss and brusquely dismissed unwanted callers. 'There's a touch of steel about Beryl,' the Labour MP Austin Mitchell was once heard to mutter. 'And it's not in her corsets.' At times it seemed as if Tebbit himself was as much in awe of her as everyone else. In 2004, when invited to a drinks party by the then Tory leader, Michael Howard, Tebbit elected to go to Goldsmith's 77th birthday instead. 'If I stand up Beryl,' he explained, 'they'd find my dismembered body in the Thames.'

Born in 1927, Beryl Goldsmith joined the Wembley Young Conservatives while still at school and soon became their chairman. Had she been 20 years younger, said *The Independent*, she would have been a formidable Conservative MP. 'But in her day, the obstacles in the way of an unmarried woman with a Jewish surname were too great even for her to overcome.' In fact, Goldsmith was shortlisted for the Conservative candidacy at the

1972 Uxbridge by-election, but the party grandees, possibly intimidated by her manner, plumped for someone else. Instead, Goldsmith threw herself into becoming Tebbit's loyal, yet far from docile secretary. In many ways, she showed an even greater relish for sticking the boot in than her boss. An assiduous letter-writer to newspapers, Goldsmith railed against a broad range of targets, any manifestation of political correctness in particular. She was also a keen advocate of the return of capital punishment for terrorists – she had been in Brighton when an IRA bomb exploded, leaving Tebbit's wife Margaret, permanently disabled.

It was Goldsmith's diatribes against Princess Diana that caused the most controversy, however. 'Why the lady continues to be regarded as hardly less than saintly by the British press remains one of life's great mysteries,' she wrote in 1993 in a letter to the London *Evening Standard* upbraiding Diana for spoiling her children. A poll in the next day's *Daily Mirror* showed that 81 per cent of readers agreed with her. But Goldsmith's fury was far from spent. Three years on, in a letter to the *Daily Telegraph*, she called Diana 'the most overrated, over-publicised, self-indulgent 'royal' since Edward VIII.

'If I stand up Beryl,' Tebbit explained, 'they'd find my dismembered body in the Thames.'

When will her blinkered fan club come down to Earth?' Tebbit was always at pains to stress what a kind and thoughtful person Goldsmith was, but she herself was under no illusions about how most people saw her. 'They wouldn't touch me with a barge pole,' she said.

Orgasmic disco diva who renounced her raunchy past

DONNA SUMMER

1948-2012

When the producer Brian Eno first heard Donna Summer's six-minute disco song 'I Feel Love' in 1977, he declared: 'I have heard the sound of the future!' And so it proved, said Neil McCormick in the *Daily Telegraph*. Although the reign of disco, with Summer as its queen, was brief, its legacy – the dominance of synthetic pop over guitar-driven rock in the charts – is still with us. Yet for many people, Summer is remembered as much for sex as for synthesizers. Her sultry 'Love To Love You Baby' (1975) caused a scandal thanks to the orgasmic moans that interspersed her singing. A rumour spread, almost certainly put about by her record company, that the singer achieved ecstasy 22 times during the recording of the song.

Summer was an 'unlikely standardbearer' for liberated sexuality, said *The Independent*. The daughter of a Boston minister, she sang in the local church, prompting the congregation to weep at the purity of her voice, or so she later claimed. Convinced that God intended her to be famous, she quit school and joined a touring production of the musical *Hair*. This took her to Germany, where she was briefly married to an actor, Helmut Sommer, from whom she adapted her stage name. Then she met Giorgio Moroder, who produced her debut album, *Lady Of The Night* (1974). When

Summer came to him with the lyrics for 'Love To Love You Baby', she jokily suggested doing a version with lots of sexy moaning. Moroder eagerly agreed, and the result became a huge international hit.

The mix of Moroder's computer rhythms and Summer's lubricious vocals became the blueprint for disco, said the *Daily Telegraph*. By the late 1970s, thanks to hits such as 'Last Dance' (1978) and 'No More Tears (Enough Is Enough)' (1979), a duet with Barbra Streisand, she had become the world's bestselling female singer. But there were tales of drug abuse, and in the early 1980s Summer, never at ease with her image as 'the first lady of lust', suffered a breakdown. When she re-emerged, it was as a born-again Christian, said *The Guardian*. She 'renounced her raunchy past' and refused to sing her more explicit hits such as 'Love To Love You Baby' (whose moans, she vehemently insisted, had not been real).

> **A rumour spread that the singer achieved ecstasy 22 times during the recording of 'Love To Love You Baby'.**

After the demise of disco, the singer developed a substantial gay following, scoring hits with 'State Of Independence' in 1982 and 'She Works Hard For The Money' in 1983. A year later, though, she alienated her new fans by claiming Aids was a punishment from God. Later, though, she managed to reconcile her religious scruples with her commercial instincts and started singing 'Love To Love You Baby' again. It was the song that 'first brought me success', Summer declared, and God 'must have known that would happen'. She died of lung cancer, caused, she believed, by carcinogenic particles released by the collapse of the World Trade Centre.

The inventor of the TV remote control

EUGENE POLLEY

1915-2012

He may not be up there with Einstein in the pantheon of science, said *The Independent*. 'But couch potatoes everywhere should give thanks to Eugene Polley.' For the American inventor was the brains behind the first ever cordless TV remote control. 'Just think!' proclaimed an advert for his gun-shaped gadget in 1955. 'Without budging from your easy chair you can turn your New Zenith Flash-Matic set on, off, or change channels. Absolutely harmless to humans…' The Flash-Matic, which worked by beaming light at photo-receivers in each of the TV's corners (one corner for on, one for off, etc), had its problems, however: if sunlight fell on the screen, the TV got confused, and Polley's invention was duly replaced by a device which used sound waves.

The son of a Chicago bootlegger, Polley couldn't afford to finish school. Instead he joined Zenith Electronics as a stock boy and worked his way up to engineer. In the early 1950s his boss became concerned that the rise of adverts would put people off watching TV, and asked his brightest minds to come up with a way for viewers to mute the screen without rising from their chairs. The first solution was the Lazy Bones, which made use of a cumbersome cord. Then there was Polley's Flash-Matic, which sold 30,000 units in its first year. It was superseded by the Space Command, invented by another employee, Robert Adler. This wasn't perfect either: the sound, inaudible to humans, set dogs howling. But it became the basis for the standard remote until the 1980s, when infra-red devices took over.

In his later career, Polley worked on the push-button car radio for the company, and an early version of DVDs. He came to feel that he hadn't received due recognition and, lacking 'an internal mute button', was forever telling people as much, said the *New York Times*. 'The flush toilet may have been the most civilised invention ever devised,' he once declared, 'but the remote control is the next most important.'

'The flush toilet may have been the most civilised invention ever devised, but the remote control is the next most important.'

The monocled eccentric who gazed at the stars

SIR PATRICK MOORE

1923-2012

It's rare for any field of science to be inextricably linked to one individual, said the *Daily Telegraph*. And yet for generations of TV viewers, 'Sir Patrick Moore was astronomy.' From the first episode in 1957 until his death at 89, he presented the BBC's *The Sky at Night* every month, which earned him a record for the longest continuous stint at the helm of a TV show. Moore's success in the role owed much to his deep knowledge of his subject, but also to his eccentric persona.

With his monocle, wild hair and oversized suits (which fitted him, one critic noted, 'as a hangar fits a VC10'), he was the epitome of the mad professor, delivering his verdicts with the staccato urgency of a machine gun, and often concluding with the violent admission: 'We just... don't... know.' On one occasion, he appeared dressed as a Martian, to make the point that aliens might exist in environments dissimilar from Earth's. 'I am surprised to see you all,' he declared with his characteristic lisp on the Rs. 'I had thought your thick atmosphere and excessive water would have prevented life from evolving here.' On another, the presenter, whose political views were extremely right-wing, illustrated the vastness of space by pronouncing that: 'Somewhere in the universe there could be a complete carbon copy of Anthony Wedgwood Benn – although I sincerely hope not.'

Moore was born in London, the son of a soldier. Schooled at home owing to a heart problem, he first conceived a love for astronomy aged 6, after stumbling on a Victorian guide to the solar system. His mother gave him a telescope and he was hooked, publishing his first scientific paper at 13, a study of a lunar crater. When war broke out, Moore was so keen to join up he persuaded a friend to impersonate him at the medical. His heart condition thus concealed, he served in the RAF until 1947. There followed five years as a prep school master; then, in 1953, he determined to become a writer. His first book was his *Guide to the Moon*, which proved a great success.

In 1957, when the BBC was looking for a sceptical, well-informed presenter for a sensationalistic programme on alien life, they decided to give Moore a try-out. He proved a natural. The show, *The Sky at Night*, ran and ran (it had the good fortune to coincide with the space race between Russia and the USA). Yet Moore was far more than just a TV personality, said *The Times*. His scholarship was impeccable. The Russians used his lunar research, for instance, when analysing the photos of the far side of the Moon taken by Lunik 3 in 1959. After Neil Armstrong took his 'small step for man' a decade later, Moore was the obvious choice to interview him for the BBC about the experience.

> **'Somewhere in the universe there could be a complete carbon copy of Anthony Wedgwood Benn – although I sincerely hope not.'**

His best book was 1970's *Atlas of the Universe* – still seen as one of the best general guides – yet this was just a fraction of his extraordinarily prolific output. The 100 books he wrote, or had a hand in writing, included *Can You Speak Venusian?* and *Space Travel for the Under Tens*, as well as the idiosyncratic *Bureaucrats: How To Annoy Them* (1982). An example of the advice in this was to spread a thin layer of candle-wax over the part of any form titled 'For official use only'. This would prevent the recipient from writing anything and probably drive him mad – a ploy that was particularly useful, the author noted, when dealing with the Inland Revenue.

Moore was a genuine eccentric, said *The Guardian*. Though far from politically correct – he once described Enoch Powell as 'Britain's most dangerous left-winger' – he was no right-wing stereotype: he deplored fox-hunting, the invasion of Iraq, and people who had quit smoking. He played the xylophone well and golf badly, and was a useful spin bowler on the cricket pitch. His definition of happiness, he once revealed, was 'bowling to a nervous batsman on a sticky wicket'.

Moore, who was knighted in 2001, was a lifelong bachelor. (He had been engaged, but his fiancée had been killed during the war.) He didn't fear death, since he didn't view it as the end. 'We go on to the next stage,' he said. 'I shall be interested to see what it is. Who knows? It might be somewhere I can learn to bat decently.'

The actor who 'played nice' and really was nice

RICHARD BRIERS

1934-2013

'There are worse fates, I suppose, than being perennially associated with a feel-good 1970s sitcom,' said Michael Billington in *The Guardian*. Yet it 'does a disservice' to Richard Briers's range as an actor that he will be remembered largely for his turn as the genial Tom Good of *The Good Life* (1975–1978), struggling for self-sufficiency in suburban Surbiton, alongside a scrumptious Felicity Kendal. A master of light comedy, when on stage Briers was 'a far more potent presence' than his TV persona suggested. This was a man, after all, who, in addition to Ayckbourn and Gray, played Chekhov and Shakespeare – though by his own admission his Hamlet was most notable for his speed of delivery. (One critic likened his performance to 'a demented typewriter'.) Relishing the verdict, Briers liked to say that his unique interpretation of the Dane enabled audiences to make it to the pub before closing time. In later life, he delivered a mercurial Lear, a moving Bottom, and a suitably neurotic Uncle Vanya. Yet he was never dismissive of comedy, describing getting a laugh as 'the best thing in the world'.

Briers was born in south London, the son of a bookmaker. The family lived over a cinema, said the *Daily Mirror*, and young Richard would listen to Humphrey Bogart's voice echoing into the street, and dream of being a star. A flop at school, he worked as a filing clerk before doing national service in the RAF. It was here where he began performing in amateur dramatics, though he wasn't an instant success. 'I was highly strung and they said I spoke too fast and no one could understand a word,' he recalled. Yet his nervous energy proved a boon after he was accepted into Rada and learnt to harness it. 'You're a great farceur,' Noël Coward once told him in his resonant tones, 'because you never, ever hang around.'

Briers's career began at the Liverpool Playhouse (where he met his wife, Ann, who was stage manager). His West End debut came in 1959 in Lionel Hale's *Gilt and Gingerbread*; his TV debut followed two years later, opposite Prunella Scales in *Marriage Lines*, about a couple adjusting to married life.

After that he was never short of offers, but the show that made his name was *The Good Life*, which was written with Briers in mind and is regularly voted one of the best-loved TV comedies of all time. 'Playing nice' is a really hard thing to pull off, said James Delingpole in the *Daily Telegraph*. Yet Briers somehow made 'boundless innocence and endless enthusiasm seem not like signs of incipient idiocy but qualities to which we should all aspire'. As John Gielgud once remarked: 'People don't realise how good an actor Dickie Briers really is.'

Briers liked to say that his unique interpretation of the Dane enabled audiences to make it to the pub before closing time.

Kenneth Branagh did. He went on to cast Briers in nine of his movies, sparking 'a glorious second coming' in Briers's career, said Billington. He was Bardolph in *Henry V* (1989), Leonato in *Much Ado about Nothing* (1993), and the following year acted alongside Robert De Niro in Branagh's *Frankenstein*. The latter was not a success, said *BBC News Online*, not least because the American's earnest Method approach did not gel with Briers's 'no-nonsense style' of learning the lines and saying them at the appropriate moment. Briers recalled on *Desert Island Discs* how at one point during filming, he had summoned the monster (played by De Niro) with the words: 'I know you're there, come in, come in.' Nothing happened. 'Don't be a fool,' Branagh had whispered in

Briers's ear. 'He's not like you. You've got to make him feel he must come in.' But Briers wasn't having any of it. 'I've read the script. I say: "Come in", and he comes in.' The film did not impress Branagh, the critics or the public.

More recently, the actor reached a new audience playing the dotty laird in TV's *Monarch of the Glen*. He was also a keen golfer and gardener but had to cut down on both after contracting emphysema from heavy smoking: Briers estimated he had got through half a million cigarettes over the years. After his death, friends and colleagues lined up to pay tribute to his talent and his fundamental good-naturedness. 'When someone dies,' Penelope Keith observed, 'people tend to eulogise them, and you always wonder if they could have been so nice. Richard was.'

A life spent in
the 'downstairs'
of grand houses

FLORENCE WADLOW

1912-2013

Anyone who has watched *Downton Abbey*, said the *Los Angeles Times*, must wonder what it would really have been like to be a servant in one of England's grand houses. And an excellent person to have asked would have been Florence Wadlow, who spent a life in service, and declared of the TV show: 'They have got it wrong. They should have talked to people like me.' For a start, the gulf between 'upstairs' and 'downstairs' was even greater than depicted in the TV series. During the entire year she spent at Hatfield House she only saw her employer, the 4th Marquess of Salisbury, during chapel services. And she never spoke to him. It was the same story at Blickling Hall in Norfolk, where for three years she worked as head cook – every day from 7am until 10pm: there she only clapped eyes on the 11th Marquess of Lothian on two occasions. 'I think he was a nice sort of gentleman,' Wadlow conjectured. 'But they weren't brought up to be friendly with the staff, were they?'

Born Florence Copeland, the daughter of a Billingsgate fish porter, she took her first job as a kitchen maid when she was 16. There was another Florence on the staff, so she was known as 'Ena': a shortening of her middle name, Georgina. At Hatfield, where the same problem arose, she was rechristened 'Jean'. The first time she ever used a fridge was at Blickling in 1936, after being promoted to head cook. 'I think his Lordship [bought the fridge because he] was a teetotaller,' she explained, 'and he loved orange juice to drink, and of course that had to be fresh oranges.' She would suggest menus to the housekeeper, who discussed them with Lord Lothian. Only once did 'Jean' enter the dining room: Queen Mary was coming for dinner and the staff were permitted to view the table settings.

After Lord Lothian was appointed ambassador to Washington, Florence worked for the Bulwer-Long family in nearby Heydon, where she met her future husband, Robert Wadlow, who worked at a lime-kiln: they had two children. Despite its hardships, Florence looked back on her career with affection, said the *Daily Telegraph*. 'Somebody asked me once if living in a big house, and seeing all the marvellous furniture and silver and everything they had, was I ever envious?' she once mused. 'I never was, really. I was always very interested but I can't remember ever wanting it.'

> **'I never was envious, really. I was always very interested but I can't remember ever wanting it.'**

The life and times of Britain's Iron Lady

MARGARET THATCHER

1925-2013

Margaret Thatcher was a 'political phenomenon', said *The Guardian*. The first woman to lead a major Western power, she was Britain's longest-serving prime minister for 150 years, and the 'most dominant and most divisive figure in British politics in the second half of the twentieth century'. She presided over the transformation of her own country, and also strode the world stage: she was a star in the USA, a heroine in many former Eastern bloc countries, and 'a point of reference for politicians in France, Germany, Italy and Spain'. By the time she left office, the principles known as Thatcherism – the belief that economic freedom and individual liberty are interdependent, that personal responsibility and hard work are the only ways to national prosperity – had won disciples across the world, said the *International Herald Tribune*. During her 11 years in office, she had made legions of enemies, too. Yet when the end came, it wasn't the Labour Party, or union might, that brought her down, but colleagues in her own party.

The grocer's daughter from Grantham grew up in a flat above the shop that had neither hot running water nor an inside lavatory. Yet young Margaret and her sister Muriel were always immaculately turned out, and were taught the virtues of hard work, self-reliance and thrift by their

Methodist father, alderman Alfred Roberts. Margaret's self-confidence was evident early on: aged 9, on accepting a prize at school, she told a teacher: 'I wasn't lucky, I deserved it.' She won a scholarship to Kesteven & Grantham Girls' School, and then studied chemistry at Somerville College, Oxford, where she became the first female president of the Oxford University Conservative Association. On graduating with a second, she worked as a chemist while trying to get selected for the Kent seat of Dartford, a Labour stronghold. Many were appalled by the prospect of a 25-year-old woman as their candidate, yet she stood in both 1950 and 1951.

After one meeting, she was given a lift home by a wealthy businessman and divorcee ten years her senior, Denis Thatcher. They were married in 1951, and in 1953 had twins – Mark and Carol. Denis would provide her with financial stability, and invaluable emotional support. (As consort, he once observed, his role was to be 'always present, never there'.) But Mrs Thatcher did not see herself in the role of full-time wife and mother. Almost immediately, she hired a nanny, and set about studying law. She was called to the Bar in 1954, yet politics still exerted an allure, and in 1959 she stood for and won the rock-solid Conservative seat of Finchley. In 1970, she was appointed education minister by Edward Heath. In that role, she presided (unwillingly) over the creation of hundreds of comprehensive schools, and became a hate figure for removing free milk from schoolchildren over 7. The controversy – which won her the nickname Milk Snatcher and a reputation for ruthlessness she never shed – caused maximum 'odium' for minimum gain, she later admitted. It was a useful lesson. She emerged tougher, said the *Daily Telegraph*, and better equipped to face down hostility.

Although she did not speak out against Heath's economic policies, Thatcher was growing increasingly convinced that Britain should put its trust in free-market economics, said *The Times*. She found an ally in Keith Joseph, who opened her eyes to Milton Friedman's monetarist views. In 1974, following a second Conservative defeat, Joseph was touted as a possible challenger to Heath. But an ill-judged speech about teenage pregnancies put paid to that, and Thatcher ended up as the focus for anti-Heath resentment, said Peter Riddell, in the same paper. Much aided by her campaign manager, Airey Neave (who was later murdered by the Irish National Liberation Army), she defeated first Heath and then several of the party's 'big beasts' in a leadership ballot in 1975. Although she and Heath didn't exchange a civil word for the next 20 years, some of the defeated contestants agreed to work with her, including Geoffrey Howe and Willie Whitelaw, who would become one of her most trusted lieutenants ('Everyone needs a Willie,' she once observed).

In opposition, Mrs Thatcher revealed a populist touch, said Andy McSmith in *The Independent*. She warned that Britain's white population feared being 'swamped' by immigrants, a comment that enraged the Left, but won her valuable working-class votes. She also startled and annoyed the Soviet authorities – accustomed to détente – by robustly attacking communism in 1976 (it was this speech that won her her treasured 'Iron Lady' epithet). But there was little in her 1979 manifesto to suggest the earthquake to come: it contained scant mention of taking on the unions, cutting public services, privatisation or reducing income tax. Rather than making promises, she sought to discredit Labour with the Saatchi campaign 'Labour isn't working'. It was a sensible approach, because the public had not warmed to Mrs Thatcher: her popularity lagged six points behind Jim Callaghan's, even when her party had a 14-point lead. In 1979, it was the Conservatives, not Thatcher, that were elected, aided by the disunity within the opposition (the Lib-Lab coalition was in tatters), and an electorate exhausted and demoralised by the crippling public sector strikes of the Winter of Discontent. On the steps of Downing Street, she famously quoted St Francis of Assisi, with a pledge to bring harmony to a troubled nation.

The new government faced almighty challenges, said the *Wall Street Journal*. Inflation and unemployment were rising, and the unions maintained their grip on industry. Her 'economic medicine' was very painful, yet she resisted calls for a softer line. In 1980, she told a Tory conference: 'To those waiting for the favourite media catchphrase, "the U-turn", I have only one thing to say: You turn if you want to. The lady's not for turning.' Unemployment rose to above three million (up from 1.4 million in 1979) and manufacturing output fell. Bankruptcies soared. Meanwhile, the top rate of income tax was reduced from 83 per cent to 60 per cent while VAT was doubled, to 15 per cent. Class and racial tensions simmered, before exploding, in the summer of 1981, into riots in Brixton, Toxteth and Moss Side.

By then, Thatcher was the most unpopular PM since polling began, said Max Hastings in the *Daily Mail*, and she seemed destined to be ousted. 'One man did more than any other to transform her fortunes –

General Galtieri', the Argentinian dictator who launched the invasion of the Falklands. Thatcher's response, to send a taskforce to recapture the islands, was decisive, and risky: 'many anticipated its failure'. But Britain triumphed. This victory 'transformed her from Milk Snatcher into Maggie the warrior queen'. In July 1982, she told an audience: 'We have ceased to be a nation in retreat. We have instead new-found confidence – born in the economic battles at home and tested and found true 8,000 miles away.'

Buoyed by military success, and aided by better economic figures and a divided opposition, she romped to victory in the 1983 election. Thus fortified, she took on what she perceived as a new enemy – the 'enemy within', as she controversially described it: Arthur Scargill and the National Union of Mineworkers. After a bruising, year-long showdown, in which police fought running battles with striking miners, the union was routed, said *The Guardian*. There followed mass closures. Thatcher's steely resolve would again be demonstrated at the Tory conference of 1984. Loathed by the IRA for her refusal to intervene in the hunger strikes that killed Bobby Sands, she became the target of an assassination attempt. Five people were killed in the bomb attack on the Grand Hotel in Brighton, and many others injured. Later that day, she delivered her speech as planned, making it clear that it was 'business as usual'. Yet a year later, she signed the Anglo-Irish Agreement, which allowed Dublin a role in Northern Ireland's affairs.

On the steps of Downing Street, she famously quoted St Francis of Assisi, with a pledge to bring harmony to a troubled nation.

On the economic front, she continued in her mission to 'roll back the state', said the *Wall Street Journal*. Council houses were sold off, boosting home ownership, but leaving an 'enduring void' in the provision of housing for the poor; and everything from BT to the water companies was privatised, transforming life in a country where it could take months to get a phone connected, and the TV listings were a state secret. Free enterprise flourished and the City was deregulated. Meanwhile, on the foreign stage, she and Ronald Reagan had identified Mikhail Gorbachev as the man to help halt the arms race, said the *New York Times*. Thatcher –

the leader whose relentless hostility to the Soviet Union, and resistance to disarmament, had stoked fears of nuclear Armageddon – helped end the Cold War.

Yet at home, discontent was growing. To her enemies, she was a woman who railed against the evils of poverty but cared nothing about the plight of the poor. But she would not compromise. She was, she liked to say, not interested in consensus: she was a 'conviction politician'. Though she was kind to junior staff (stories of her dragging ministers into kitchens to thank the cooks, or consoling clumsy waitresses, are legion), and could be maternal (Ferdinand Mount recalls her insisting on interrupting a meeting to fetch him some cough medicine), her manner was often brisk, argumentative and even dictatorial. 'There's not much point being a weak and floppy thing in a chair, is there,' she once announced. On another occasion, said Hastings, she opened a ministerial meeting by slamming her handbag down on the table and declaring: 'Well, I haven't much time today – only enough time to explode and have my way!' But while her appetite for conflict and her imperious manner ('No! No! No!') entranced some, it alienated many.

'To those waiting for the favourite media catchphrase, "the U-turn", I have only one thing to say: You turn if you want to. The lady's not for turning.'

In her third term, her administration began to unravel over the hated 'poll tax' and her anti-Europe stance. Early on, her 'handbag-swinging negotiating style' in Brussels had paid dividends, said *The Independent*, when, for instance, she secured a reduction in the UK's contribution to the EC budget. But her distrust of Europe would be her undoing. In 1989, a bitter internal row over the Exchange Rate Mechanism led to chancellor Nigel Lawson's resignation. Weeks later, Anthony Meyer mounted a leadership challenge and won enough votes to show that there was a real discontent in the party. But it was Geoffrey Howe – the last remaining member of the 1979 line-up – who delivered the final blow when, in November 1990, he too stepped down, and used his resignation speech to urge his party to push for change. A few days later, Michael Heseltine stood against her – and the unthinkable happened: she failed to win outright in the first ballot.

In retirement, Thatcher travelled the speaking circuit, sat in the House of Lords, and found herself feted by New Labour (the creation of which, she once said, was her greatest achievement). Following Denis's death in 2003, she withdrew from public life. Later, it became clear that her mind was failing her. A devoted team looked after her in her five-storey house in Belgravia, until – early in 2013 – she moved into a suite at the Ritz.

Mrs Thatcher, the wife and mother

From the beginning of her premiership, Thatcher liked to portray herself as a housewifely figure. She would claim that managing the economy required the same skills as running a household, and for every photograph of her driving a tank, there was another of her pottering around a food factory in a hairnet. Yet even her close friends would admit that this Boudicca in a power suit was a better politician than a mother, said Francis Elliott in *The Times*. Though she patently cared for her two children, politics was her preoccupation. The twins were sent to boarding school before the age of 10, and Carol Thatcher has claimed that she did not miss her mother because she had never seen much of her. But relations with Carol were often fraught, said the *Daily Mail*. The more approachable of the twins, she made a more favourable impression on the public than her brother, but it was Mark who was allegedly their mother's favourite. Colleagues reported that her voice softened when his name was mentioned, and when he went missing in the Sahara in 1982, she was paralysed by worry, and shed tears in public. 'We are a grandmother,' she proudly proclaimed when he had his first child.

By the time she entered Downing Street, the children were grown up, and it was the ever-loyal Denis who provided her with 'emotional guy ropes'. After a fraught day at Downing Street, he would be waiting upstairs with a glass of whisky, shrewd counsel and a consoling ear. 'He's about as much good as a one-legged man in an arse-kicking competition,' he'd say, of whichever of her rivals had upset her. She was devastated by his death in 2003, by which time both her children were living abroad. In old age, she acknowledged the sacrifices she had made to pursue her career. She wished she saw more of her children, she said. But 'you can't have everything. It has been the greatest privilege being prime minister of my country… I can't regret.'

Darkly imaginative novelist hailed as 'two of our best authors'

IAIN BANKS

1954-2013

When Iain Banks's debut novel, *The Wasp Factory*, appeared in 1984, it met a torrent of abuse. One reviewer found it 'repulsive'; another 'silly' and 'sadistic'; a third referred to it simply as 'a work of unparalleled depravity'. Sensing an opportunity, its publisher at Macmillan put the scabrous comments on the paperback's cover. It duly became a bestseller. Banks never looked back. Producing a book a year, he displayed a knack for winning artistic acclaim while selling a great many copies. Not only that, he also enjoyed success as a writer of sci-fi under the name Iain M. Banks. (His fans liked to say that he was 'two of our best authors'.) Banks later came to regret the division of his work into two distinct genres, said the *Daily Telegraph*. All his books share a black sense of humour, Left-leaning politics and a penchant for shock tactics. A good example of the latter is the opening sentence of his 1992 novel *The Crow Road*: 'It was the day my grandmother exploded.'

Banks was born in Fife, the son of an Admiralty officer. After studying English, psychology and philosophy at Stirling University, he took a range of jobs – clerk, dustman, hospital porter, to name but a few – while in his spare time pursuing his ambition to be a writer. It was ten years before he struck gold with *The Wasp Factory*, the twisted tale of a 16-year-old named Frank living in near-isolation on the coast of Scotland, who gets a kick out of torturing animals. In 1987 he published his first sci-fi book, *Consider Phlebas*, which conjured up a world controlled by The Culture, a network of benign but all-powerful machines with liberal sensibilities similar to the author's own. It was the first of a series in this vein. Banks alternated these with works with more familiar settings: novels such as *Espedair Street* of 1987 – hailed as one of the best novels about rock music – and *The Crow Road*. In the case of each book he followed a strict regimen: three months working out the plot as he went hill-walking, three months writing (observing office hours), then six months off.

Latterly, however, his output had slowed. Critics felt that some of his later novels, such as *Dead Air* (2002), lacked focus, said *The Guardian*, and served too much as pulpits for his astringent political views. (When Tony Blair invaded Iraq, Banks tore up his passport and sent it to him. On the day his neighbour Gordon Brown took over as PM, he applied for a replacement.) Yet his works continued to sell, and his earlier books, particularly *The Wasp Factory*, acquired classic status. He began to crop up in lists of the best British authors of the twentieth century.

Banks always said that he had few professional regrets, but that he did regret the pain he had caused to others through selfishness.

As his fame grew, the bearded, leather-jacketed novelist discovered that the publishing industry was filled, as he ruefully put it, with 'young, smart, attractive women'. His first marriage collapsed under the strain of his affairs. Banks always said that he had few professional regrets, but that he did regret the pain he had caused to others through selfishness. Earlier this year, he revealed online that he was 'officially Very Poorly' with inoperable gall-bladder cancer. He promptly proposed to his girlfriend Adele, asking her with mordant wit if she would consent to be his widow. To the prospect of death he brought the common sense that had characterised his writing, said *The Scotsman*. He relished the 'little immortality' of literature, he said, but predicted his own would last no more than a few decades.

The modest farmer's son who became Ireland's Ted Hughes

SEAMUS HEANEY

1939-2013

'By his death, the veil of poetry is rent and the walls of learning broken.' Seamus Heaney's tribute to his fellow poet Ted Hughes could equally well have applied to himself, said *The Times*. A literary titan, who won the Nobel Prize in Literature in 1995 (an experience he likened to being hit by a 'mostly benign avalanche'), he was at one point responsible for an astonishing two-thirds of poetry sales in the UK. This level of success seemed to rile some of the critics. The poems of 'famous Seamus' were too easy, they said (as if clarity were a vice); and in his native Ulster, critics on both sides of the sectarian divide attacked what they saw as his 'culpable ambiguity' on the Irish question. In the circumstances, it's remarkable that he went on producing his volumes of sage and sonorously grounded verse (each of which was a literary event on publication) without losing his cool. That refusal to take himself too seriously was characteristic of the man, said Lachlan Mackinnon in the *Sunday Telegraph*. 'One of my favourite memories is of the way he reacted when a stranger walking his dog waved at him as we made our way out of a Dublin graveyard. "Thanks for the poetry!" cried the stranger. With a characteristic twinkle in his eye, Seamus waved back. Then, out of the corner of his mouth, he turned to me and murmured: "I hire them.'"

Heaney was raised on a farm in County Derry. He was brought up to respect a man who could wield a spade, yet after taking a first in English at Queen's University, Belfast, realised that he himself wasn't cut out to be a farmer. As he wrote in the poem *Digging*: 'Between my finger and my thumb / The squat pen rests. / I'll dig with it.' In the early 1960s an editor at Faber spotted some of his poetry in the *New Statesman* and wrote asking for a manuscript. It was like receiving 'a letter from God', Heaney said. His first collection, *Death of a Naturalist*, won instant acclaim when it appeared in 1966. Its facility for rich rustic imagery – whether it was the mould on blackberries or bullfrogs squatting like 'mud grenades' – led some to see him as an Irish Ted Hughes. (He was once dubbed 'the laureate of the root vegetable'.) His stature grew with each new volume, culminating in 1975 in what many see as his finest work, *North*. Inspired by P.V. Glob's book *The Bog People*, it was full of allusions to the Troubles. Heaney wasn't overtly political, said the *Daily Telegraph*, but there was little doubt of his allegiance. Finding himself included in an anthology of 'British' verse, he wrote to the editors: 'My passport's green / No glass of ours was ever raised / To toast the Queen.'

'Spared the dissipation of Dylan Thomas, the emotional isolation of Philip Larkin or the personal turmoil of Hughes, Heaney led a rather tame and domestically stable life,' said the *Washington Post*. The wildest thing about him, it was once noted, was his shock of white hair. He doted on his wife and muse, Marie, and when not fulfilling lecturing duties at Harvard in the 1980s, or Oxford, where he served as Professor of Poetry in the 1990s, devoted himself quietly to his art. His fine translation of *Beowulf* in 1999 transformed that dour tale into an unlikely bestseller. He was unflaggingly kind to others – the novelist Andrew O'Hagan used to play a parlour game, which he never won, trying to get Heaney to be harsh about someone – and for all the accolades, his modesty never failed him. Asked to cite a line from his poetry that might serve as his epitaph, he chose – from his translation of Oedipus at Colonus (2004) – the words spoken by the messenger of the old king: 'Wherever that man went, he went gratefully.' And his own last words were sent in a text message to his wife minutes before he died. '*Noli timere*.' Do not be afraid.

The heroin addict who changed the face of rock

LOU REED

1942-2013

The music producer Brian Eno once remarked that not many people bought the first album by The Velvet Underground, but that those who did formed a band. Certainly, no rock group has ever been so unsuccessful in its day yet had such a huge influence, said Neil McCormick in the *Daily Telegraph*. Every rock star who has favoured noise, experimentalism and wearing dark glasses at night over ordinary commercial criteria owes a debt to the Velvets, and above all to their frontman Lou Reed.

His discography includes 'Heroin' (a paean to drug abuse); 'I'm Waiting For The Man' (ditto); 'Venus In Furs' (about sado-masochistic love); and his solo single 'Walk on the Wild Side' (about gay prostitution). Hardly surprising, you might think, that these songs didn't fly off the shelves – although in fact the last one did. It was his only top ten UK hit, and only then, no doubt, because most people at the time had no idea what 'giving head' meant.

Lewis Allan Reed was brought up on Long Island, the son of an accountant. In his teens, he was subjected to electroconvulsive therapy (ECT) to 'cure' him of his homosexual tendencies. The experience left him profoundly emotionally damaged, said Nick Hasted in *The Independent*.

After studying English and philosophy at Syracuse University, where he immersed himself in transgressive literature, he moved to New York and wrote pop songs for a record label. Yet what he really wanted, said Hasted, was to express his rage, wielding his guitar like an ECT treatment directed at 'those who, similarly afflicted, needed such musical shock therapy'.

He got the chance after teaming up with a Welshman with a talent for the electric viola called John Cale. His wailing instrument, combined with Reed's affectless New York drawl, formed the core of the new band they founded, The Velvet Underground. The brutality of the music, so out of keeping with the flower-power era, attracted the admiration of Andy Warhol, who produced their first album, *The Velvet Underground & Nico* (1967). Sadly, his patronage didn't convert into sales. After the release of their second album, *White Light/White Heat* (1968), Cale fell out with Reed – the tensions exacerbated by Reed's drug use – and quit the band.

> **His definition of misery, Reed said, was 'being interviewed by an English journalist'.**

The next two albums, on which Reed opted for a lighter tone, are less revered by fans, despite containing such gems as the wistful 'Pale Blue Eyes' and raucous 'Sweet Jane'. Then the band split. Reed disappeared, only re-emerging two years later in London. (It transpired that he had been working for his father for $40 a week.) He then embarked on a solo career, and his second album gave him his first taste of fame. Produced by David Bowie, *Transformer* (1972) contained 'Walk on the Wild Side' and the deceptively simple 'Perfect Day'.

Reed was on the brink of stardom, so what did he do? He released *Berlin*, an album of fraught, suicidal angst. The critics panned it (though many later changed their minds), inflicting on the singer the second major trauma of his life. It set the pattern for the rest of his career: an album of relative accessibility, followed by the wilfully obscure. The nadir was *Metal Machine Music* (1975), consisting almost entirely of feedback. But woe betide any critic who dared question his decisions, especially if he were English, said Ludovic Hunter-Tilney in the *Financial Times*. (His definition of misery, Reed said, was 'being interviewed by an English journalist'.)

In the 1980s he cleaned up his act, disavowing drugs, booze and bisexual promiscuity, and instead living healthily and practising the martial art t'ai chi. He could still be thoroughly unpleasant in interviews, but achieved a measure of contentment in later life with his third wife, Laurie Anderson. There were acclaimed albums, too, such as *New York* (1989) and *Magic and Loss* (1992).

The critics said his glory years were behind him, but Reed feigned indifference to critical opinion. 'I'm told I'm a parody of myself, but who better to parody?' he demanded to know. 'I can do Lou Reed better than most people, and a lot of people try.'

The voice that helped us make sense of the Thatcher years

JOHN COLE

1927-2013

'The coat, the accent, and, above all, the insight. All combined to make the inimitable John Cole,' said Nick Robinson on *BBC News Online*. When he took over as the BBC's political editor in 1981, there were some who thought him ill-suited to the role. His herringbone overcoat, which he wore whenever addressing the cameras on a cold night outside Westminster, was deeply unfashionable. His thick Belfast brogue required a little tuning-in: *Private Eye* mocked him in its 'Hondootedly' column, which invariably had Cole addressing the then PM with the words: 'Hondootedly, Mossis T'atcher.' For all that, he won the trust of the public with his blend of warmth and wit, integrity and expertise, and it was his voice they relied on to make 'sense of the drama and the upheaval of the Thatcher years; of the rise of Major and the fall of Foot and Kinnock'.

John Morrison Cole was born into a Protestant family in northern Belfast, the son of an electrical engineer. He left school at 17, went to work for the *Belfast Telegraph* and soon pulled off his first big scoop when he accosted Prime Minister Clement Attlee on his way home from a holiday in County Sligo. Was it true, he asked, that Attlee intended to end partition in Ireland, as an English paper had claimed? It wasn't, and the cub reporter's story made the front pages. Not long after, Cole took a job with the *Manchester Guardian* (as it then was), rising to become its labour correspondent – a hugely important role in those days of union power – and later its deputy editor.

Cole was 'a wonderfully awkward colleague', said Michael White in *The Guardian*. He would never let anyone get away with 'sloppy facts' or 'sloppy opinions'. But his independence of mind often left him isolated: an Ulster Protestant, his progressive views put him at odds with fellow Unionists, while his 'adhesion to the right wing of the Labour Party and the TUC' gave rise to clashes over *Guardian* editorial policy. Cole was distraught when his main rival, Peter Preston, won the editorship in 1975, and moved to *The Observer*, where for six years he served as deputy editor. But in 1981 he enraged the paper's owner, Roland 'Tiny' Rowland, by giving evidence against him at the Monopolies Commission. Cole's career seemed doomed. Then, out of the blue, the BBC offered him the job of political editor. 'I ended up on telly by accident,' he recalled. 'Us modern Presbyterians don't believe in predestination, but on this occasion I thought I'd give it a whizz.'

> **'I ended up on telly by accident,' he recalled. 'Us modern Presbyterians don't believe in predestination, but on this occasion I thought I'd give it a whizz.'**

In the 1980s you couldn't call yourself famous until you had been immortalised by the satirical puppet show *Spitting Image*, said the *Daily Mail*. And Cole gave the puppet-makers plenty to work on thanks to his 'fast-paced' Ulster brogue and his huge spectacles. Cole hated his puppet: he felt it made him look a fool, whereas he saw himself, in his own words, as 'a pretty serious journalist', said Peter Preston in *The Observer*. He wasn't alone in that estimation. Even Tory politicians, aware of his Labour sympathies, were impressed by his 'manifest integrity'. Though Margaret Thatcher once dismissed him as 'an old socialist', it was his microphone she sought out from a crowd of journalists the morning after she escaped the Brighton IRA bomb, said Michael Leapman in the *Belfast Telegraph*. It was to him that, in 1987, she confessed her desire to go 'on and on and on', and it was Cole who was among the first to predict her downfall in 1990. In that, as in other scoops, he was tipped off by sources who knew they could trust him not to reveal their identity.

Only after he retired, two years later, did the broadcaster reveal the depth of his detestation of Thatcher. Above all, he abhorred what he called her 'enamelled certitude', her 'immanent sense of being right'. Indeed he went further, naming her as the worst-ever British PM. In later life, he lived modestly in his pebble-dash home in Surrey with his wife Madge. In 1993 he refused a CBE, citing a rule that *Guardian* journalists shouldn't accept a gift that couldn't be consumed within 24 hours. Often in the street, a member of the public would mistake him for the TV weatherman Ian McCaskill, and ask him what the weather would be. His answer was always the same: 'Sunny with a slight risk of showers.'

Reluctant feminist icon
of the 'sex war'

DORIS LESSING

1919-2013

One day in 2007, the novelist Doris Lessing arrived at her home in West Hampstead to find a crowd of photographers waiting outside. She assumed they were filming a soap, until one asked if she realised that she'd been awarded the Nobel Prize in Literature. 'Oh, Christ!' she muttered, adding that they no doubt wanted her to make 'uplifting remarks of some kind'. The footage of this down-to-earth, grey-haired old woman seated on her doorstep, batting aside questions from importunate journalists, duly became a hit on YouTube, with a new generation of fans praising the author's 'cool' attitude, said Lisa Allardice in *The Guardian*. 'But Lessing was just being herself. She really didn't give a damn about what the world thought.' After decades of being shortlisted, she assumed the Swedish academy had chosen to honour her, because, at 87, it wouldn't be long before she 'popped off'. In any case, she had won every other literary award going, she pointed out – though it was nice to complete a 'royal flush'.

Lessing was brought up in rural Rhodesia. Her father Alfred Cook Tayler – a bank clerk who lost a leg in the Great War – had moved there in the hope of making a fortune growing maize. The money never materialised. Contemptuous of her mother's conventional aspirations for her, the rebellious Doris left school at 14, went to work as a telephone operator in the capital Salisbury (now Harare), got married aged 19, and before long had abandoned her husband and, without qualm, apparently, her son and daughter, too. An active member of the local communist party, she soon remarried – feeling it her 'revolutionary duty' – to a prominent communist, Gottfried Lessing. That union also foundered ('I do not think marriage is one of my talents,' she once confessed), not least because her husband didn't take seriously her ambition to be a novelist. In 1949 she left him and travelled to London with little more than £20, her second son Peter, and the manuscript of a novel, *The Grass is Singing*. An account of an affair between a frustrated Rhodesian housewife and her black houseboy, it became a literary sensation the following year.

Lessing then embarked on her five-novel autobiographical sequence, *Children of Violence*, starting with *Martha Quest* (1952) and closing with *The Four-Gated City* (1969). Midway through she also wrote *The Golden Notebook*, an account of a woman's descent into madness that was hailed as a feminist masterpiece when it appeared in 1962. Lessing was taken aback, said Elaine Showalter in the *Washington Post*. She had wanted to explore the psychological wounds created by a collapse of faith in communism, only to find herself lumbered with what she described as a feminist 'albatross'. So she goaded feminists by refusing to stay on-message: 'The sex war,' she insisted, 'isn't the most important war going on.' This contrariness extended to her choice of genre, said Boyd Tonkin in *The Independent*. Thus she dismayed fans of her social realism by turning to sci-fi in the late 1970s with books such as *The Making of the Representative for Planet Eight*. In the 1980s she released two novels under a pseudonym just to see how they fared without her name attached. Not well, it turned out, though some said this was because they were not up to her usual standard.

Whatever the genre, said Tonkin, the thread of continuity in Lessing's work is the theme of a woman's quest for 'one-ness', whether through political commitment, transcendentalism, or the creation of 'alien, more advanced civilisations'. It was Lessing's own quest too, which she pursued both in her personal life (she was attracted in recent years to Sufi teachings) and in her novels. Her reply on being asked what she considered her most substantial achievement, was instant. 'To go on writing, through thick and thin. I've met girls who say: "My mother told me to read you, and my grandmother." That really is something, isn't it?'

'The only genuinely global hero'

NELSON MANDELA

1918-2013

A few days before the Rugby World Cup final in 1995, the relatively newly installed President Mandela appeared at a meeting of ANC hardliners, sporting a peaked cap in the colours of the Springbok side, said John Carlin in *The Independent*. His audience was mystified. Rugby was the oppressors' sport; the Springboks had come to symbolise the brutality of apartheid rule; the team's players were almost all white, its fans Afrikaners. In Soweto, they celebrated Springbok defeats. But fist clenched, arm aloft, Mandela told the crowd: 'The cap I am wearing is to honour our boys. I ask each and every one of you to stand behind them, because they are our pride, they are my pride, they are your pride.' His message was clear: the Boks belonged to all South Africa now; their victory would be everyone's victory. His audience began to like what he was saying. And when he told them: 'We want to win the World Cup because we are a new nation,' they erupted in cheers.

But Mandela didn't just work his magic on the ANC. White South Africa was similarly confused, and then delighted, when Mandela – the old 'communist terrorist' – appeared on the pitch before the final against the All Blacks, wearing a Springbok shirt. 'Nelson, Nelson, Nelson,' thundered thousands of Afrikaner rugby fans, when he appeared again, at its end, to celebrate South Africa's victory. Presenting the trophy to captain Francois Pienaar, he said: 'Thank you, Francois, for what you have done for our country.' To which Pienaar replied: 'No, Mr President, thank you for what you have done.' Even in Soweto, they danced; the Rainbow Nation was born.

It was certainly the 'happiest day of Nelson Mandela's political life', said Carlin – and one that reflected his many extraordinary qualities as a man, and as a political strategist: Mandela understood the potency of symbols; he knew the importance of reconciliation; and had harnessed the power of forgiveness. 'If politics is essentially about persuading, winning over, capturing hearts and minds, no one has done that better.' Mandela emerged from 27 long years in jail to 'pull off not one but two political feats'. He convinced his black followers to turn away from vengeance; and he won the trust and love of white South Africans too. In so doing, said David Blair in the *Daily Telegraph*, he averted a civil war that seemed inevitable, inspired millions, and became 'perhaps the only genuinely global hero'.

Nelson Mandela was born in 1918 in a village in the rolling hills of the rural Transkei. A member of the family of the paramount chief of the Thembu people, he grew up with a 'strong sense of both tribal pride and the responsibility of leadership', said Paul Vallely in *The Independent*. His forename was Rolihlahla, which meant, as he liked to point out, 'troublemaker' in the language of his Xhosa tribe; it was a teacher at his local Methodist school who called him Nelson, after the great military leader from across the sea. When Nelson was 12, his father died, and he moved into the house of the chieftain himself, said the *New York Times*, 'not as an heir to power, but to study it'. Later, his friends would credit his regal self-confidence – and occasional autocratic behaviour – to his years in the royal household. 'Unlike many black South Africans, whose confidence had been crushed by generations of officially proclaimed white superiority, Mandela never seemed to doubt that he was the equal of any man.' One of the political lessons he absorbed in the Thembu capital, said David Beresford in *The Guardian*, was the value of listening. 'I have always ventured to listen to what each and every person in a discussion had to say before venturing my own opinion,' he once explained. 'Oftentimes my own opinion will simply represent a consensus of what I heard in the discussions.'

At the University College of Fort Hare, Mandela studied law, and fell in with Oliver Tambo, another leader-to-be of the freedom movement. He enjoyed university, but in 1940 he and Tambo were all-but expelled for leading a student protest against poor-quality food. Returning home, Mandela found that a bride had been chosen for him. Rather than marrying a woman he didn't love, he fled to Soweto, where he was introduced to Walter Sisulu, and the African National Congress. Years later, Sisulu recalled that on meeting Mandela, with his aristocratic bearing and confident gaze, he felt his prayers had been answered. Mandela, Sisulu and Tambo soon began forming an ANC youth league, with a view to replacing its staid leadership. Meanwhile, Mandela found work as a clerk in a law firm. Always conscious of appearances, he dressed up for work in a smart suit, said Richard Stengel in the *Daily Mail*: in a suit, he knew he could command respect.

In 1944, he married a nurse, Evelyn, who was Sisulu's cousin. They had four children, one of whom died in infancy, but Mandela was already too engrossed in politics to pay much attention to his family. Handsome, charming and something of a dandy, he was also a lady's man. The marriage ended abruptly in 1956; Evelyn, who died in 2004, would later accuse Mandela of cruelty and neglect. Not long after, he met an attractive, strong-willed medical social worker named Winifred Madikizela. Mandela was smitten: he said on their first date that he would marry her, and in 1958, he did exactly that.

In 1948, the Nationalist Party had won a whites-only general election, after which it began implementing a policy of apartheid – separation – across South Africa, said Richard Dowden in *The Times*. The new state was designed only to serve white interests. In more than 40 laws passed by the whites-only parliament, black South Africans were removed from their land; dumped in townships or remote 'homelands'; and arrested if found in white areas without a permit in their pass book. Influenced by Gandhi's example in India, Mandela and others reacted by calling for boycotts and strikes. In so doing, said Vallely, they made common cause with the communists, though Mandela refused to join the party. In 1953, he and Tambo set up South Africa's only black legal practice, to help victims of white oppression. But as the government became increasingly repressive, it became clear that their strategy was not working: protests were intensifying, but so were mass arrests. 'A freedom fighter learns the hard way that it is the oppressor who defines the nature of the struggle, and the oppressed is often left no resource but to use methods that mirror those of the oppressor,' he wrote. 'At a certain point, one can only fight fire with fire.' In 1956 Mandela and 155 others were arrested for high treason. The case proved hard to mount, however, and it was still dragging on when – on 26 March 1960 – 69 people demonstrating against 'pass laws' were shot dead by police at Sharpeville. In the massacre's wake, the ANC was banned. Mandela co-founded its military wing, Spear of the Nation, and went underground, becoming known as the 'Black Pimpernel' as he travelled the country in disguise.

From a base at a farm near Rivonia, outside Johannesburg, Mandela began planning the first stage of the armed struggle – sabotage. The idea was to hit power plants and communications, wrote the late Anthony Sampson for the *Sunday Telegraph*. This, Mandela hoped, would discourage inward investment, putting pressure on Pretoria, which was already facing international calls to abandon apartheid. In 1962, Mandela was smuggled out of the country. In London, he forged links with, among others, Labour's Hugh Gaitskell, and David Astor, the editor of *The Observer*.

> **'Hating clouds the mind. It gets in the way of strategy. Leaders cannot afford to hate.'**

But back in South Africa, the game was up. He was captured, and charged with fostering revolution. At the conclusion of the 'Rivonia' trial, he gave a four-hour speech, ending with: 'I have cherished the idea of a democratic and free society in which all persons live together in harmony and with equal opportunities. It is an ideal I hope to live for and to achieve. But if needs be, it is an ideal for which I am prepared to die.' Narrowly avoiding the death sentence, Mandela and his co-accused were given life terms. He was 44 when he was sent to Robben Island; he would be 71 by the time of his release.

Conditions on Robben Island were harsh. Black prisoners were given reduced rations; Mandela and fellow inmates were forced to quarry in a mine; he slept on the floor of a tiny cell, and suffered the humiliation of being made to wear short trousers (black men were considered children). In 1969, he was refused permission to attend the funeral of his son, who had been killed in a car crash; meanwhile, his beloved Winnie was being persecuted on the outside. Yet Mandela remained focused on the cause – and used his time productively, said the *New York Times*. Convinced of the need to understand his enemy, he learnt Afrikaans, read up on Afrikaner history, and absorbed the views and attitudes of Afrikaner guards. He kept fit – his daily routine included hundreds of fingertip press-ups – studied law, debated ideas, and honed his powers of persuasion on prison staff, many of whom were won over by his quiet authority, his dignity and his restraint.

Mandela made it his business never to lose his self-control, and concealed whatever pain or anger he might be feeling, said Ahmed Kathrada, a fellow prisoner, in *The Independent*. He was unflappable, and inscrutable. He also had a stubborn streak: when he ran out of his favoured hair oil, he harassed the authorities for weeks, and even complained to the sympathetic MP Helen Suzman. Among inmates, this became known as 'the Pantene crisis', and we were relieved, said Kathrada, when a supply was located. He would also say that he learnt not to hate. 'Hating clouds the mind,' he said. 'It gets in the way of strategy. Leaders cannot afford to hate.'

By the 1980s, the Pretoria government was becoming increasingly isolated; sanctions were biting; and, in Britain, a 'Free Nelson Mandela' campaign was escalating. In secret, white leaders began meeting the prisoner in Robben Island – and were bowled over by his charisma, charm and obvious integrity, said Carlin. Kobie Coetsee, the minister of justice under apartheid, would weep when he recalled his negotiations with Mandela. Niel Barnard, the feared head of the National Intelligence Service, spoke of Mandela as if he were his own father. Thus, eventually, Mandela was let out of prison, to seek a negotiated settlement with the black majority.

On 11 February 1990, Mandela walked to freedom. What would Madiba, as he was known in South Africa, be like, after 27 years in jail? The man who emerged was surprisingly sprightly – and ready for business. Deploying 'his 1,000-volt smile', he set about persuading a doubtful, angry ANC that apartheid could not be overthrown by force; and persuading fearful whites – many of whom regarded him much as many Americans regarded Osama bin Laden – that he would protect them. Risking the fury of his supporters, he described apartheid's President F.W. de Klerk as a 'man of integrity' at his first press conference; and professed himself delighted finally to meet a senior political reporter from *Die Burger*, apartheid's *Pravda*.

It was an incredible start, but his battle was only just beginning: extreme violence – incited by the security forces – broke out in the townships, and political negotiations were fraught. In his personal life, too, there was sadness, as he realised his marriage to the fiery Winnie was over. But, finally, democratic elections were planned for April 1994. The ANC emerged victorious, and at 75, Nelson Mandela became his country's first black president. While leaving much of the administration to his deputy, Thabo Mbeki, Mandela carried on his mission of reconciliation: he made a high-profile visit to the whites-only enclave of Oriana, to meet the widow of Hendrik Verwoerd, the architect of apartheid; and invited several former apartheid leaders to tea. He was determined, among other things, to prevent a destabilising 'white flight'.

At the same time, he launched his Truth and Reconciliation Commission. 'We hated it at first,' said Justice Malala in *The Guardian*. 'We testified about years of unbearable suffering at the hands of the white majority, and wanted to look the killers and torturers in the eyes. None came. Instead they sent their lawyers and spokesmen. Mandela insisted we persevere – and he was right. It wasn't about them, but about us, confronting our emotions, and being healed. How do I remember Mandela? In the George Orwell story, a young policeman in Burma walks towards an elephant that has just killed a villager. He is the only man with a gun; 2,000 people are following him, urging him on. He knows it's wrong to kill the elephant, which is no longer a danger, but he is scared of looking weak, so he shoots it. When Mandela came out of prison, there were millions of us shouting at him to shoot the elephant. He had the courage and wisdom to refuse.'

After five years in office, Mandela did something rare among African presidents: he stood down, as he had promised to do. By now, he was loved around the world: he was on first-name terms with the Queen (no one else addressed her as 'Elizabeth') and had become a magnet for celebrities. In his later years, said Richard Stengel, Mandela swapped his suits for colourful shirts: to command respect he no longer needed to dress as a white man. He retired from public life in 2004. By then he had made a happy third marriage to Graça Machel, but the activities of his feuding, and apparently grasping, offspring overshadowed his final years. Mandela had never been a good parent; his children had been sacrificed for a greater cause. It was, he said, his chief regret – but only one of many emotions he concealed behind his dazzling smile.

Index of subjects